THE TWENTIETH-CENTURY AMERICAN CITY

THE AMERICAN MOMENT
Stanley I. Kutler, Consulting Editor

The Twentieth-Century American City
Jon C. Teaford

American Workers, American Unions, 1920–1985
Robert H. Zieger

The Twentieth-Century American City

PROBLEM, PROMISE, AND REALITY

Jon C. Teaford

THE JOHNS HOPKINS UNIVERSITY PRESS
Baltimore and London

The Johns Hopkins University Press
701 West 40th Street
Baltimore, Maryland 21211
The Johns Hopkins Press Ltd, London

*The paper in this book is acid-free and meets the
guidelines for permanence and durability of the
Committee on Production Guidelines for Book
Longevity of the Council on Library Resources.*

LIBRARY OF CONGRESS CATALOGING-IN-PUBLICATION DATA

Teaford, Jon C.
    The twentieth-century American city.

    (The American moment)
    Bibliography: p.
    Includes index.
    1. Cities and towns — United States — History — 20th
century. 2. Urbanization — United States — History —
20th century. I. Title. II. Series.
HT123.T43   1986   307.7'64'0973   85-24214
ISBN 0-8018-3094-X (alk. paper)
ISBN 0-8018-3096-6 (pbk.: alk. paper)

Contents

Editor's Foreword

Jon Teaford is a distinguished historian of urban America. His earlier work reconceptualized in a significant way the study of urban American history by emphasizing the legal dimension of the city's personality. In this new work, *The Twentieth-Century American City,* Teaford has incorporated more of the social and non-political aspects of urban problems. The result is a description of the twentieth-century American city as a microcosm of the tensions characterizing so much of modern American political and social life.

Teaford's tightly-drawn study contrasts the city's promise and reality. As the twentieth century opened, new and established Americans alike turned to the promise of urban life, a promise of a richer, fuller, more orderly, and less demanding life than that offered by the vanishing Agrarian Ideal. The city was to offer community, work, and human satisfaction. Instead, of course, social ills, such as poverty, disease, and crime, took on new forms. New issues, new ways of governance, preoccupied Americans. The concentration of population seemed to magnify problems, problems that demanded solutions, yet provoked widely divergent approaches that only widened community rifts.

Teaford demonstrates that, rather than creating community, political and social fragmentation dominated the pattern of urban history throughout the twentieth century. The great American city is now sometimes reduced to dozens of suburbs in search of a city. The changing physical and demographic patterns accelerated decay and disintegration, with the result that cities have become pitiful giants, immobilized like Gulliver in Lilliput. Since 1945, the plight of the cities has been one of the major domestic problems in the United States. Led by the national government, enormous expenditures of capital and political energy have been expended in massive, yet often misdirected, efforts to salvage and revive the American city. As we approach the end of the century, that transformation remains uncertain. Indeed, as Teaford suggests, recognizing and accommodating fragmentation perhaps offers the only plausible course for the future of the city.

THE AMERICAN MOMENT is designed to offer a series of narrative and analytical discussions on a variety of topics in American history. Books in the series are both topical and chronological. Some volumes will survey familiar subjects — such as Puritanism, the American Revolution, the Civil War, the New Deal, and the Cold War — and blend necessary factual background with thoughtful, provocative interpretations. Other volumes — with topics such as women and reform movements, urban affairs, ethnicity, sports, and popular culture — will chart new or less familiar terrain. All will provide narrative and interpretation to open significant new dimensions and perspectives on the American past.

Stanley I. Kutler
UNIVERSITY OF WISCONSIN
MADISON, WISCONSIN

Preface

By the close of the 1970s urban "euthanasia" and central-city "triage" had entered the vocabulary of students of the American metropolis. Even casual observers of the aging, beleaguered metropolises of the Northeast and Midwest found the phraseology of the terminal ward and battlefield hospital appropriate to discussions of America's cities. To the south and west, cities like Houston, Phoenix, and Los Angeles evoked less morbid language, but even in the booming Sunbelt, smog, traffic congestion, ethnic tensions, and the disparity between rich and poor tarnished the image of urban life. Moreover, the problems of the city were not new. Throughout the century, journalists, politicians, and social scientists had been writing and speaking about the ills that plagued America's cities. During the age of Theodore Roosevelt as well as the era of Lyndon Johnson and Jimmy Carter, Americans perceived the city as the nation's chief domestic dilemma.

The following pages deal with the problems of the city, the panaceas proposed to remedy these ills, and the often discouraging reality that stymied the plans of many well-meaning Americans. The narrative focuses on the nation's largest cities, the giant metropolises splintered by the social and economic divisions endemic to American life. Thus New York, Chicago, and the other leading urban hubs are the chief characters in this drama of dreams and frustrations. The less striking stories of smaller cities receive short shrift. Since there were few large cities in the South and West at the beginning of the century, Sunbelt cities that later ranked among the nation's urban giants do not figure into the picture in the early pages. In 1900 only two cities of the former Confederacy, New Orleans and Memphis, had over 100,000 people, and Memphis, having only 102,000, barely earned this distinction. West of New Orleans and south of San Francisco the largest city was Los Angeles, which also boasted 102,000 residents. During the first decade of the twentieth century, metropolitan America and the Sunbelt were, therefore, almost mutually exclusive, overlapping in only a few instances.

This account of the twentieth-century metropolis builds upon my past work in urban history. Beginning with the publication of my first book in 1975, I have attempted to describe and interpret the evolution of urban government in the United States. My three previous books have examined the development of the municipal corporation during the first two hundred years of white settlement in North America, the dilemma of governmental fragmentation in metropolitan America during the late nineteenth and early twentieth centuries, and the structure and functions of city government between 1870 and 1900. In the present volume, I move beyond this focus on government and attempt to deal more fully with life in America's metropolitan areas. Thus I describe public policy as a counterpoint to the rifts, conflicts, and conundrums of the private sector, an often ineffectual element in the compound of twentieth-century urban development.

As in my previous books, I owe much to the editor of this series, Stanley I. Kutler, of the University of Wisconsin–Madison, and to the senior social sciences editor at the Johns Hopkins University Press, Henry Y. K. Tom. I also acknowledge the assistance of Joyce Good and her office staff, who ably and faultlessly typed the book manuscript. They have been invaluable in the preparation of this volume.

THE TWENTIETH-CENTURY AMERICAN CITY

Problem,
Promise,
and Reality

At the dawn of the twentieth century virtually all observers agreed that the age of the city had arrived. Speaking for reform-minded clergy, Reverend Josiah Strong preached that "the new civilization is certain to be urban; and the problem of the twentieth century will be the city." Likewise, the economist Richard T. Ely warned that Americans had "to prepare for the coming domination of the city, and for an extension of urban conditions even to rural communities." And the civic reformer Frederic C. Howe proclaimed more optimistically that "the city is the hope of the future. . . . Here the industrial issues, that are fast becoming dominant in political life, will first be worked out." Whether hopeful or despairing, Americans recognized that New York City, Chicago, and San Francisco, not the myriad of dreary hamlets strung along the railroads or the dozing county seats dotting the map of America, would determine the destiny of the nation. Commercial growth, industrialization, and the labor-saving mechanization of agriculture all seemed to ensure that urbanization would be the inevitable wave of the future.

Having witnessed the dynamic urban growth of the late nineteenth century, few Americans could deny that the tide of population was surging in the direction of the city. In 1850 only six American cities had over 100,000 inhabitants; by 1900 thirty-eight cities could claim this distinction. In 1850 only 5 percent of the American population lived in urban places of more than 100,000 inhabitants; by 1900 it was up to 19 percent. In 1850 Chicago was a town of 30,000 residents; by 1900 it boasted a population of 1,700,000. During the second half of the nineteenth century, the population of New York City increased sevenfold, as did that of Saint Louis; San Francisco's rose tenfold, and Detroit's soared fourteenfold. City streets were reaching out miles from the metropolitan centers, and acre after acre of farmland was succumbing to urban development. Thousands of miles of new streetcar tracks and water, sewer, and gas mains accommodated the expanding population

along the metropolitan fringes. Evidence of urban growth was everywhere, and politicians, academics, journalists, and preachers could not
ignore it. All had to recognize the onslaught of urbanization.

Most Americans at the turn of the century also agreed, however,
that the city was the overriding problem of the present and the future.
With its striking contrasts between wealth and poverty, its debilitating
congestion, its ethnic diversity, and its crime and vice, the city was the
nation's greatest social problem. New York's crowded tenements were
monuments to the economic inequities of urban America, whereas Vic-
torians viewed Gotham's brothels and saloons as badges of the city's
moral depravity. Moreover, the jumble of immigrants who congregated
in the cities, speaking foreign tongues, practicing strange customs, and
adhering to alien religions, appeared to threaten the very unity of the
nation. It seemed as if the nation's problems had gravitated to the urban
centers even more rapidly than had its people. Many native-born
Americans thought nostalgically of the rural past and the homogeneous
village life of an earlier America. The city of the present and the future,
in contrast, seemed threatening and ominous. Already, reformers like
Jacob Riis were exposing the evils of urban slums, and novelists like
Stephen Crane were composing tales about the victims of the heartless
city. By 1900 the list of books and articles on urban ills was lengthening
rapidly.

Moreover, urban pathologists continued to examine the city during
the succeeding decades of the twentieth century, diagnosing previously
undiscovered maladies and prescribing new nostrums for longstanding
problems. In the first and second decades of the century, self-styled
reformers battled slumlords, party bosses, and streetcar magnates,
decrying the political and economic injustices of the city. By the 1920s
the advent of the automobile was beginning to pose new problems for
America's urban areas, and in the 1930s economic depression brought
the dilemma of poverty again to the forefront. From 1900 to 1940 the
mass of printed matter describing urban problems continued to increase
with unrelenting regularity as one generation of social workers, city
planners, municipal reformers, and concerned citizens yielded to the
next.

World War II momentarily diverted attention from the domestic
problems of the city, but after 1945 a new wave of concern swept the
nation as Americans looked about them and discovered pervasive urban
blight. The central cities were decaying, shoppers were avoiding the central business districts, and the slums seemed to be spreading. Even
smaller cities, which had previously been immune to "urban" problems,
fell prey to blight as outlying shopping malls stripped Main Street of its

business, leaving rows of empty storefronts. Big-city social reformers called for more public housing, but the completed housing projects soon became objects of scorn. Soulless high-rise structures for the poor seemed to breed more crime, delinquency, and antisocial attitudes than the dilapidated slums they replaced. During the 1950s planners lobbied for urban renewal, and block after block of aged buildings fell before the wrecker's ball. By the close of the 1960s, however, urban renewal was anathema among progressive planners; like public housing, it was as much a problem as a solution.

During the postwar era new migrants from the southern states and Latin America congregated in the nation's cities, and many public officials and students of modern metropolitan life perceived them as yet another urban problem. Puerto Ricans in New York City, blacks in Chicago, white Appalachians in Cincinnati, all were newcomers to the city, and like previous newcomers they adjusted only gradually to the urban environment. Assimilation was slow and unsteady, marked by riots that unnerved middle-class whites and by rising crime rates that seemed to endanger the safety of established urbanites. By the 1960s, newspaper editors, television commentators, and academic experts were all referring to an "urban crisis." Although racism and poverty were at least as prevalent in rural as in urban America, the city became synonymous with the nation's domestic ills. In the chaotic 1960s "urban" became a code word for all that was troubling the nation on the home front.

In the 1970s urban problems continued to make news. New York City virtually went bankrupt, as did Cleveland, and Detroit and Boston were not far from insolvency. Again the problems of the city grabbed the nation's headlines, and, as in earlier decades, there was no shortage of articles, books and symposia on urban ills. In the 1970s, as in the first decade of the century, the city was a baffling problem for the nation. How to achieve the good life in the metropolis? This seemed to be the perpetual dilemma of the twentieth century.

Yet for every criticism and exposé there was a suggestion for improvement, a scheme for realizing the elusive goal of harmony and contentment in the city. Americans did not surrender before the barrage of urban problems. Instead, the perceived problems of the city seemed to fuel the American imagination, resulting in a long list of urban panaceas. The city thus offered much promise. Many believed that through the application of Christian precepts, advanced technology, good government, enlightened planning principles, and ample federal funds the city could provide a better way of life for millions of Americans. The correct compound of public policy and private endeavor could supposedly bridge the ethnic divisions within urban society, eliminate the economic inequities of the city, and reduce threatening tensions and hostilities.

To realize the promise of city life, planners offered a perpetual stream of proposals for urban betterment. The Chicago architect Daniel Burnham spoke on behalf of the City Beautiful; Britain's visionary Ebenezer Howard thought utopia lay in the Garden City; France's Le Corbusier sponsored a scheme known as the Radiant City; and the great American architect Frank Lloyd Wright proposed an "ideal" plan known as Broadacre City. Each scheme was a supposed panacea for the century's urban ills. Decade after decade, commentators devoted thousands of pages to harsh critiques of the existing city, exposing its flaws and shortcomings. But they also presented utopian visions of what the city could be. The city could be gleaming skyscrapers set amid green parks, or it could be a self-sufficient hub ringed by a greenbelt of forest and farms, offering the advantages of town and country. Then, in the 1960s, a New York foe of urban renewal, Jane Jacobs, ridiculed the old panaceas and offered some of her own. The city of Jane Jacobs's dreams was a place of vitality and excitement, inhabited by vibrant throngs who appreciated the density and diversity of the metropolis. The hopes and imaginations of urban commentators seemed to know no bounds.

Others offered solutions for some of the specific social and political ills that plagued the city. At the beginning of the century, settlement houses provided a cheery, wholesome alternative to the saloon and tenement and a means for instilling middle-class American values in immigrants. In the wake of World War I proponents of Americanization programs in the public schools also promised assimilation of the immigrant masses and a new national unity. Throughout the twentieth century proposals for upgrading housing conditions among the poor followed one after another at a dizzying pace. During the first two decades of the century, enforcement of building codes would supposedly ensure the light, air, and breathing space necessary for a decent life. Between 1930 and 1960 giant slum clearance and public housing projects seemed to promise a better existence for deprived city dwellers. Then it was the small public projects, rent subsidies, and the transplantation of low-income residents to the suburbs that appeared to be the solution for metropolitan housing ills. Likewise, social workers, welfare activists, and proponents of community action programs all sponsored panaceas for the urban poor. Meanwhile, the commission government, city manager rule, the strong-mayor plan, and neighborhood power all took turns as popular answers to the dilemma of city government. Each would supposedly end irresponsible rule and realize the goals of effective, democratic government in the metropolis.

In response to every urban problem there were a dozen proposals promising a better future. Scholars, architects, planners, and civic-minded citizens did not throw up their hands in exasperation and conclude that the unsatisfactory status quo was the best of all possible worlds. Instead, a degree of optimism and a willingness to adapt and reform prevailed during the twentieth century, and a long line of political leaders promised a better urban life. By the 1970s, the nation's presidents were diligently issuing urban policy statements, each a litany of promises intended to demonstrate concern for the suffering cities.

The twentieth century, then, has been a period during which Americans have recognized and accepted as inevitable the triumph of the city. But it has also been an era dedicated to confronting the flaws in this inescapable reality and to righting the wrongs of metropolitan life. This recognition of urban dominance and the accompanying belief that life in the metropolis can and must improve are hallmarks of the twentieth century. Nineteenth-century America was a rural nation, and there were no national campaigns or policies aimed at upgrading the quality of life in the cities. Local leaders in the various cities took steps to better the urban environment, but not until the 1890s did urban reformers organize national associations to deal specifically with metropolitan problems. Moreover, in the nineteenth century the federal government failed to battle perceived urban maladies, and state action was erratic at best. Not until the close of the nineteenth century did political scientists, social workers, landscape architects, and engineers classify and analyze the problems of the city and lay the foundations for modern urban planning and urban studies. In the twentieth century, unlike the nineteenth, the problems of the city became a thriving industry for scores of scholars and reform-minded experts.

Many of the publicized promises and policies of academics, planners, and politicians, however, have had only a marginal impact on the development of the twentieth-century American city. Despite all the visionary schemes proposed and all the data collected and analyzed, urban life has not proceeded according to any grand reform plan. Various policies have backfired, and other schemes have stimulated much discussion but little action. No master blueprint has determined the nature of the twentieth-century city in the United States; instead, urban America has evolved in response to new technology, changing lifestyles, and demographic trends as well as often conflicting policies and programs. The city has developed as a motley patchwork of demands, desires, interests, and schemes — an ugly creation in the eyes of those sponsoring neat panaceas. Although a long list of reformers has sought to heal the economic and ethnic divisions in urban America and to ease the social tensions, the fissures have not disappeared. Generations of planners have sought to curb sprawl and harness the forces of urban growth, yet makeshift, uncoordinated development has predominated. Seemingly oblivious to the best-laid plans of urban experts, the city has continued to spawn the divisions, tensions, and inequities antithetical to harmony and cooperation.

Thus the reality of the twentieth-century American city has deviated markedly from the promises and programs of reformers and planners. Most reform-minded urban experts have conceived of the ideal city as a cooperative, planned commonwealth. The actual twentieth-century American metropolis, however, has been an uncoordinated mass of clashing social and ethnic fragments. American urban history is a tale of unwilling accommodation rather than harmonious cooperation. It is the story of diverse groups vying for territory, income, and power, of barriers that arose between those sometimes hostile groups and the bargaining and brokerage necessary to reduce their conflicts. Despite the hopes and promises of reformers, this scenario of division and fragmentation describes the reality of the city during the first eight decades of the twentieth century. Throughout the era, the metropolis has remained socially, economically, and ethnically fragmented, each fragment in search of its own happiness and on guard against the threatening advances of the others. Although many have dreamed of the city as a cohesive community, the dream has not been realized. In the twentieth-century metropolis the parts have triumphed over the whole.

The Century Begins, 1900–1919

In 1900 America's cities housed a diverse body of persons drawn to the metropolis by the promise of profit, excitement, and success. Lithuanians and Poles gravitated to Chicago's stockyards and Pittsburgh's steel mills, expecting to find work and money; daughters of native-born midwestern farmers migrated to Kansas City and Indianapolis to make a living from typing and shorthand and to experience a freedom denied them in the country town; and ambitious Yankees from Vermont and New Hampshire teemed into Boston's State Street and New York's Wall Street seeking their fortunes in the world of finance. The farm no longer provided sufficient employment or excitement for the world's masses, so they turned to the urban hubs of manufacturing, commerce, culture, and amusement. Migrants from the peasant villages of Europe and Asia, and from the declining farms of New England and the Midwest, converged on the largest metropolises, a motley collection of humanity who together committed their fate to the American city.

With such a diverse population, the city of the early twentieth century more closely resembled a patchwork quilt than a tightly woven fabric. Social, economic, and ethnic divisions split the city into neighborhood fragments. Some lived on the right side of the railroad tracks and others on the wrong side, and the world of the tenement was an alien culture to wealthy mansion dwellers. The spires of conflicting congregations accented the urban skyline, advertising the religious diversity of the metropolis. And in the largest cities presses printed the news in Italian, German, Yiddish, Polish, German, and Czech as well as in English. The American city was a mass of segregated and unassimilated humanity.

To understand the city of the early twentieth century, then, one must examine its diverse parts. Its divisions were at once a source of vitality and of conflict. And for those who sought to reform the city and who spoke of a unifying civic ideal, the social and economic cacophony of urban America was a clarion call to action.

THE DOWNTOWN

The economic nucleus of the city was the central business district, or "downtown." This was the common center of those diverse masses thrown together in pursuit of an income. Many urban neighborhoods had a distinct ethnic identity; there were Jewish ghettos, black districts, and Polish zones. Other neighborhoods had a definite economic identity. But the central business district was the knot uniting the various strands of the city. In the downtown area the diverse ethnic, economic, and social strains of urban life were bound together, working, spending, speculating, and investing. Along the downtown thoroughfares wealthy financiers passed by grubby beggars, rubbed shoulders with horny-handed porters and draymen, and jostled for space with clerks and stenographers. In the socially and culturally fragmented city, the central business district was the one bit of turf common to all.

The transportation network of the early twentieth century ensured that the downtown area was the unifying focus of metropolitan life. In New York City, Boston, Chicago, and throughout the nation streetcar and rapid transit lines converged on the central business district, carrying millions of people to the city center each day. During the first decade of the twentieth century only the very wealthy relied on private automobiles or carriages for their transportation. For the great bulk of urban Americans, the trolley, elevated railroad, and subway were the chief means of travel within the city. All of these transit lines centered on the downtown. An occasional cross-town line linked sections of the metropolitan periphery without passing through the urban hub, but nowhere was the transit web so tightly woven as in the central business district. According to the novelist William Dean Howells, trolleys clattered along tracks imbedded in the street surface while elevated "trains roar[ed] and shriek[ed] and hiss[ed] on the rails overhead, and a turmoil of rattling express-wagons, heavy drays and trucks, and carts, hacks, carriages, and huge vans roll[ed] itself between and beneath the prime agents of the uproar." At the beginning of the century the downtown was clearly the raucous crossroads of the city.

No means of transit was as important as the electric streetcar. In 1902 there were almost four hundred miles of streetcar track in New York City, and the trolleys transported more than 400 million people annually. Chicago boasted over seven hundred miles of track and almost 300 million passengers, whereas Philadelphia's system transported 325 million fares. Each workday millions of Americans jammed into the electric streetcars and traveled at a pace of five to ten miles an hour to and from the office, store, or factory. For most people it was an unpleasant experience, and the British essayist Arnold Bennett was shocked by the spectacle of proper Bostonians "buffetted and flung about . . . in [street] cars which really did carry inadequacy and brutality to excess." Lucky commuters grabbed seats, but many stood, clutching straps as the trolley jolted to its destination. Adding to the displeasure of the jangled passengers were the persistent rumors that city councilmen had been bribed to award unduly favorable franchise terms to the streetcar companies, thereby sacrificing the welfare of the transit customer. Many could nod their head in agreement when novelist Theodore Dreiser described Chicago's streetcar network as "the parasite Gold Thread" linking the city's neighborhoods and draining the pockets of its citizens.

In the largest cities the elevated railroads offered an alternate means of transportation to the city center. With the surface thoroughfares clogged to capacity with trolleys, vans, carts, and pedestrians, some enterprising late-nineteenth-century capitalists decided to exploit the air space above the streets and build rail lines overhead. New York City's elevated lines had been carrying commuters since the 1870s, and by the beginning of the twentieth century 200 million people each year traveled on the city's overhead trains. More than one hundred miles of ugly tracks darkened the city streets below, testifying to New Yorkers' preference for mobility over beauty. In the 1890s Chicago followed New York's example, constructing a railway on stilts. In fact, the famous elevated "loop," completed in 1897, was to give downtown Chicago its nickname. Like the streetcars, the elevated lines converged on the Loop, transporting 100 million people annually at the dawn of the century.

By the first decade of the twentieth century, a new means of rapid transit, the subway, was pouring millions of additional commuters into the already congested urban centers of New York City, Boston, and Philadelphia. Boston pioneered underground transportation in the United States, opening its first subway line in 1897; New York City followed suit in 1904 and Philadelphia in 1905. Subway trains clearly outpaced surface trolleys, averaging fifteen miles an hour for local service and twenty-five miles an hour on express runs. As a result, an increasing number of commuters eschewed the surface lines, opting for travel overhead or underground. In 1912, some 665 million passengers traveled on the subways and elevated tracks of New York City, 50 percent more than the number that patronized the streetcars.

Yet complaints did not cease. Even with three levels of transportation, New Yorkers griped about the difficulty of traveling through the metropolis. "In view of the terrible conditions now existing on surface, elevated, and subway lines during rush hours," wrote an exasperated correspondent to the *Times* in 1910, "it is reasonable to predict that before relief comes conditions will be so appalling as to make city travel so vile and dangerous that none but the most hardy and reckless may attempt it." New York City, Boston, Chicago, and Philadelphia had the most technologically advanced and expansive transit facilities in the world; in each of these cities the populace enjoyed a rapid transit alternative to the surface streetcar. But each new advance in public transportation was met by an ever-greater demand. Although the populations of New York City and Chicago each increased only about 30 percent during the first decade of the twentieth century, the number of public transit passengers in these cities soared almost 100 percent. So, despite new facilities, the crowding persisted. And a large proportion of this commuting mob converged on the transportation hub of the city, the downtown.

Intercity railroads were another important channel to the central business district. During the first decades of the twentieth century, the railroad dominated long-distance transportation in the nation, and in most major cities the principal rail terminals were in or near the business core. These rail depots were the chief portals to the city for millions of visitors arriving on the endless stream of trains. By the close of the first decade of the century, Union Station in Saint Louis was handling 322 trains daily, Philadelphia's Broad Street depot recorded 574 each day, and the combined total of trains scheduled daily for Boston's North and South terminals was almost 1,400. At the peak period, between 7:00 and 8:30 A.M. each weekday when the commuter and overnight Pullman trains both converged on the city, Cincinnati's terminals handled seventy-four trains, approximately one per minute.

To accommodate this massive flow of traffic, the railroad companies constructed giant depots, monuments to the preeminence of the iron horse in American life. The greatest of these were the two New York giants, Pennsylvania Station, built 1906–10, and Grand Central Station, built 1907–13. Modeled after the Roman baths of Caracalla, Pennsylvania Station included an enormous waiting room, which was 800 feet long and had giant Corinthian columns supporting a vaulted ceiling that rose to a height of 150 feet. Grand Central Station was also a spacious temple to railroad travel, with a monumental vaulted waiting room and sixty-six tracks for passenger traffic, a number unequaled in the United States. Like Pennsylvania Station, it was an appropriately grand gateway to the nation's greatest city.

Leading into the urban terminals and skirting the central business districts were the railroad freight yards, and concentrated nearby were numerous factories, warehouses, and wholesalers. Such businesses needed to cluster near railroad yards or sidings, for the railroads delivered the raw materials and finished goods essential to their trade. Freight transfers by horse-drawn wagons were expensive, and as late as 1910 there were only eight hundred motor-driven trucks in all of Chicago. Therefore, proximity to the railroad lines meant transportation savings for the manufacturer and wholesaler, and nowhere did more freight lines meet than at the edge of the central business district. Some giant works could afford to locate in the suburbs and maintain their own freight yards, but for many entrepreneurs the central industrial zone adjacent to the downtown business district and the main railroad terminals proved the most profitable and desirable location.

The concentration of railroad lines in the city center also determined the location of the major hotels. Since most visitors arrived by rail, those in the hotel business naturally desired a site downtown with easy access to the depots. Suburban or rural retreats might attract summer tourists seeking an escape from the city, but the commercial traveler wanted a room near the rail terminals and near the downtown offices of prospective customers, clients, partners, or investors. Thus the early twentieth century was the heyday of the downtown hotel, and many hostelries vied for business by offering the ultimate in comfort and luxury. When New York City's Astoria Hotel opened its doors in 1897, the *Times* reported that guests "will be lodged and fed amid surroundings as gorgeous as those of king's palaces." The ladies reception room was "striking in its dainty Venetian columns," with curtains "in rich golden-brown velvet, embroidered à la Louis XV," and chairs "covered with cinnamon velvet and embroidered with the heavy gold designs of the First Empire." The main dining room was "strictly in the style of the Italian Renaissance with carved pilasters and columns of marble," and the walls were "paneled in rose Pompadour silk." In 1904 the new St. Regis Hotel challenged the magnificence of the Astoria. According to one reporter, the St. Regis was the "most richly furnished hotel in America"; it boasted a Palm Room "lighted by a skylight, supported by great marble arches," and along the walls were "rare tapestries and wonderful mural decorations." But few travelers were willing to pay the rates at the St. Regis, $8.00 a day and upward for a room and bath. After all, at Cleveland's first-rate Hotel Euclid, with a "long distance 'phone in every room," the rates for room and bath began at only $2.00 a day, and the Hotel Jefferson, "the largest and most fashionable hotel in St. Louis," charged $2.50 and up per day.

One of the great events in the hotel business during the first decade of the century was the construction of the massive LaSalle Hotel in

Chicago. Twenty-two stories high, it boasted 1,172 rooms and claimed to be the largest hotel building in the world. Together with Cleveland's Euclid and Saint Louis's Jefferson, Chicago's LaSalle serviced the millions of rail-borne visitors to the business core of America's cities. Catering to travelers from across the nation, each hotel contributed to the excitement and vitality of the downtown.

Adding to the glamor of the central business district were the theaters and vaudeville houses located within a few blocks of the leading hotels. With virtually all transit lines meeting downtown, no place was so accessible to the hordes of urban entertainment seekers as the city center. By 1910 thirty-eight theaters clustered in the vicinity of Broadway between Thirtieth and Forty-seventh streets in midtown Manhattan, attracting theater fans from the Bronx and Brooklyn as well as out-of-town visitors. That year theatrical producers offered the New York public a choice of 102 new nonmusical plays, 26 musical comedies, and 13 Shakespearean revivals. For those not attracted to the English bard, Florenz Ziegfeld presented his yearly "Follies." According to the *New York Times* reviewer, the 1911 version featured, as usual, "girls and glitter, music and rapid action," plus a blockbuster number set amid a "pretty vista of a California poppy field, with animated wheat shocks, and some extremely human-looking bumble bees."

Such theatrical fare was not limited to the nation's largest city. Cleveland claimed to have the largest and most beautiful theater west of New York City, the Hippodrome, seating 4,500. On opening night in 1907, the Cleveland mammoth offered "two big hippodramas," but it was constructed to handle everything from circuses to vaudeville shows to grand operas. Advertisements in the *Chicago Tribune* during Christmas week 1907 informed pleasure seekers of the vaudeville show at the Majestic, featuring the comedienne Elizabeth Murray, "the prima donna laughteroso of vaudeville," and Radie Furman, "the German comedienne, with broken language to burn, and consequently laughter a-plenty." Those seeking more serious entertainment could attend Chicago's Garrick Theatre and experience William Vaughan Moody's *The Great Divide,* proclaimed by critics as "the great American play." That same week in 1907, ads in the *Washington Post* attempted to entice capital-city theatergoers to "a melodrama of business life" entitled *Edna, The Pretty Typewriter* or to the "jolly Christmas bill" at Chase's Polite Vaudeville House.

Whereas the theaters were magnets attracting audiences to the city center each evening, the department stores exerted a similar pull on female shoppers during the day. Large retailers eager to maximize their patronage clustered near the transit crossroads of the city. At the beginning of the twentieth century most of this patronage was female: women made an estimated 80 percent of the retail purchases, whereas few adult male customers wandered beyond the men's clothing departments of the large stores. "Give the Lady What She Wants" was the slogan of Chicago's Marshall Field and Company, and such a philosophy proved profitable for giant retailers throughout the nation.

To attract women customers, the greatest retailers of the early twentieth century built magnificent stores with displays and facilities that were intended to make shopping a pleasure rather than a chore. In 1902 New York's Macy's opened its new store, offering twenty-three and a half acres of floor space, thirty-three elevators, escalators capable of transporting 40,000 people an hour, and a restaurant that seated 2,500 tired, hungry shoppers. Five years later Chicago's Marshall Field's opened its new building; with thirty-five acres of selling space it ranked as the nation's grandest emporium. Topping the six-story rotunda was a 6,000-square-foot Tiffany glass dome containing 1,600,000 pieces of iridescent glass; one art critic claimed it was "in a class with the nave of St. Peter's in Rome." At the gala grand opening the interior was festooned for an ancient-Roman-style "Feast of the Seasons." According to the store's advertisements in the *Chicago Tribune,* "the Main Aisle and Rotundas [will be] arranged as a 'Temple of Mercury'" and "the Window Displays, representing the principal historical periods of decorative art, will be by far the most beautiful we have ever shown, and of unusual educational and artistic interest." Completed in 1911, the new Wanamaker's Store in Philadelphia rivaled the grandeur of the Chicago giant. Its Grand Court surpassed the Field's rotundas in size, soaring 150 feet. An immense eagle from the Saint Louis World's Fair of 1904 decorated the Wanamaker court, and above in the gallery was one of the world's largest organs, with over thirty thousand pipes and the potential power of twenty-five brass bands. Like Marshall Field's, Wanamaker's was not simply a place to shop, it was a commercial palace glorifying the art of buying and selling.

The grandeur of Marshall Field's or Wanamaker's was primarily for the benefit of middle-class women with money to spend. For those less fortunate females who had to clerk at the giant emporiums, a day at the department store was a less pleasant experience. This was especially true of the cheaper, less reputable department stores, which were anxious to reduce overhead by cutting wages. At the turn of the century the Chicago sociologist Annie Marion MacLean worked two weeks during the Christmas season at two department stores and described the privations of the "working girl." For an average of only four to five dollars a week, saleswomen worked from 8:00 A.M. to 6:00 P.M. six days a week, and during the Christmas season MacLean and her colleagues stayed at the store "till eleven at night, with the exception of Christmas eve, when we worked until twelve." According to MacLean, many of the clerks turned to prostitution to supplement their meager incomes, and "the girls themselves said that more than a third of them were leading lives of shame."

While thousands of women tended department store counters, many others were finding employment as clerks and stenographers in the offices of the central business district. White-collar employment was booming in the banks, corporate headquarters, newsrooms, law offices, and accounting firms of the urban core; the number of stenographers and typists almost tripled between 1900 and 1910. To house the expanding offices, new buildings rose on every block of the central business district, some of them soaring twenty or thirty stories. The advent of steel-frame construction had ushered in the age of the skyscraper, and during the first decades of the twentieth century, these towering behemoths transformed the profile of downtown America.

As early as the 1890s, Chicago journalist George Ade observed that "there is nothing new in the prophecy that some day . . . every building in the business region will be at least twelve stories high, the streets will be so many cañons and the sunshine will filter down through crevices in the vast area of flat roofs." This prophecy was soon realized. By 1906, when the novelist Henry James sailed into New York harbor, the skyscrapers of Lower Manhattan already formed a striking if disorderly panorama. According to James, "the multitudinous skyscrapers standing up to the view, from the water," were "like extravagant pins in a cushion already overplanted, and stuck in as in the dark, anywhere and anyhow." In 1900 only six buildings in Manhattan rose more than 300 feet and none more than 400 feet. Eight years later the newly completed Singer Building soared more than 600 feet above the streets and work had begun on the 700-foot Metropolitan Life Tower. In 1913 the 792-foot Woolworth Building opened its doors; this gothic tower dominated the New York skyline until 1930. Nicknamed "the Cathedral of Commerce," the Woolworth Building, like the Metropolitan Life and Singer towers, was actually a monument to American competitive enterprise. Metropolitan Life wished to surpass the Singer tower in order to advertise the grandeur of its insurance business; Frank Woolworth sought to advertise his five-and-ten-cent stores through an even taller and more striking building. The jagged skyline of the city was a testament to the business aspirations of America. Each corporation sought to top the others, and each embodied its dreams in a soaring skyscraper.

But among the by-products of the skyscraper was stifling congestion. Thousands of workers toiled in the offices of each enormous
tower, and at rush hour the flow to and from the structures jammed
downtown thoroughfares. When an insurance company submitted
plans for a sixty-two-story, 909-foot skyscraper, one New York critic
complained that the building would generate such crowds that "people
would have to walk in three layers, one above the other." Moreover, the
structures cast long shadows, depriving nearby buildings of light and
air. With the convergence of transit lines in the central business district,
downtown congestion was already among the miseries of metropolitan
life. The skyscraper only stuffed ever greater numbers within the narrow confines of the clogged urban core.

Among the buildings standing within the shadow of the soaring
skyscrapers was City Hall. The complaints about skyscrapers were mild
compared to the scathing criticisms of those occupying offices in the
municipal building. In 1888 the British observer James Bryce had
claimed that "the government of cities is the one conspicuous failure of
the United States." Sixteen years later the journalist Lincoln Steffens
seconded Bryce's condemnation, referring to corrupt municipal government as "the shame of the cities." At the dawn of the century, few topics
generated so much discussion and so many editorials as city government.

Of all those occupying the chambers of City Hall, perhaps the most
maligned were the city councilmen. Elected by wards, the councilmen
were usually neighborhood politicians who devoted the bulk of their
time to winning favors for constituents. Outside of their wards, they enjoyed little social or economic distinction, and middle-class devotees of
good government viewed many councilmen with contempt. According
to Steffens, a grand jury investigating corruption in Saint Louis
reported that a number of that city's municipal legislators were "utterly
illiterate and lacking in ordinary intelligence. . . . In some, no trace of
mentality or morality could be found; in others, a low order of training
appeared, united with base cunning, groveling instincts, and sordid
desires." In truth, however, most were very ordinary small businessmen, no better or worse than the mass of the urban citizenry.

By the beginning of the twentieth century, in most major cities
the discredited council had lost ground to the executive branch headed
by the mayor. A figure of some citywide repute, the mayor enjoyed a
prestige that the council lacked, and he and his appointees were usually
the source of policy initiatives. Yet in some cities tales of corruption and
dirty politics even tarnished the mayor's office. In San Francisco,
Mayor Eugene Schmitz was under the thumb of the city's leading
political operator, Abe Ruef, and public utility companies eager for

favors from Schmitz and his cronies lined Ruef's pockets with bribes. New York City's mayor in 1900, Robert Van Wyck, was a toady of the Tammany political machine headed by Boss Richard Croker, and it was generally acknowledged that Croker and not Van Wyck ran the city. Van Wyck's successor, Seth Low, was a model of reform propriety and a foe of Tammany bossism. But he was also an icy patrician, unable to attract enough votes to win a second term as mayor. When, in 1903, the people of New York rejected Low and elected the candidate of the Tammany Democrats, a disgusted Theodore Roosevelt observed, "the dog has returned to his vomit."

Less vilified than the mayor or council was the emerging corps of professional bureaucrats entrenched at City Hall. Some municipal employees were political hacks enjoying a public salary only because of their devotion to the party machine. But many others were dedicated professionals whose first loyalty was to their bureau and not to any political party. By the first decade of the century the most powerful of these career civil servants could successfully stave off all political forays. In 1907 local newspapers regarded Seattle's city engineer, Reginald H. Thomson, as that city's "most powerful citizen," who could "make or unmake councilmen" and "even bring the mayor of the city on his knees, begging favors." Likewise, Boston's longtime health commissioner, Dr. Samuel H. Durgin, ruled his domain absolutely, and according to one contemporary, in clashes between the mayor and Durgin, "the mayor has invariably retreated and the head of the Health Department has remained unmolested if not undisturbed." San Francisco's park superintendent, John McLaren, also broached no political interference during his more than half a century in office. He boasted that "the parks of San Francisco were built by gardeners and not by politicians." Each of these figures was an appointed official with a firm and unbending devotion to achieving his professional goals. Although the spotlight of public scrutiny was more often focused on such elected leaders as the mayor or the councilmen, these bureaucrats were among the most significant molders of municipal policy.

The mayor, the councilmen, and the bureaucrats all gathered at City Hall, and from that command post in the heart of the city coordinated the complex government of the metropolis. They were in charge of the thousands of miles of sewer lines, the reservoirs, pumping stations, and mains that constituted the municipal water system, and the thousands of persons employed in the fire department, police force, and sanitation corps. Amid the chorus of complaints, few citizens expressed an appreciation of the magnitude of municipal efforts or the quality of the services provided. There were rumors of payoffs, and, in the eyes of upper-middle-class advocates of good government, the plebeian municipal legislators seemed vulgar and uncouth. But water flowed from distant reservoirs into urban kitchens and bathrooms, fire brigades extinguished thousands of fires each year, urban residents could enjoy the pleasures of municipal parks each summer weekend, and municipal libraries put books into the hands of millions of readers. At the beginning of the twentieth century City Hall was the headquarters for an array of vital and impressive services.

City Hall, soaring skyscrapers, Marshall Field's and Macy's, glittering theaters, mammoth hotels, cavernous rail terminals, and a dense tangle of streetcar lines – all were part of the downtown scene. In the early twentieth century, the downtown was truly the business heart of the metropolis, the source of the city's commercial lifeblood, pumping income into the pockets of urban householders. It was also the center of city government and the place where public policy was made. And it was the transportation hub, where managers, workers, shoppers, and pleasure seekers from all sections of the metropolis crossed paths. This hub belonged to no single class or group; it was nobody's neighborhood. For some the department store displays, gilded theaters, and luxurious hotels were treasures for the hope chest of ambition, to be enjoyed once the striving dreamers had made their fortunes; for others the riches of Marshall Field's and the pleasures of the Astoria Hotel were immediately attainable symbols of the prosperous life. For many the skyscraper was a vertical factory, consuming the daylight hours of each workday; for Frank Woolworth it was a monument to personal success. But no matter what the perspective, the downtown was a shared experience, holding together the varied fragments of the metropolis. Beyond the railroad yards and the ring of wholesale houses and factories on the downtown periphery lay another facet of urban America – the diverse neighborhoods, clashing chords of a dissonant city.

THE NEIGHBORHOODS

At the turn of the century, a tour through the city's neighborhoods offered the visitor a startling array of sights, sounds, smells, and experiences. On leaving the central business district one found a social, economic, and ethnic checkerboard with some squares rich and others poor, some squares black and others white, some squares German and others Czech. Flophouse transients clustered along skid row, only a few short miles from the mansions of the nation's wealthiest families. Saloons and brothels lined streets in lower-class districts, whereas middle-class purity and sobriety prevailed in nearby suburbs. In the city's neighborhoods the cultural fissures in urban society were obvious. Railroad tracks, rivers, and ravines often marked the boundaries of districts that had little in common. To cross these barriers and move from one neighborhood to the next was to travel between alien worlds.

For those who reaped the economic bounty of urban America, the city offered imitation castles along tree-lined boulevards. In every major city there was a mansion district, where local millionaires lived in massive stone residences vaguely reminiscent of French chateaus, Norman keeps, or baroque palaces. The mile and a half of upper Fifth Avenue between Fifty-ninth and Ninetieth streets was millionaire's row in New York City. Along this avenue lived the who's who of American business — the Astors, Goulds, Fricks, Whitneys, and Carnegies. The most grossly magnificent of the mansions was the ostentatious white granite pile built by copper king William Clark. With 130 rooms, it offered all the living space and pretentious ornament a millionaire could desire. Commenting on the flamboyant vulgarity of the Clark mansion, one critic observed: "If . . . architecture is frozen music, this edifice is frozen ragtime discord." A block north of Clark's palace was Harry Payne Whitney's residential tribute to enormous wealth. Completed in 1900, the Whitney house could count among its treasures a seventeenth-century ballroom imported from France and eleven marble bathtubs, including one in rose pink.

The hub of New York society, however, was Mrs. William Astor's chateau at Sixty-fifth Street and Fifth Avenue. Mrs. Astor was the queen of New York's elite, and the high point of the social season was her annual ball on the second Monday of each January. For example, in 1905 about six hundred of New York's elite descended on the Astor mansion after attending the opera or dinner parties. Arriving between 11:00 P.M. and midnight, they passed through the huge foyer in which, according to the *New York Times,* "scarlet blossoms of the poinsettia . . . and Easter lilies were banked, while the tall, round columns had palms at their bases, and higher were encircled by innumerable clusters of white or pink roses." Guests proceeded to the French drawing room, where Mrs. Astor received them dressed in "an exquisite French creation of deep purple velvet" and bedecked with a diamond tiara, a diamond "dog collar" around her neck, "a large corsage ornament of diamonds," and a diamond stomacher once owned by Marie Antoinette. After an hour of dancing in the famous Astor picture gallery, supper was served at 1:00 A.M., followed by the cotillion at 2:00 A.M. In the course of the evening the guests received special party favors that included everything from "decorated Directoire canes" to "May poles trimmed with ribbons" to "decorative auto horns." It was full night for New York's wealthiest, but they came away from the event knowing they had enjoyed the social imprimatur of the city's haughtiest hostess.

New York, however, had no monopoly on "society." During the late nineteenth century Chicago's Prairie Avenue between Sixteenth and Twenty-second streets on the near south side was a haven of wealth comparable to New York's Fifth Avenue; socialite Arthur Meeker referred to it as "the Sunny Street that held the Sifted Few." At the turn of the century such millionaires as Marshall Field and George Pullman, of Pullman sleeping car fame, still resided on this plutocratic avenue, but the center of society was shifting to the north side thoroughfares along the shore of Lake Michigan. In 1882 real estate tycoon Potter Palmer chose the north side as the site for his extravagant castle, and during the next two decades the French chateaus of other millionaires arose nearby along Chicago's Gold Coast.

Ushering in a new era in ostentatious living, Chicago's first apartment house for millionaires opened in 1906 along Lake Shore Drive on the near north side. It contained eight apartments, each with twelve rooms, five bathrooms, a greenhouse, a silver vault, and a wine closet. Each apartment rented for $4,200 a year in an age when most laborers made no more than $500 annually and when handsome middle-class houses sold for $5,000. Yet at first some of Chicago's elite regarded apartment living as déclassé. Even after World War I Meeker's upper-crust family had some doubts about tenancy in a multiunit tower: "In the beginning Father didn't like it; he felt that, in spite of twelve rooms and five baths, it was a step down in the world to share a roof and front door with seven other families." But "Mother liked it very much; she said it was like living in an hotel; enjoyed exploring her kitchen, a room she'd never seen before, and took to coming in a négligée to the breakfast table." For scores of wealthy Chicagoans doubts about apartment living had vanished by the close of the century's second decade, and a file of luxurious high rises along Lake Michigan testified to the popularity of the new lifestyle.

Although not every urban area could claim the wealth of New York or Chicago, cities throughout America boasted their own versions of the Gold Coast or Fifth Avenue. In Saint Louis the rich clustered around the city's exclusive "places." Massive and forbidding gates marked the entrances to these places, warning plebeians that plutocratic territory lay beyond. Within the gates mansions lined a semiprivate median park jointly maintained by the place's residents. To ensure that only the wealthy could build within the privileged subdivisions, the developers of Westmoreland and Portland places fixed the minimum cost of houses at $25,000 and the minimum frontage of building lots at one hundred feet. Writing in *House and Garden,* one admirer of these restricted enclaves of wealth claimed that the place "imparts a measure of privacy to home life that is highly desirable in these days of glaring publicity, and serves to protect a neighborhood from the many annoyances that necessarily surround localities where restrictions do not obtain."

Elsewhere, gateways did not mark off the neighborhoods of the wealthy, but the social boundaries within the city were just as evident. At the beginning of the century, Boston's Back Bay remained synonymous with wealth, although some Brahmins were already leaving for the suburbs. Likewise, Philadelphia's Rittenhouse Square was still the geographic center of riches in Pennsylvania's largest city, although it, too, would lose much of its eminence by World War I. In Atlanta, the homes of the wealthy lined Peachtree Street; in Cleveland, Euclid Avenue housed the plutocrats at the turn of the century; and in Buffalo, Delaware Avenue was the fashionable address. In every city there was a "Sunny Street that held the Sifted Few," a district that denoted material success and social standing. And in every city there were clubs, balls, banquets, and teas where the sifted few gathered. The plutocratic subculture of urban America was alive and well at the beginning of the twentieth century.

Yet there were millions of Americans who were financially comfortable but not rich enough to pass through the social sifter and enter the front door of Mrs. Astor's mansion. These coarser grains formed the middle class. Doctors, lawyers, dentists, accountants, smaller merchants, and modest manufacturers could all be found along the avenues of middle-class neighborhoods in the early twentieth century. Some were on the verge of "society," whereas others were only one step from the working class, but they shared certain common characteristics. They held white-collar positions and their income was sufficient to enable them to purchase a home or rent a comfortable apartment. Moreover, they sought to protect their well-appointed households from "undesirable" influences, preferring an ethnically and morally pure environment for themselves and their children. But unlike the very wealthy, they did not enjoy independent means, nor did they maintain their own private carriages or possess that plaything of the rich, the motorcar. Like the working class, they had to go to work each weekday, and during at least the first decade of the twentieth century they were still dependent on public transit lines. Therefore, the ideal middle-class neighborhood was a district of owner-occupied, detached homes convenient to transit lines providing easy access to the central business district, yet free of the saloon, the brothel, and the working-class alien.

For many middle-class Americans the emerging ring of suburbs seemed best fitted to these requirements. According to the Draper Realty Company's advertisements in the *New York Times,* "Oakland," a "restricted residential park" in the borough of Queens, offered much for those in the upper middle class. Formerly "the fine old country estate of Effingham Lawrence — a Country Gentleman," it provided "small country estates from one-fourth to one acre" for those who yearned to be country gentlemen but could not quite afford the privilege. Moreover, it was only "a cool, comfortable 18 minute trip from Herald Square on the new Penn. R.R. Just long enough for running through the morning paper." Its promoters believed that "no other location has so many advantages to offer in natural beauty, exclusiveness or accessibility to the business centre of Manhattan." And beauty, exclusiveness, and accessibility were all that members of the upper middle class desired.

In the real estate listings of the *Tribune,* middle-class Chicagoans could likewise read about the advantages of suburban neighborhoods. In 1906 the Proviso Land Association in the "ideal suburb" of Maywood offered six- to nine-room houses at prices "so reasonable that any man now paying $25 or more per month rent can in a short time own his own home." Moreover, the land association advertised that "building restrictions protect purchasers against flats or squatters' huts." The Maplewood subdivision in suburban Riverside also offered "lots with uniform building restrictions" only twenty-three minutes by train from the Loop. And the River Forest Land Association urged middle-class Chicagoans to build their own homes "under the great oaks and magnificent elms" of River Forest, a community of "good schools" only a five-cent fare from the heart of the city.

The sales pitches of the Draper Realty Company, the Proviso Land Association, and other developers found a ready audience during the first decades of the twentieth century, and many thousands migrated outward to the new suburban neighborhoods. Between 1900 and 1915 the population of the island of Manhattan in the heart of New York City increased less than 16 percent, whereas the population of the borough of Queens soared 160 percent. From 1900 to 1910 the population of the core area of Boston known as Boston proper rose only 9 percent, whereas the number of persons living in the outlying neighborhood of Dorchester soared 52 percent, and the populace of the independent suburban municipality of Brookline increased by almost 40 percent. Similarly, during the first decade of the century the population of that "ideal suburb" of Maywood rose by almost 80 percent, while thousands of other Chicago area residents transplanted themselves to the shaded streets of Oak Park or to Evanston, the "city of homes."

But the happiness and tranquillity of the urban middle class depended on the continued purity of their neighborhoods. The presence of the saloon, with its clientele of undesirable foreigners, could supposedly ruin a residential district, destroy property values, and endanger the morality of middle-class youth. Thus middle-class urbanites fought to exclude corrupt influences from their neighborhoods and in the process divided the metropolis into distinct zones of morality.

Chicago's Hyde Park Protective Association was among the most vigorous groups dedicated to ensuring neighborhood purity. Hyde Park was an upper-middle-class district on Chicago's South Side, and at the turn of the century 60 percent of its population was born in the United States of native-born American parents, double the proportion for the city as a whole. Under the state's local option laws prospective liquor dealers in Hyde Park had to secure the approval of a majority of the property owners, tenants, and businesses on both sides of the street in the block where the saloon was to operate. With dogged devotion the protective association tried to guarantee that no rum seller seeking to locate in Hyde Park obtained sufficient signatures. Largely successful, the protective association spawned antiliquor efforts in other Chicago neighborhoods, and from 1894 the Chicago City Council passed a series of ordinances defining certain residential districts as off-limits to saloons. According to a leader of the Hyde Park Protective Association, even saloonkeepers wanted to keep the barroom away from their homes and families. In a letter printed in the *Tribune,* this foe of alcohol claimed that one liquor dealer had admitted to him: "If I had a family to raise I would go ten miles to raise it in a prohibition district. There is no influence so bad for children as the saloon and the people who frequent it."

Many Americans were traveling ten miles each day to avoid living in communities subject to the taint of the saloon. One of the attractions of the independent suburban municipalities ringing the major cities was that they were usually "dry," whereas the central cities were "wet." With the exception of working-class Chelsea, every suburban municipality surrounding Boston prohibited saloons. If the residents of Newton, Brookline, and Cambridge had wanted to frequent a barroom, they would have had to board a streetcar and head for Boston, where whiskey taps still flowed at the corner tavern. Likewise, the suburban municipalities adjoining Chicago generally excluded alcohol, and the suburb of Evanston was the headquarters of the Women's Christian

Temperance Union. Middle-class Americans moved to elm-lined suburban streets in the hope of raising their families away from the uglier side of urban life. For the sake of their children and their property values, they did not want the barroom or bordello to follow them to their shaded retreat.

Most urban Americans, however, did not have the option of buying a single-family dwelling in a restricted outlying neighborhood free of saloons, apartments, and squatters' huts. In fact, home ownership was a privilege enjoyed by only a minority of urban householders. In 1900 in Chicago, Baltimore, Pittsburgh, and Minneapolis, 25 to 30 percent of all homes were owner-occupied, whereas the unusually high figures for Detroit, Cleveland, and Milwaukee ranged from 35 to 40 percent. By contrast, owners occupied 12 percent of New York City's homes. The great majority of urban Americans, especially those in the working class, rented living space; they could not afford to do otherwise.

Thus working-class urbanites did not migrate to owner-occupied homes in the new suburban "Parks," "Heights," and "Gardens" that were proliferating along the metropolitan fringe. Most remained nearer the heart of the city so that some family members could walk to work while others took advantage of the denser web of transit lines crisscrossing the older, more centrally located neighborhoods. Although some workers were able to purchase modest inner-city dwellings, most lacked the requisite capital, so they rented their rooms instead.

Many of the working-class neighborhoods had a distinctive ethnic identity. During the first decade of the twentieth century the Pilsen district on Chicago's west side was almost entirely Czech. Here Czech-language newspapers were published, church services were conducted in Czech, and restaurants offered Czech food. Yiddish was the common language in the Chicago neighborhood centering on the corner of Halsted and Maxwell streets; about 90 percent of the residents of the surrounding blocks were Jewish. More than forty Orthodox synagogues clustered in the district, caring for the spiritual needs of the residents. Meanwhile, the jam of peddlers, stalls, and pushcarts along Maxwell Street served the commercial wants of the Jewish neighborhood. According to social worker Edith Abbott, "On Sunday the [Maxwell Street] market became a fair, with peddlers of all sorts thronging into the streets at sunrise, and dealers buying stocks from rag-pickers and hucksters. . . . Stall after stall was piled with strange garments supplied from dark basement storerooms." As one traveled north on Halsted Street, Yiddish gave way to Italian, and by 1910 one could also hear a smattering of Greek. Here there were no synagogues, only the Roman

Catholic parishes of Guardian Angel Church and Our Lady of Pompeii. Here residents turned to *L'Italia* and *La Tribuna Italiana Transatlantica* for their news. Here were the lodges of the Unione Siciliana and the meeting places of scores of Italian mutual aid societies that ensured their immigrant members help in time of illness as well as a proper funeral and burial.

During the first decades of the twentieth century, however, this bastion of Italian culture was gradually forced to accommodate a growing number of Greek newcomers. In the vicinity of Halsted Street, on the near west side, the Greek district known as the "Delta" was expanding; it would become the largest Greek settlement in the United States. According to one visitor to the neighborhood, "practically all stores bear signs in both Greek and English, coffee houses flourish on every corner, in dark little grocery stores one sees black olives, dried ink-fish, tomato paste, and all the queer, nameless roots and condiments which are so familiar in Greece." A trip along Chicago's Halsted Street offered a Cook's tour of the world's cultures. One witnessed the life of refugees from Eastern European Jewish ghettos, passed on to the alien culture of Italy, and proceeded to the Greek Delta, where yet other strange sights, sounds, and smells assaulted the senses. Nowhere was the polyglot nature of the American city so evident.

Traveling down South State Street in Chicago, one entered the neighborhood of yet another ethnic minority, the blacks. This was the territory of the Olivet Baptist Church and the Bethel A.M.E. congregation, and residents here read the *Chicago Defender,* an outspoken organ of racial protest. In 1910 only 2 percent of Chicago's population was black compared to almost 9 percent of Russian birth or parentage and 20 percent of German birth or parentage. But the black population was growing more rapidly than the white, increasing by 46 percent between 1900 and 1910 and 148 percent between 1910 and 1920.

Other cities could match the ethnic diversity of Chicago. The Lower East Side of Manhattan housed thousands of immigrants from eastern and southern Europe. Hester Street, New York City's version of Maxwell Street, was the heart of the Jewish quarter, with a multitude of stalls and pushcarts known to the outside world as the Pig Market because anything could be purchased there but pork. In 1910 only 91,000 blacks lived in New York City, compared to an estimated 1,050,000 Jews and 544,000 Italians. Yet, as in Chicago, the rate of black migration from the South was increasing, and during the second decade of the twentieth century the Harlem district of Manhattan became the center of Afro-American life in the nation's largest city. In Philadelphia there were three main areas of Jewish settlement on the city's near north and near south sides, and the focus of Philadelphia's black community was immediately southwest of the central business district. Meanwhile, in Milwaukee, Poles dominated the south side, Germans prevailed on the west side, and the minority of Milwaukeans born of English-speaking parents were most commonly found on the east side. In some major cities, such as Columbus, Indianapolis, Kansas City, and Los Angeles, a majority of the residents were native-born and of native parentage. But most of the nation's largest cities were agglomerations of people from throughout the world, speaking in foreign tongues and only partially adapted to Yankee customs.

Few working-class immigrant neighborhoods were ghettos, where newcomers to America remained trapped from birth until death. Instead, many immigrants left the old neighborhoods, moving to better housing in areas where they accommodated the culture of the "old country" to the lifestyle of America. Between 1905 and 1915 an estimated two-thirds of the Jews living on New York's Lower East Side left the neighborhood, migrating to the northern reaches of Manhattan, to the Bronx, or to Brooklyn. After 1910 blacks, Slavs, and Italians began to encroach on Chicago's Maxwell Street area, and the neighborhood's Jews quickly dispersed to new hubs of settlement farther from the city's center. Elsewhere, Germans were giving way to Czechs, and Czechs to Italians and Poles. Some static centers of ethnic culture remained where the old language and lifestyle resisted outside encroachments. But the ethnic map of America's cities was not unchanging, and for most groups ethnic diversity did not result in a fixed pattern of neighborhood apartheid.

For one group, however, the barriers to residential mobility were especially formidable. During the early twentieth century blacks did conquer Harlem, pushing Jewish residents farther north. They were also able to claim other territorial acquisitions. But black pioneers dedicated to expanding the frontiers of Afro-American settlement had to summon all their ingenuity, perseverance, and courage to combat those whites who found black mobility especially threatening and undesirable. For example, white residents of Chicago's Hyde Park neighborhood not only sought to exclude liquor, they also fought the influx of Afro-Americans. Organized in 1908, the Hyde Park Improvement Protective Club pressured real estate agents to sell property in white-occupied blocks only to whites. The club's president announced emphatically, "The districts which are now white must remain white. There will be no compromise."

The city council of Baltimore agreed with such sentiments and in 1910 enacted an ordinance forbidding any black person from moving into a block where a majority of the residents were white. That year four black families had taken up residence in a previously all-white block of McCulloh Street in Baltimore. According to the author of the ordinance, white hoodlums from the neighborhood had rampaged, and "window-glasses of the negroes' houses were broken with stones; skylights were caved in by bricks, descending bomb-like from the sky; there were mutterings of plots to blow up the houses; in short we were on the verge of riot." Supposedly to avoid such violence, Baltimore's council enacted the residential segregation ordinance, bolstering the city's racial divisions with the force of law. Within a few years, the city councils of Louisville, Atlanta, Birmingham, Richmond, Dallas, and New Orleans followed the example of Baltimore. In 1917 the United States Supreme Court held the residential segregation ordinances unconstitutional, but the actions of Baltimore's city fathers were indicative of the obstacles to black mobility.

Whether because of racial discrimination or economic necessity, many urban Americans were forced to live at least temporarily in drab, decaying neighborhoods near the urban core. In the eyes of most middle-class observers, these less-fortunate urbanites suffered from deplorable overcrowding and shocking sanitary conditions. In 1900 New York City's Tenth Ward on the Lower East Side comprised 109 acres and housed 76,000 tenement dwellers, or 700 people per acre. Five- and six-story tenements covered 80 to 90 percent of the ground space of the narrow city lots, and most of the windows opened on narrow air shafts that transmitted odors from floor to floor but provided little light or ventilation. Accounts of sanitary conditions in the crowded buildings shocked many middle-class citizens accustomed to modern plumbing and devoted to cleanliness. According to the *First Report of the Tenement House Department,* one New York inspector investigated the odors emanating from a tenement and found the "entire cellar floor covered with a putrid slime; imbedded therein were various kinds of organic matter in every stage of decomposition, together with dead cats, dead rats, and the skeleton remains of several small animals." Another reported that "the woodwork around the sinks in the apartments [was] so foul, rotten and saturated from long usage that it was absolutely impossible for me to remain more than three minutes, on account of the stench that emitted therefrom."

In other places the findings were similar. Although Chicago's tenements were typically only two stories tall, an investigator of housing conditions in that city claimed that the population density in the Polish quarter was "three times that of the most crowded portions of Tokyo, Calcutta, and many other Asiatic cities." Three or four people vied for sleeping space in tiny tenement rooms, and Chicago housing reformers discovered cases of "five people sleeping in one bed." A student of housing in Philadelphia reported primly: "It may be asserted that a fairly large part of the working classes is compelled to use toilet accommodations in a condition of which the rest of the world would be unwilling to hear in full." An investigator in Baltimore was more specific when she reported on a block occupied by 330 people: "There are no toilet accommodations in the block beside the 30 yard privies, the vaults of which were in thirteen instances recorded as 'full.'" And she found that "for five houses on Hughes street only four [privies] were provided. The two families in the fifth house have to use the privies of the adjacent houses, or, as an inmate expressed it, 'We ketches what we can.'"

Not only did middle-class observers view with horror the sanitary conditions of many working-class neighborhoods, they also found the moral climate of such districts disturbing. In 1890 the crusading New York journalist Jacob Riis said of the saloon, "Wherever the tenements thicken, it multiplies. Upon the direst poverty . . . it grows fat and prosperous." Others also complained of the prevalence of saloons in poor neighborhoods. At the turn of the century sociologist Charles Bushnell found that there were over 500 saloons for the 120,000 working-class residents of Chicago's Stockyard district, but in upper-middle-class Hyde Park, a nearby neighborhood of 65,000, there were only 21 drinking establishments. Bushnell suggested disdainfully that "men who strike for higher wages, without any resolve to reform their drink habits, would sometimes do well to reflect on this situation." Another pioneering sociologist, Royal Melendy, studied the 163 saloons in Chicago's working-class Seventeenth Ward and uncovered "the appalling fact that 34½ percent of the saloons in this district are stall saloons" with "private 'wine-rooms,' which . . . are used by prostitutes as places of assignation." Moreover, "almost without exception the saloons exhibit pictures of the nude."

Yet Melendy recognized that the neighborhood saloon offered workers relaxation and enjoyment, a refuge from the squalid tenement or lodging house, and relief after a day at the mill. At the saloon workingmen could play cards, shoot pool, discuss politics, gather for trade union or fraternal meetings, obtain information about job openings, and, at some of the larger establishments, enjoy a vaudeville show. In addition 111 of the 163 saloons in Chicago's Seventeenth Ward offered free lunches as a lure to attract customers. The free lunch counters served bread, cheeses, vegetables, and several kinds of meat. Much of the fare was salty or highly spiced to cause thirst, but for workers living on a meager wage the free lunch was a popular feature of the saloon.

At the turn of the century, working-class saloons often were centers of neighborhood politics. As the principal meeting place of the male electorate, the saloon was a prime site for politicking. Even an upper-class politician such as Cincinnati's William Howard Taft advised young men interested in politics to "get acquainted . . . with the saloonkeepers. . . . In the city [the saloonkeeper] is the proprietor of the social club of his neighborhood." A disproportionate number of saloonkeepers actually entered politics, and at the turn of the century one-third of Milwaukee's city councilmen operated bars, as did about a third of Detroit's aldermen. During the first decade of the twentieth century, reform foes of the liquor interests attempted with some success to check the political clout of the rum seller, but at the neighborhood level the saloon remained a popular site for partisan activity. And in the minds of middle-class reformers the saloon remained a symbol of the often disreputable character of ward politics.

The sins of the average neighborhood saloon were mild, however, compared to the evils lurking in the vice districts of America's major cities. New York City's Tenderloin and Bowery, Chicago's Levee, and San Francisco's Barbary Coast were representative of the red-light districts found throughout the nation. Just as the Astors and their friends resided in one segment of the metropolis and the middle class and working class each could claim its own neighborhoods, so the prostitutes, pimps, and gamblers inhabited a distinctive enclave within the city. In the diverse, fragmented metropolis of the early twentieth century, every element possessed a domain.

Chicago's Levee was probably the most notorious red-light district in the nation. Lying a mile south of the Loop, it offered virtually every form of bawdy and illicit entertainment. Gambling houses, dance halls, saloons, pawnshops, and penny arcades lined the streets, but the chief attraction was the more than two hundred brothels, including such establishments as the French Elm, where mirrors covered the walls, and the House of All Nations, which offered patrons women of a dozen nationalities. The showplace of the Levee was the Everleigh Club, an elegant brothel operated by two southern belles, Ada and Minna Everleigh. Dedicated to providing quality service, the sisters demanded high standards of etiquette from their young women and instructed them to "be polite and forget what you are here for." Visitors to the Everleigh Club could revel amid the exotic elegance of Moorish, Japanese, Egyptian, and Chinese parlors or enjoy the opulence of the Silver, Copper, or Gold rooms, the last annually refinished in lustrous gold leaf. The Everleigh sisters did not lavish these surroundings on any lustful male who sought admittance; they firmly refused to deal with the "rough element, the clerk on a holiday or a man without a checkbook." And when the German Kaiser's brother visited Chicago he was guest of honor at a dinner at the Everleigh Club.

New Orleans's Storyville district ranked with the Levee as a fount of illicit pleasure. Concerned about the spread of vice throughout the city during the 1890s, New Orleans's reform alderman Sidney Story sponsored an ordinance restricting prostitution to a specifically defined area adjacent to the central business district and the French Quarter. Much to Story's disgust, the district soon bore his name. More than seven hundred prostitutes, both black and white, plied their craft in this district, and some of the finest brothels rivaled the Everleigh Club. The Arlington, for example, advertised that it was "absolutely and unquestionably the most decorative and costly fitted-out sporting palace ever placed before the American public," and within its walls were "the work of great artists from Europe and America" as well as "curios galore."

In the minds of many observers, the gilt and curios of the brothels only thinly masked the hideous reality of the vice district. Robert Hunter, a middle-class student of Chicago's poor, described the habitués of the Levee as "morally insane," persons "who fail utterly in conceiving a single thought which is not vile, or an image which is not unspeakable." Near the lavish Everleigh Club were the "opium dens or hop-joints . . . hidden away behind Chinese laundries or in dark and apparently empty basement rooms under the pavements." Likewise, there were "five and ten cent museums with highly colored pictures, of an immoral sort, or illustrative of some horrible monstrosity" intended to arouse the "interest of the jaded, callous, and deadened denizens and visitors of the district." Sneak thieves and pickpockets abounded. The Rand McNally guide wisely suggested that tourists entrust their "valuables with the clerk of [their] hotel" before embarking on an expedition to the Levee. For high-minded investigators from Hyde Park or the North Shore, the Levee was the darkest blot on the reputation of the Windy City.

Equally depressing to many were the skid row neighborhoods of America's cities. In these cheap lodging-house districts gathered the losers of the economic game, men and women forced to sleep in missions, in five-cent-a-night flophouses, and on the sidewalks or in doorways. On a research expedition, Royal Melendy spent the night in a large flophouse dormitory with "100 two-story iron bedsteads," a night of "indescribable horror" made memorable by the "groans and occasional piercing cries of the wretched victims in the first clutches of the tremens, the hacking cough of the consumptive," and "the unbearable stench of the syphilitic." Likewise, Robert Hunter visited a lodging house that rented beds for two cents a night. The beds were actually wooden shelves where men slept together on the bare boards without any covering. According to this envoy from the comfortable life of middle-class America, "the animalism and despicable foulness and filth made one almost despair of mankind." In Chicago alone an estimated thirty-thousand impoverished transients lived in such conditions, and in every major city there were thousands more who endured similar hardship.

Yet these transients slept only a few miles from the Potter Palmer mansion and "the Sunny Street that held the Sifted Few." In fact, within a radius of a dozen miles were neighborhoods representing every rung on the social ladder. There were the gilded quarters of the wealthy, the shaded avenues of the comfortable, the raucous street markets of immigrant Jews, the parishes of the Poles and the Italians and the brothels of the madams. Ill-assorted and clashing, the diverse neighborhoods of the city clustered around a downtown hub, linked to it by the centripetal transit lines that tied the metropolis together.

The city was thus segregated, with each fragment pursuing its own social, religious, and cultural life. But the disparities among the fragments troubled some citizens, who dreamed of an urban community that shared more than a transit system, a central business district, and a common waterworks. The goal of these concerned individuals was to create a city free of poverty, prostitution, alcohol, ignorance, corruption, congestion, and ugliness — a homogenized community cleansed of wrong that would share a vision of the good life. During the early years of the century, righting the urban wrongs became a passion of these earnest reformers.

RIGHTING THE URBAN WRONGS

Historians have labeled the first two decades of the twentieth century the Progressive Era, an age of enthusiasm for reform as many Americans sought to right the wrongs of a newly industrialized society. Nowhere was this flowering of reform so evident as in the large cities. In New York City, Chicago, and San Francisco, the problems of irresponsible wealth and devastating poverty were juxtaposed in such glaring contrast, and the ethnic, cultural, and moral divisions were so sharply drawn, that reform-minded people felt compelled to take action. Rapid urbanization and unprecedented industrialization had produced a city of ill-fitting parts, but many who enjoyed the comfort, security, and self-confidence associated with middle- or upper-class status believed that they could refashion the city, creating a better, less divided urban community. Their efforts resulted in that series of projects, programs, and policies known as urban progressivism.

Among the most idealistic and influential of the progressive projects was the settlement house. Settlement houses were community centers in the slums with living accommodations for middle-class volunteers who hoped not only to teach their impoverished neighbors but also to learn from them. According to its constitution, New York City's University Settlement aimed "to bring men and women of education into closer relations with the laboring classes for their mutual benefit," and a Chicagoan viewed his settlement as "a common center where representatives of the masses and classes could meet and mingle as fellow men." In other words, the settlement was an attempt to bridge the widening gap between the middle class and the working class by making both groups aware of the concerns and merits of the other. To achieve this goal, settlement workers provided the slum dwellers with an attractive haven from tenement life where they could organize clubs, hold meetings, enroll in classes, or gather for informal socializing at the settlement's alcohol-free coffeehouse. Once the poor were attracted to the warmth and comfort of the settlement, the more affluent volunteers could become better acquainted with them and acquire an understanding of the working class that was not available along Fifth Avenue and Prairie Avenue or in Hyde Park and Brookline.

In 1886 an idealistic Amherst graduate, Stanton Coit, founded the first settlement in the United States, New York's Neighborhood Guild. Three years later a young Wellesley English instructor, Vida Scudder, was instrumental in the establishment of the College Settlement on Manhattan's Lower East Side, and in that same year the most famous settlement worker, Jane Addams, introduced the settlement house idea to Chicago, where she founded Hull House. By 1900 there were more than one hundred settlements across the country; five years later the number exceeded two hundred; and in 1910 there were over four hundred.

Many members of the growing corps of settlement workers used their new-found knowledge of working-class problems to lobby for reform legislation aimed at upgrading factory conditions, improving housing standards, and limiting the power of corrupt ward bosses. Moreover, labor union organizers used the settlements for their meetings, and leaders like Jane Addams defended the rights of laborers seeking higher wages and shorter working hours. Yet settlements also encouraged the organization of social clubs that aped the manners of the middle and upper classes and adopted such romantic names as the Rosebud, the Lady Aroma, the Lady Belvedere, and the Four Hundred

Social. Some criticized the prolabor sentiments of the settlement worker, but the Four Hundred Social and the Lady Aroma hardly posed a threat to bourgeois preeminence.

In fact, many who believed in more radical action attacked the tea-and-sympathy approach of the settlement. One critic described the settlement as "young ladies with weak eyes and young gentlemen with weak chins flittering confused among heterogeneous foreigners offering cocoa and sponge cake as a sort of dessert to the factory system." The caustic economist Thorstein Veblen claimed "the solicitude of settlements . . . is in part directed to enhance the industrial efficiency of the poor . . . but it is also no less consistently directed to incubation . . . of certain punctilios of upper-class propriety in manners and customs." Describing Jane Addams and her colleagues as members of "a race of successful and predatory bipeds who stand between the worker and his wages," the Socialist novelist Jack London said of settlement workers that "beyond relieving an infinitesimal fraction of misery and collecting a certain amount of data . . . , they have achieved nothing." But many thousands of volunteers and donors felt otherwise; they willingly gave their time and money in the hope of forging new links between the social fragments of the metropolis.

While settlement workers sought to create a pleasant refuge from the slum dwelling, other reformers concentrated on upgrading the physical condition of the lower-class abode. In New York City the Tenement House Committee of the Charity Organization Society and its dynamic secretary Lawrence Veiller led the movement for housing reform. To arouse public concern Veiller organized a tenement exhibition in 1900, complete with charts, tables, maps, diagrams, photographs, and a cardboard model of an entire tenement block on the Lower East Side. For those comfortable New Yorkers who had never visited the city's slums Veiller's maps pinpointing the location of tuberculosis victims and charity applicants graphically demonstrated the problems of the other half of society. The following year, partly because of Veiller's exhibition, the New York state legislature enacted a more stringent tenement house law. Under the revised law, the traditional narrow air shafts were no longer permissible; instead, builders of new tenements had to provide courts admitting light and air to every apartment. The law also required future tenements to include a private toilet for each apartment, and both future and existing tenements had to provide adequate fire escapes, hallway lighting, and waterproof cellars.

Meanwhile, in Chicago the City Homes Association was fighting the battle against bad housing. In 1901 it was instrumental in the founding of the Municipal Lodging House, an institution that provided shelter for vagrants who had formerly slept on the streets or in police stations. After registering at the lodging house, impoverished guests surrendered their clothing for fumigation, bathed, retired for a night's sleep on a stark iron bedstead, and then awakened to a breakfast of coffee and bread. The management also tried to place the inmates in jobs, and those refusing to work were barred from the institution. Few could accuse the lodging house of excessive hospitality, but it did offer an alternative to the worst horrors of skid row. In 1902 the City Homes Association won its greatest triumph with the passage of a tenement ordinance similar to the New York law enacted the previous year. Like the New York measure, Chicago's ordinance sought to guarantee adequate light and air for tenement residents, imposed certain minimum plumbing standards, and attempted to limit the danger posed by fire.

Elsewhere reformers also voiced the need for stricter housing codes. In Baltimore two charity organizations appointed a special housing committee that conducted a survey of slum conditions and recommended such building regulations as should "insure light, air and sanitary surroundings for the wage-earner compelled by force of circumstance to make his home in the more congested sections of the city." Philadelphia's Octavia Hill Association lobbied at the state capital in support of legislation requiring quarterly inspection of tenements by the city health department. Buffalo's Tenement House Committee fought to guarantee enforcement of the state tenement house law, exposing violators and forcing the city to require improvements or order evictions. Such vigilance not only threatened the profits of landlords but also raised the rents of tenants, and in 1906 Frederic Almy, a leading Buffalo charity worker, admitted that "as a consequence of the improvements there has been a perceptible increase of rent for the tenement house population." But in Buffalo as elsewhere housing reformers were confident that they knew what was best for the lower classes.

Commitment to enforcing the new building codes varied from city to city. Inspired by the spirit of reform, New York City housing inspectors like Mary Sayles were excited by the opportunity to "know life at its barest and hardest, to grapple with cold physical facts, to stand on a common footing with those who have had no special advantages." Similarly, housing reformer Emily Dinwiddie expressed her "distinct pleasure in getting to the bottom of the difficulty in an involved case of bad plumbing." But New York's Tenement House Department was understaffed and underfunded, and turnover of personnel was high. The same was true of the Building Department and Sanitary Bureau of Chicago. In addition, Chicago inspectors were supposedly not above accepting bribes from dishonest landlords and builders. Still, housing reformers could claim some achievements. From 1902 through 1914, New York City's tenement department responded to more than half a million tenant complaints and reported 193,000 code violations. Moreover, in cities across the nation flush toilets became a more common fixture in working-class homes, the number of dark, windowless rooms declined, and the number of serviceable fire escapes increased.

Some housing reformers, however, felt that restrictive building codes alone were not sufficient to right the wrongs of the slums. They favored the construction of model tenements, limited-dividend housing superior to that built by profit-hungry landlords. In Washington, D.C., General George Sternberg organized the Sanitary Improvement Company, which erected 310 two-family flats and reaped no more than a 5 percent annual return on its investment. In 1911 the philanthropist Jacob G. Schmidlapp of Cincinnati began construction of model working-class dwellings, erecting 88 houses for 326 families during the next ten years. By 1917 Philadelphia's philanthropic Octavia Hill Association owned 179 houses and managed 224 more. But such groups made a scarcely perceptible dent in the nation's housing problem; a few thousand units could not house millions of working-class families. In 1910 Lawrence Veiller observed that model tenements constructed during the previous forty years housed only 3,588 Manhattan families, whereas tenements built for profit during the same period sheltered 253,510 households. "In other words," Veiller concluded, "for every 13 people who have been provided with model tenements, 1000 others have been condemned to live in insanitary ones."

Thus Veiller and most of his fellow reformers believed that building codes were the primary instruments for upgrading low-income housing and closing the gap in living standards between the working class and the middle class. Through state laws and municipal ordinances, housing reformers could enforce middle-class standards of minimal decency throughout the metropolis. Perhaps Polish immigrants in Buffalo would have to pay higher rents; reformers had at least outlawed the worst features of slum housing.

Housing reform did not, however, ensure an acceptable level of moral decency throughout urban America. To achieve moral purity, reformers needed to launch a frontal attack on the vice districts. Recognizing this, opponents of the saloon, gambling den, and brothel mobilized their forces for an all-out assault on sin. And during the first two decades of the century they would win some victories.

Nowhere were the crusaders against sin more active than in Chicago. Leading the forces of moral reform in the Illinois metropolis was Arthur B. Farwell, president of the Chicago Law and Order League. To acquaint themselves with the sins of the city, Farwell and his fellow reformers explored the Levee, visiting the notorious Freiburg's dance hall. As dance hall manager Ike Bloom later recalled: "I order the drinks all around — lemonade; and when they ask for the center of the dance floor to kneel down and pray and sing 'Washed in the Blood of the Lamb' I give it to 'em. I give 'em my jazz band too, which plays their accompaniment and plays it mighty damned well." Others also invaded the red-light district. In 1909 the English evangelist "Gypsy" Smith led a crowd of thousands into the Levee and held prayer meetings in the street, seeking repentance from the woeful souls of the neighborhood. But by 1910 prayers and hymn-singing no longer satisfied the moral reformers. Eager for action, they convinced Chicago's mayor Fred Busse to create the Chicago Vice Commission, which included a number of prominent clergymen, physicians, and educators.

Reporting the following year, the commission attacked prostitution as "the greatest curse which today rests upon mankind" and stated flatly that "the overwhelming majority of the citizens of Chicago and the fathers and mothers of its children never will countenance the recognition or legalization of a commercial business, which spells only ruin to the race." Consequently, it proposed creation of a morals commission to suppress the evil. To placate the forces of moral reform, in October 1911 the mayor took well-publicized action, ordering the police to close the notorious Everleigh Club. Owner Minna Everleigh accepted the defeat with good grace, saying, "I'll close up my shop and walk out of the place with a smile on my face." A year later Chicago's police closed down the entire Levee, forcing prostitu to go underground. Finally, in 1914, the Chicago city council at d the permanent morals commission that had been recommended three years earlier.

Other cities also joined in the campaign against prostitution. In 1900 a select committee of prominent members of the Chamber of Commerce investigated vice in New York City, and two years later it published its findings in a report entitled *The Social Evil.* In 1911 the Saint Louis Civic League organized a Committee on Public Morals, and within three years every known brothel in the city had closed its doors. Farther west, in Kansas City, prominent business leaders, members of the Council of Women's Clubs, and clergymen belonging to the Church Federation joined forces and coerced city officials to suppress local houses of prostitution. In Minneapolis reform clergy were proclaiming suppression to be "the only sane and safe method of correcting the depraved passions of the human heart." Likewise, a representative of the Cincinnati Vigilance Society argued that the continued existence of "evil resorts" was "not only a menace to civilization, but was sacrificing hundreds of the boys and girls of the city each year." Between 1910 and 1917, forty-three cities sponsored investigations of the vice problem, and in 1916 the American Social Hygiene Association claimed that forty-seven cities had closed their red-light districts. The following year the suppression of Storyville in New Orleans added one more to this number.

The suppression of the Levee and Storyville did not halt prostitution in the city, however. According to one moral reformer, after the closing of the brothels in Kansas City, "the town soon became overrun with . . . girls plying their trade on the street." Following the crackdown in Baltimore, investigators found that of the two hundred dispossessed prostitutes who could be traced, seventy-eight were still engaged in the trade or were living with men out of wedlock, and another forty-three had left town and might well have been soliciting in other cities. Moreover, in 1918 the Chicago Law and Order League sadly reported that "all of the houses of ill repute did not remain closed and from that time [1912] to this it has been a constant contest by the city . . . to see to it that these houses are kept closed." Sensing the task before it, this organization concluded that "one of the greatest problems of life is this sex problem and to solve it we need all the power of heaven and earth." The moral reformers had, however, destroyed the geographical enclaves of sin in the city and imposed a uniform standard of middle-class morality throughout metropolitan America. They had established their views as the official policy of the city if not as the universal rule of behavior.

By 1915 another issue was moving to the forefront of the moral reform agenda. Many middle-class urbanites had fought for decades to exclude saloons from their residential neighborhoods, and a vocal contingent had attacked liquor as a threat to the welfare of the working class. During the second decade of the twentieth century, however, those advocating prohibition of the manufacture and sale of alcohol throughout the nation were gaining new political clout. Urban Americans were less likely to favor prohibition than rural dwellers, but in some major cities foes of alcohol could muster a formidable army of voters. In 1916 a Michigan prohibition proposal won the support of a majority of the electorate in both Flint and Grand Rapids and lost in Detroit's Wayne County by less than fourteen hundred votes. The following year Los Angeles residents voted overwhelmingly to ban saloons from their city and to prohibit the sale of distilled liquor. Chicago's moral crusader Arthur B. Farwell also favored the reform, leading prohibition forces in the Windy City. Finally, in 1919, Farwell and his friends proved successful with the ratification of the Eighteenth Amendment to the federal constitution. A new experiment in moral uplift had thus begun.

By curbing the influence of the liquor interests, reformers also sought to uplift the standards of urban politics. Improving the quality of municipal rule ranked with moral reform, housing reform, and the settlement house as one of the great crusades of the age. To many middle-class reformers, the saloonkeeper–ward boss and the corner gin mill were symbols of all that was wrong with the government of the city. Unprincipled persons with little education or social rank seemed to be exploiting urban government for the sake of personal profit and favors for constituents. Character and merit too often seemed unimportant to local party leaders, and ward bosses appeared to be indifferent to the need for efficiency and expertise in government. Thus during the first two decades of the twentieth century good-government reformers stepped up their efforts to unseat the ward boss and his barroom cronies from the throne of power and fought to enhance the clout of expert bureaucrats and honest officials with correct middle-class credentials.

In some cities reform crusaders successfully brought corrupt officials to the bar of justice. Joseph Folk of Saint Louis prosecuted those accused of giving and accepting bribes for the sale of public utility franchises. In 1902 he brought indictments against twenty-four individuals, and eventually he sent eight members of Saint Louis's municipal legislature to prison. Francis Heney played the role of chief prosecutor in San Francisco. Heney was a fiery lawyer who had been expelled from the University of California during his freshman year for fighting a duel, and later in frontier Tucson he had killed a man in a scuffle at high noon before the courthouse. In 1905 he swore to put San Francisco's political chief, Abraham Ruef, and Mayor Eugene Schmitz behind bars, and during the next three years he hounded them relentlessly. Heney and his fellow reformers uncovered evidence that the mayor and Ruef had received bribes from public utility companies and had extorted sums from San Francisco's "French" restaurants, establishments which served respectable diners on the first floor but which maintained private dining rooms with beds upstairs for clandestine gourmands eager for something more than a meal. The crusading prosecutor convicted Schmitz and Ruef after a series of bizarre trials during which an explosion blew the front off the home of a key witness, a vengeful dismissed juror pumped a bullet into Heney's head, and the chief of police disappeared mysteriously in San Francisco Bay. Heney survived his wound, but Ruef went to San Quentin.

Prosecution of dishonest officials might momentarily cleanse the city of scoundrels, but reformers believed that only changes in the structure of government would bring permanent relief. For example, many thought that it was necessary to eliminate the plebeian ward alderman, a figure traditionally regarded as dishonest and narrowly preoccupied with neighborhood concerns. Boston's charter of 1909 abolished ward representation, creating a nine-member council elected at large; two years later an at-large council took charge in Pittsburgh; in 1914 Columbus voters eliminated ward-based municipal legislators; and in 1919 Detroit also adopted a small, at-large council. Meanwhile, the framers of municipal charters were shifting power from the council to the executive, and in a number of cities the mayor no longer needed to obtain council confirmation for the appointment or removal of executive officers. In a few major cities like Chicago and Minneapolis the city council remained formidable, but in most of the largest municipalities the trend was toward enhanced executive authority.

Some mayors used their strengthened office as a political pulpit from which to harangue the evil forces supposedly blighting urban government. The most famous mayoral crusader was Tom Johnson of Cleveland. As Cleveland's executive from 1901 to 1909 Johnson declared holy war on municipal misrule, and the special focus of his wrath were the privately-owned public utility corporations, most notably the local streetcar company. Although Johnson himself was a former streetcar magnate, he opposed all who profited from legally protected monopolies, referring to these fortunates as "Privilege." According to Johnson, "the greatest movement in the world to-day may be characterized as the struggle of the people against Privilege." Thus he battled continuously for a reduction of the streetcar fare from five cents to three cents and thereby won the allegiance of thousands of embittered voters who hung from straps on the crowded trolleys each morning and evening. Ultimately Johnson favored municipal ownership of the privileged streetcar, electric, gas, and telephone utilities. Chicago's Mayor Edward Dunne also campaigned for municipal ownership, and many rising politicians realized that attacks on streetcar companies could garner votes from suffering commuters. But the courts and state legislatures generally sided with privately owned utilities, and Johnson and Dunne generated more rhetoric than results.

Although some mayors wielded their authority effectively in the battle against corruption and favoritism, many friends of good government felt that structural reforms enhancing mayoral powers were not sufficient to remedy the municipal malady. These reformers believed that the entire mayor-council scheme hallowed by tradition had to be scrapped in favor of a new model of urban rule. In 1901, in the wake of a devastating tidal wave that killed one-seventh of the city's population and left the local government in shambles, business leaders in Galveston, Texas, drafted a commission plan of municipal rule. Discarding the mayor and council, the new plan provided for government by a board of commissioners, with each commissioner responsible for an executive department. Gradually adopted in other cities during the next decade, the commission plan eliminated ward representation and supposedly made it simpler for voters to locate responsibility for government incompetence. If the sewers backed up, voters could fix the blame on the commissioner of public works and defeat him in the next election. Moreover, with its superficial resemblance to the directorate of a business corporation, the executive commission appealed to those favoring more businesslike, efficient municipal rule.

Proposals for commission rule proved most popular in smaller cities, but a number of municipalities with populations of more than 100,000 adopted the scheme. Between 1910 and 1917 Memphis, Oakland, Birmingham, Omaha, New Orleans, Jersey City, Portland, Oregon, Saint Paul, Buffalo, and Newark all accepted the reform plan. During its crusade in support of commission rule, the *Kansas City Star* summarized the views of many reformers when it observed that, "Commission government is the application of modern business methods to the conduct of municipal affairs." A prominent advocate of the plan in Buffalo emphasized that the scheme encouraged expertise and efficiency and compared it to "the staff system of the German military administration which has been so highly recommended for large business in this country by efficiency experts." Commission rule seemed to promise efficiency, accountability, and an end to the ward divisions that fragmented the American municipality. For some big-city voters, especially middle-class residents enamored with business-like administration, this promise was appealing.

Yet reform enthusiasm for commission government was fleeting, and by 1915 structural reformers were already transferring their affections to a new scheme, the city manager plan. In 1908 the city of Staunton, Virginia, hired a "general manager" to discharge "all the executive and administrative duties now appertaining to the city council." This innovation soon caught the fancy of Richard Childs, a wealthy young advertising man whose hobby was municipal reform. During the following half-century Childs was the chief publicist for city manager government, lauding it as a means for realizing efficient, expert rule. Whereas commission government suffered from a division of executive authority among a number of commissioners, the manager scheme concentrated supervision of executive and administrative responsibilities in one figure. Whereas the commissioners were elected amateurs, the manager was a full-time professional administrator hired by the city council. In the eyes of many reformers, commission rule was good, but city manager government was better. By 1917 eighty-one cities had already adopted the manager plan, but Dayton, Ohio, was as yet the largest municipality to accept the scheme. At the onset of World War I Childs's panacea was just beginning to transform local government in the United States.

Some favored manager government and others preferred commission rule; some spoke on behalf of municipal ownership of utilities and others saved their rhetoric for highly publicized prosecutions of dishonest officials. The stream of municipal reform flowed through many diverse channels during the Progressive Era. But Richard Childs, Tom Johnson, Francis Heney, and Joseph Folk all agreed that something had to be done. The old system which allowed streetcar companies, ward aldermen, and political bosses to pursue their own interests without regard for the larger community no longer seemed acceptable. According to Progressive reformers, it was time for the disparate selfishness of the past to yield to a higher civic ideal. A new community spirit was called for, a spirit that would ensure a common striving for effective and responsible rule.

To translate this abstract civic ideal into the concrete reality of the cityscape was the responsibility of the emerging corps of urban planners. In 1909 an assortment of architects, public officials, civic leaders, and landscape architects met at the First National Conference on City Planning. This conference was the culmination of a decade of optimistic agitation for the beautification of the city. During this first decade of the twentieth century, enthusiasts claimed that "civic art" and municipal improvements engendered pride in the city and excited a common loyalty among all urban classes. Through the physical planning of the city, many believed a new civic spirit was possible, a spirit of harmony and order as opposed to chaotic, individualistic striving or disruptive social and ethnic conflict. Just as housing and moral reformers sought to apply some common middle-class standard of decency and morality to the entire city, city planning enthusiasts wanted to extend their standards of beauty throughout the metropolis. The entire city, and not just a few privileged residential neighborhoods, should be an object of pride, a harmonious aesthetic whole worthy of the wealthiest nation in the history of the world.

No one was more dedicated to this goal than planner-architect Daniel Burnham. During the first decade of the century he was the leading practitioner of City Beautiful planning. The City Beautiful movement included various groups, each with its own special focus, but basically they all agreed that the city could and must be made beautiful, usually through the creation of additional parks, landscaped boulevards, plazas, statuary, and monumental classical architecture. As chief of construction of the Chicago World's Fair of 1893, Burnham had created a dazzling collection of white, neoclassical palaces lining shimmering pools and ornamented with gargantuan sculpture. Burnham's handiwork thrilled millions of visitors to the fair and heightened the desire for civic improvements. In 1901 Burnham joined the Senate Park Commission for the beautification of Washington, D.C., and designed a monumental union terminal, thereby ridding the mall leading to the capitol of unsightly railroad tracks. Four years later Burnham drafted a comprehensive proposal for San Francisco, complete with boulevards radiating from imposing plazas, vast new parks, and a neoclassical civic center. Eight months after Burnham submitted his plan, an earthquake and fire devastated San Francisco, and the stricken city sacrificed beauty to the necessity of rebuilding as quickly as possible. Burnham's scheme thus remained only a vision, a never-realized source of inspiration for planners and civic leaders.

More successful was Burnham's plan for a civic center in Tom Johnson's Cleveland. A young devotee of Johnson's expressed the hopes of both the Progressive mayor and the City Beautiful planner when he envisioned Cleveland "as a city planned, built, and conducted as a community enterprise . . . a unit, a thing with a mind, with a conscious purpose, seeing far in advance of the present." Designed in 1903, the civic center was to be the keystone of this united visionary city. According to Burnham's plan, a grand colonnaded railroad terminal was to stand at the head of a grassy esplanade bordered by the city hall, county courthouse, federal building, and public library. The civic center commission under Burnham's leadership provided that all the buildings were to be in the neoclassic style with a uniform cornice line, "resulting in beautiful designs entirely harmonious with each other." Harmony and order was all important, for, according to the commission, "the jumble of buildings that surrounds us in our new cities contributes nothing valuable to life . . . [but] disturbs our peacefulness and destroys that repose within us that is the basis of all contentment." Gradually over the next two decades, Cleveland was to carry out this harmonious scheme, except for the railroad terminal which was never constructed.

The Cleveland scheme was, however, a small-scale project compared with Burnham's comprehensive plan for his hometown of Chicago. In 1907 Burnham enjoined planners to "make no little plans;

they have no magic to stir men's blood," and in his Chicago plan, submitted two years later, he lived up to his own words. It was a big plan which proposed the redevelopment of the entire Chicago area within a sixty-mile radius of the city center. Burnham's plan mapped a metropolitan system of parks and boulevards and recommended the creation of a waterfront park running for twenty miles along the Lake Michigan shore. Moreover, it proposed the construction of a grandiose civic center on the city's near west side. Throughout the emphasis was on harmony and order. In the introduction Burnham stated that, "Chicago in common with other cities realizes that the time has come to bring order out of chaos incident to rapid growth, and especially to the influx of people of many nationalities without common traditions or habits of life." The plan would supposedly create not only an aesthetic harmony but also a social harmony among the city's diverse population. For example, Burnham believed that the proposed city hall would be "a monument to the spirit of civic unity," its "towering dome . . . vivifying and unifying the entire composition." The proposed civic buildings would symbolize "in concrete form the feeling of loyalty to and pride in the city" and would accomplish Burnham's long-term goal of "cementing together the heterogeneous elements of our population." In succeeding years Chicago realized many of Burnham's suggestions — such as the lakefront park — although the unifying civic center remained only a paper dream.

Others shared Burnham's faith in planning the city as an orderly, harmonious whole. According to these planning reformers, the city needed to move forward in a single direction rather than grow irrationally in response to a multitude of private pressures. In 1909 Benjamin C. Marsh, an early advocate of urban planning, summed up the thinking of many when he wrote, "A city without a Plan is like a ship without a rudder." The great publicist of the City Beautiful movement, Charles Mulford Robinson, likewise preached the benefits of comprehensive planning and emphasized, "the great need . . . of obtaining one underlying plan . . . which shall weld together in a harmonious system the street plotting of the different districts, shall mark the course of present and future improvements with entire assurance, and shall put before the people a tangible goal to work toward."

Like the settlement worker, the housing reformer, the moral crusader, and the good-government advocate, the planning reformer was, then, attempting to apply a common standard for the motley city. American cities had sailed through the nineteenth century without a rudder, lacking any unifying social, moral, political, or planning goals. Individual enterprise had molded urban America, and it had produced a city of social, economic, moral, and political diversity and conflict. At the dawn of the century, the city included great wealth and great poverty, opulence and deprivation, sin and sanctimony, politicians dedicated to personal profit and politicians committed to civic virtue, ugly zones of commercial exploitation and enclaves of lovely shaded streets. Progressive reformers sought to unite this diverse metropolis by supplanting the individual greed of the past with a new civic spirit, a spirit that would emphasize the communal welfare over private desires or special group interests. In accord with this new civic spirit, middle-class settlement workers attempted to reach out to their working-class compatriots, and housing reformers sought to provide decent dwellings for all urbanites, even though the profits of landlords might suffer. Foes of the brothel and saloon tried to guarantee a decent moral environment, and political reformers endeavored to cleanse the city of the organized greed of the party machines. Moreover, urban planners sought to create a physical plan that might offer a common goal for the community as a whole and arouse a shared pride in the city. The goals and standards of the Progressive reformers were middle-class goals and standards, reflecting the social origins of settlement workers, housing crusaders, and good-government advocates. But these self-confident individuals of comfortable status believed their civic vision was one all others might reasonably share.

During the first two decades of the twentieth century, many were confident that this new civic spirit could prevail in the long run and that the fragmented metropolis of autonomous individuals and clashing groups would yield to a unified community. Progressive reformers had presented an alternative to the atomistic city characterized by machine politicians, madams, bejeweled society matrons, and real estate speculators. Only succeeding decades would prove whether or not the Progressive promise would become a reality.

Promises Thwarted: The Twenties

During the 1920s, the progressive civic ideal collided head-on with the social and political realities of America's cities, leaving a wreckage of reform. Before World War I urban reformers had sought to realize a unifying civic vision that would ensure minimal standards of morality, housing, and political decency for persons throughout the metropolis. Thus they had closed the brothels, restructured municipal government, enacted building codes, and established settlement houses in the slums. After World War I, however, Americans witnessed the fruits of these reforms and they were not impressed. Gangsters reaped unprecedented wealth from the moral weakness of urban Americans; politicos offensive to middle-class reformers adapted the new structures to their own ends; and the gaps separating rich and poor, foreign-born and native, black and white, did not diminish and perhaps even widened. Moreover, the advent of the automobile and gasoline-powered truck enhanced divisions within the metropolis by freeing urban dwellers and employers from the centripetal forces of the railroad and streetcar. Both the inherited conflicts of the past and the emerging technology of the future seemed at odds with the promise of civic harmony.

THE FAILURE OF MORAL REFORM

In no city was the failure of moral reform more evident than in Chicago. Before World War I Arthur Farwell and his law and order league spearheaded the crusade against prostitution and lent support to foes of the saloon. In response, authorities shut down the Levee, and in January 1920 the prohibition amendment went into effect. But booze and brothels did not disappear from Chicago. Instead, gangster chieftains built illicit empires that supplied forbidden pleasures and earned Chicago a notorious reputation.

At the beginning of the 1920s one of the kingpins of Chicago crime was Big Jim Colosimo. A large flashy man with a diamond on every finger, a huge diamond horseshoe on his vest, and diamond-studded belt and suspender buckles, Colosimo was a veteran of the Levee where he married a leading madam and supplied prostitutes to the local brothels. In 1920, just as prohibition offered a new outlet for his talents, a bullet from an unknown assailant cut short his career of empire building. But Big Jim's top lieutenant, Johnny Torrio, succeeded him and created a multimillion dollar network of bootlegging, prostitution, and gambling.

An efficient administrator who personally eschewed smoking, drinking, profanity, and illicit sex, Torrio was responsible for adapting the world of vice to the new age of the automobile. With Chicago's authorities periodically cracking down on crime and with the growing number of automobiles reducing the travel time from the urban core to the outlying fringes, Torrio shifted much of his gambling and prostitution business to suburban roadhouses. A string of independent municipalities ringed Chicago and in some of the less reputable communities the mayor and police chief were willing to cooperate with gangsters in exchange for payoffs. Thus Torrio captured the dismal southern suburb of Burnham, a town that had the added advantage of bordering on the state of Indiana. If the Illinois authorities raided the Burnham houses, the prostitutes and gamblers could readily flee to safety across the state line. The malodorous village of Stickney, bordering Chicago's giant sewage canal, also succumbed to Torrio, and in that community the gang leader established his largest bordello, the sixty-woman Stockade. But Torrio's greatest acquisition was the suburb of Cicero, Chicago's largest satellite and a working-class community of 50,000 inhabitants. On election day 1924 Torrio's forces, led by his henchman Al Capone, ensured that the gangster ticket would triumph at the polls. According to the Illinois Crime Survey: "Automobiles filled with gunmen paraded the streets. . . . Polling places were raided by armed thugs and ballots taken at the point of gun from the hands of voters waiting to drop them in the box." Henceforth, Cicero was criminal territory, with 160 saloons and gambling houses running night and day, the drinking and gambling only interrupted by periodic gangland violence. Local wits claimed that it was easy to tell when one crossed the line from Chicago into the west side suburb — "if you smell gunpowder, you're in Cicero."

Thus during the 1920s the Chicago area remained a moral checkerboard with some squares reserved for sin and others for sanctity. Just as in the prewar era, such upper-middle-class zones as Hyde Park and Evanston remained off-limits to liquor and prostitution, and such sylvan north shore sanctuaries of wealth as Kenilworth, Winnetka, and Lake Forest never sold out to Torrio, Capone, or their likes. But working-class suburbs such as Cicero, Stickney, and Burnham were wide open to illicit activities, and a short spin in the automobile would transport one from the restricted neighborhoods of the north shore to the tawdry Babylons on the west and south sides. Arthur Farwell and his allies had closed the Levee, but they had not suppressed vice nor established a uniform standard of morality throughout the metropolis.

In fact, the forces of crime and corruption were enjoying a heyday as millions of dollars poured into their coffers from the purses of thirsty Americans. Chicago's Genna brothers placed home stills in hundreds of Italian households on the near west side, creating a highly lucrative cottage industry. By 1925 their gross liquor sales amounted to $350,000 per month, with $150,000 monthly profit. In 1924 the North Side Gang leader Dion O'Banion was supposedly making almost a million dollars a year from his liquor trade; his successor, Hymie Weiss, was also a millionaire. But the Torrio-Capone syndicate was the wealthiest of the Chicago gangs, reaping a gross annual income in the late 1920s estimated at between $100 million to over $300 million.

With so much money at stake, the competition was fierce and violent. In 1924 gangsters working for Torrio and Capone murdered the flower-loving O'Banion in the florist shop that he had purchased with his ill-gotten gains. Two months later O'Banion's gunmen retaliated, pumping five bullets into Torrio. The gang leader survived, but recognizing the health hazards of his occupation, he wisely retired, turning the syndicate over to Capone. A year later Hymie Weiss's men loaded into eleven automobiles, drove out to Cicero, and poured more than a thousand bullets into Capone's headquarters. Capone was not injured, but twenty days later ten machine gun bullets mowed down the troublesome Weiss. And on St. Valentine's Day 1929 Capone's mobsters slayed seven men at the North Side Gang's headquarters, a massacre that confirmed Chicago's reputation for violence and lawlessness. In all, an estimated five hundred Chicago gangsters died in the mob warfare between 1924 and 1929.

Elsewhere the story was much the same. In Detroit the Purple Gang battled the Licavoli Gang for control of the huge liquor traffic from Canada, cutting short the life of many Detroit mobsters. Like their Chicago brethren, Detroit gangsters soon recognized the advantages of independent suburban municipalities beyond the jurisdiction of central-city authorities. The working-class suburb of Hamtramck became the Detroit counterpart of Cicero, a wide-open town of corrupt officials and illicit pleasures. Saloons, brothels, and gambling dens crowded within the municipal boundaries, winning Hamtramck a reputation as "the wild west of the middle west" and "a cancer spot and crying disgrace." Municipal office in Hamtramck was a stepping stone to the penitentiary, and one political figure after another ended up behind bars. Mayor Peter Jezewski and his commissioner of public safety spent two years in Leavenworth for authorizing Hamtramck police to convoy liquor shipments through the city. The president of the city council was sentenced to seven years in prison for manslaughter. In the early 1930s Mayor Rudolph Tenerowicz was convicted of accepting bribes from brothel keepers and was succeeded in office by former Mayor Jezewski who had returned from his sojourn in the federal penitentiary. Henry Ford may have ensured that his factory suburbs of Dearborn and Highland Park remained free of saloons and vice resorts; but each Ford rolling off the assembly lines offered new mobility to Americans and placed the sins of Hamtramck within easy reach of residents throughout southeastern Michigan.

Even in the City of Brotherly Love, drinking and vice were rampant and law enforcement ineffective. In 1923 Pennsylvania's governor estimated that 1,300 saloons operated in Philadelphia, and the following year the mayor appointed General Smedley Butler of the United States Marine Corps as Director of Public Safety with responsibility for battling the forces of demon rum. Nicknamed "Hell's Devil Butler," the feisty marine had triumphed over the insurgent Filipinos, the fanatical forces of the Boxer Rebellion, and the armies of the Kaiser, but the task of purifying Philadelphia proved insuperable. On taking office Butler ordered his lieutenants to close the saloons within forty-eight hours or suffer immediate demotion. Within the next few days, police raids did temporarily close almost one thousand establishments, but Butler soon discovered that local magistrates and juries lacked the time or inclination to apply the full force of the law against those arrested for liquor violations. In 1925 less than 4 percent of the persons arrested in Philadelphia for operating speakeasies suffered any punishment more serious than a light fine. Moreover, enthusiasm for Butler's crackdown waned among the city's "respectable classes" when the authorities raided a formal ball at the swank Ritz Carlton Hotel, seized bottles of champagne, and ordered the hotel padlocked. Soon after extending his crusade beyond the beer-drinking classes to Philadelphia's champagne society, Butler was dismissed from office. The vanquished marine correctly concluded that "law enforcement on an absolutely even basis has not had the support of the people of Philadelphia and does not have it now." A Philadelphia newspaper observed that the dismissed safety director "was 100 percent honest," but it also noted that "we are doing the Mayor no injustice in expressing the belief that this was a little more than he had counted on." Many Philadelphians might have lauded a cosmetic cleansing of their community, eliminating the worst blotches on the city's reputation. But few were willing to tolerate a thorough moral scrubbing of metropolitan social life.

Throughout the nation the struggle to enforce prohibition was faltering. In 1929 New York City police reported that there were 32,000 speakeasies in the metropolis, twice the number of drinking establishments in preprohibition days. Congressman Fiorello LaGuardia estimated that in order to enforce the prohibition laws New York City would need 250,000 policemen plus an additional 200,000 agents to police the honesty of the police. Cleveland's Lonardo and Porello gangs battled throughout the 1920s for control of the alcohol brewed in the city's Italian households while others freighted Canadian whiskey across Lake Erie. In Kansas City John Lazia bossed the gambling and bootlegging operations until his murder in 1934; in San Francisco "Black Tony" Parmagini was kingpin of both the liquor and narcotics traffic. In every American metropolis minor-league Capones gunned their way to a share of the illegal profits. Some teetotalers pointed out the supposed salutary effects of prohibition, and one researcher claimed that owing to the Eighteenth Amendment arrests for profanity in New York City had dropped 80 percent and arrests for operating brothels had plummeted 97 percent. But most urbanites found such claims doubtful. New Yorkers were still swearing, liquor-dispensing nightclubs continued to enliven the Manhattan scene, and visitors and residents alike had no difficulty finding their way to resorts of commercial vice.

By the close of the 1920s, it was evident that the dream of imposing a new standard of virtue on all urban dwellers was becoming a nightmare. The moral fragmentation of the city persisted as some districts were open to commercial sin whereas in "better" neighborhoods middle-class residents consumed alcohol privately but opposed the open flouting of standards of decency. Thugs and gangsters were gaining a level of power and wealth undreamed of in preprohibition days, and respect for the law seemed at a new ebb. Al Capone himself summed up the failure of moral reform when he complained, "They say I violate the prohibition law. Who doesn't?"

THE FAILURE OF POLITICAL REFORM

Moral corruption was not only evident in the nightclubs and brothels of metropolitan America but also in the city halls. Despite reform efforts, the promises of purified government foundered during the 1920s, and the civic ideal of disinterested rule for the good of the entire community remained an unrealized dream. In cities across the nation, newspaper headlines continued to decry the chicanery and incompetence of mayors and councilmen. By the close of the decade even the panacea of city manager government had lost its reform luster as experience had proven its shortcomings. In 1930 the goal of civic virtue seemed as elusive as the realization of a liquor-free America.

No figure deviated so clearly from the reform ideal as did Chicago's Republican chief executive William Hale Thompson. Mayor from 1915 to 1923 and 1927 to 1931, "Big Bill" Thompson became famous for his buffoonery, his tolerance for gangsterism, and his general willingness to offend reform sensibilities. Soon after assuming power, Thompson embarked on a campaign to undermine the Morals Squad of the police department, and by 1918 he had convinced the city council to cut off funds to this branch of the police and had abolished the office of morals inspector. Henceforth, Thompson's political followers were able to extort protection money from gamblers, speakeasy operators, and brothel keepers without fear of police interference. In 1921 one Chicago newspaper reported that the liquor, gambling, and prostitution interests had paid more than one million dollars to the Eighteenth Ward William Hale Thompson Men's Club, and those who failed to contribute to this political organization could not continue in business. By the close of his second term in 1923, Thompson was being sued for accepting kickbacks and illegal payments from the construction of public works projects, and the mayor's appointees on the board of education and the Republican party mastermind "Swede" Lundin were under indictment for defrauding the school treasury of more than a million dollars. Moreover, patronage politics flourished, and jobs and favors went to those who had loyally served the Thompson machine.

Thompson's outrageous personality also offended advocates of honest, efficient government. With his penchant for wearing sombreros, his raucous voice, and his profane language, "Big Bill" hardly presented the image of businesslike administration that reformers desired. Moreover, he was an outspoken isolationist who opposed America's entry into World War I, attacked any friendly overtures to Great Britain, and never missed an opportunity to express his contempt for the king of England. When the city's newspapers accused him of a lack of patriotism, he characteristically responded, "If Bill Thompson has got to jump to his feet and sing 'God Save the King' to please the *Tribune* and the *News,* then they can both go straight to hell!"

Faced with charges of corruption, Thompson chose not to seek reelection in 1923, and the Democratic reform candidate won the mayor's office with a pledge to close down the liquor, gambling, and vice resorts in the city. For four years Chicago experimented with respectability to the despair of many thirsty citizens. Meanwhile, in order to capture the voters' attention and remain in the public eye, "Big Bill" announced that he was embarking on a voyage to the South Seas to hunt tree-climbing fish, fish that the ex-mayor claimed could "live on land, will jump three feet to catch a grasshopper and will actually climb trees." Amid much fanfare, Thompson set sail from an amusement park along the shores of Lake Michigan, but before the ship reached New Orleans "Big Bill" was on his way back to Chicago to continue his political career.

Reentering Chicago politics, "Big Bill" ran again for mayor in 1927 and clearly proclaimed his allegiance to the "wet" forces opposed to prohibition. He told Chicago's voters: "Read Bill Thompson's platform — you can't find anything wetter than that in the middle of the Atlantic." Attacking the Democrats for having closed "businesses," i.e., speakeasies, Thompson promised, "When I'm elected we will not only reopen places these people have closed, but we'll open 10,000 new ones." Appreciative gangsters flocked to his support and on Al Capone's bulletproof office walls were portraits of George Washington, Abraham Lincoln, and William Hale Thompson. When "Big Bill" returned to the mayor's office in 1927, it was a signal to the gangs that Chicago was again open to plunder.

But Thompson Republicans were not the only Chicago politicians with gangland connections. "Big Jim" Colosimo backed the Democratic First Ward machine of aldermen Michael "Hinky Dink" Kenna and "Bathhouse John" Coughlin. And although Johnny Torrio was a member of the William Hale Thompson Republican Club and Al Capone likewise favored the GOP, both continued to work with Kenna and Coughlin and to use their muscle to guarantee Democratic majorities in the First Ward. Chicago's good-government reformers might have had the upper hand from 1923 to 1927, but throughout the 1920s gangsters had useful friends in both political parties.

In New York City political reformers also proved unsuccessful during the 1920s. The Tammany Democratic political machine continued to rule, handing out jobs and contracts to loyal party workers. Devotion to the party machine and personal gain seemed of highest priority to the Tammany nabobs, yet the voters returned Tammany to power each election. During the early 1920s the ponderous John F. Hylan was Tammany mayor of the nation's greatest metropolis. Humorless and socially inept, with a speaking style that induced slumber in his listeners, Hylan inspired few New Yorkers and achieved little of significance. In 1925, however, New York's voters elected Tammany's James J. Walker to succeed Hylan, and Walker ushered in an era of municipal rule that delighted many of the public but horrified serious good-government advocates.

Jimmy Walker was a songwriter-turned-politician who produced one big hit while serving the muses of Tin Pan Alley, the romantic "Will You Love Me in September as You Do in May?" Fond of show business and the bright lights of Broadway, Walker frequented the leading speakeasies and night clubs where he drank the illegal whiskey of bootleggers and courted pretty chorus girls. In fact, the dapper mayor was more faithful to his barber and his tailor than to his wife, more concerned about the cut of his suit than the state of city finances. But Walker's debonair manner garnered him the support of New York City's voters, and in 1929 he easily won another four-year term as mayor.

His slick charm, however, masked the corrupt practices of the Walker administration. In the early 1930s investigators subpoenaed Walker's financial records and found that many doing business with the city had helped finance the playboy mayor's carefree lifestyle. A bus company seeking a franchise from the city had given Walker a $10,000 letter of credit to pay for one of his much-publicized expeditions to Paris; a Wall Street broker with a large interest in a taxicab company dependent on the city's favor deposited $26,000 in bonds in the mayor's account; another business figure gave Walker $247,000, supposedly out of friendship for the mayor; and his honor's financial agent had deposited almost a million dollars from undisclosed sources in a secret brokerage account during Walker's term in office. Faced with these revelations, in 1932 Walker resigned the mayor's chair and immediately departed for Europe, far from the jurisdiction of the New York courts.

Elsewhere, as well, reformers wrestled with public officials of unsavory reputation. In Boston Mayor James Curley ruled the city, lavishly spending municipal funds for public works projects. Earlier in his career Curley had served sixty days in jail for having helped a loyal but ignorant wardheeler by taking his civil service examination for him, and in the 1920s Curley continued to refer contemptuously to good-government reformers as "goo-goos." Dedicated to old-fashioned ward politics, Boston's mayor advocated the "direct method" of rule, "even if you have to break a few laws and tear up red tape." Meanwhile, in the Middle West a jury found the mayor of Indianapolis guilty of corrupt practices and sentenced him to prison, and six Indianapolis council members were indicted and fined for accepting bribes. On the west coast San Francisco's former mayor Eugene E. Schmitz made a comeback and served two terms on the city's governing board of supervisors. Ignoring his previous convictions for extortion, the voters of San Francisco rallied behind the tarnished politician in a display of loyalty that sickened devotees of honest government.

Even the panacea of city manager government proved a partial failure during the 1920s. The number of cities adopting the scheme continued to grow so that by 1930 there were 430 municipalities across the country which had turned to the manager plan. But the scheme seemed best-suited for small and medium-sized cities and homogeneous suburban retreats. In municipalities of ten to twenty-five thousand inhabitants, where city officials faced nothing more divisive than spats over the location of a fire station or petitions for street resurfacing, professional public administrators found a climate most suitable to their survival. In the largest cities, however, with their diverse populations and clash of interests, a college-trained manager would not suffice to lead the motley populace. Instead, by the 1930s many students of city government had conceded that an elected executive versed in the skills of politics was needed at the helm of municipalities like New York City, Chicago, and Philadelphia. Such cities seemed to require not only professional administrators but also full-time political brokers who could piece together the social, ethnic, and economic fragments of the metropolis into some pattern of accommodation and compromise.

During the 1920s the true litmus test of the city manager scheme was Cleveland. In January 1924 the Ohio metropolis began an experiment with manager rule, the largest city up to that date to adopt the scheme. Ranking fifth in population among the nation's municipalities. Cleveland was representative of metropolitan America, and its success or failure under city manager government would be a signal to other large cities vainly seeking a better structure of urban rule. Unfortunately for city manager proponents, the signal proved negative. Seven years of manager government did not eliminate corruption, enhance the quality of the city council, or imbue the electorate with a unifying civic spirit. No matter the form of government, Cleveland politics seemed to move along well-trod paths.

During the first stages of implementation, it was evident that the rosy visions of reformers were unrealistic. High-minded, nonpartisan councilmen did not select the city's original manager; instead this task fell to the leaders of the Republican and Democrat party organizations. Fearing the reformers, the boss of the majority Republicans made a deal with the chief of the minority Democrats to cooperate in the selection of a manager and to split the patronage under manager rule, with

60 percent of all jobs going to Republicans and 40 percent going to Democrats. Thus party bosses chose Cleveland's first "nonpartisan" administrator.

Traditional politics also continued to dominate the city council. Writing in *Collier's Magazine,* one observer said that the first council elected under the new plan "was as full of politics and politicians as a snake is full of poison," and the same was true of the succeeding councils as well. Moreover, councilmen continued to concentrate on serving their districts and their constituents rather than focusing on the legislative needs of the city as a whole. In 1925 a council leader observed, "every councilman is knee-deep in taking care of the interests of the neighborhood voters who put him in office. How can he direct the affairs of the entire city?" Personal gain motivated some municipal legislators, and in 1929 a councilman was sent to the penitentiary for conspiring to sell land to the city at three or four times its market value. As in the past, politics, parochialism, and corruption all characterized the Cleveland city council. Under the manager plan, as under mayoral government, the pull of party loyalty and ward interests seemed stronger than the attraction of the reform ideal.

After a few years of manager rule, the ethnic minorities and labor organizations within Cleveland became especially critical of the plan. Excluded from the city's business elite and unable to exercise as much personal clout as the downtown bank president or streetcar magnate, these groups depended on the ballot to influence government. With executive power vested in a nonelected manager, however, the importance of the ballot diminished, depriving these groups of significant leverage over the city's administration. In the minds of those beyond the pale of Cleveland's social and economic elite, manager government thus seemed an unacceptable violation of democratic principles. In 1927 the Cleveland Federation of Labor issued a pamphlet stating that "the City Manager Plan is un-American, undemocratic and autocratic and should not be tolerated by anyone who desires to conserve the liberties of the people." That same year Cleveland's most widely circulated Czech-language newspaper urged its readers to "restore Cleveland's government to the hands of the people" and argued that "great banking interests have joined forces in support of the city manager system . . . providing for a lifelong dictator and making it impossible for you to perform your inalienable civic rights." Two years later it continued to call for "a resumption of democratic rule in Cleveland's city hall," urging Czechs "to overthrow the autocratic regime." Meanwhile, many Poles had joined in the opposition, claiming that under manager rule "treatment of us was worse than the Negro, for a Negro was chosen to a position as commissioner of civil service, though already that position had been promised to a Pole."

Blacks, however, saw little evidence of their favored status under the scheme. The black community's newspaper fervently opposed manager government, and in 1927 its editor wrote: "Not only are Afro-Americans given less attention under the city manager plan than when a chief executive, elected by the people, presided over the destinies of the city, but this same thing is true of the great mass of poor people, without reference to class or race." That same year the Baptist Ministers' Conference endorsed a restoration of mayoral government, and one prominent black clergyman claimed that "our present city government is tending towards autocracy, which I resent because of the autocracy of our southern states." And in 1929 the local bishop of the Colored Methodist Episcopal Church attacked the manager scheme in similar language, arguing that "it deprives the people of Cleveland of the privilege of choosing their ruler just as effectively as though they were excluded by the Constitution."

Cleveland's manager plan narrowly survived a series of repeal campaigns in the late 1920s before succumbing in a referendum in 1931. Thus, after an experiment of seven years, Ohio's largest city rejected manager government. Under the reform scheme, patterns of behavior typical of mayor-council government survived with party leaders still grasping the levers of power and ward representatives still catering to the city's neighborhood fragments. Yet the executive was no longer elected, and this change proved especially offensive to those excluded from the city's elite inner circle. Many Czechs, Poles, blacks, and union members favored an executive who would have to serve the various voting blocs or face defeat in November. By 1931 they had succeeded in returning Cleveland to the more traditional path of an elected executive.

Meanwhile, in Kansas City, Missouri, the manager plan was hardly proving a panacea for municipal ills. In 1925 the Pendergast Democratic organization backed the reform scheme, ensuring its adoption by the electorate. Boss Tom Pendergast then installed a loyal party worker in the office of the city manager, and the new manager soon shattered reform hopes for nonpartisan rule when he announced that his administration would be "a Democratic administration, that wherever possible Democrats will be appointed to positions in the departments." Until Pendergast's conviction for income tax evasion and insurance frauds in 1939, his machine controlled Kansas City, proving that the city manager plan like the mayor-council structure was amenable to boss rule.

Moreover, in manager-ruled Kansas City as in mayor-ruled Chicago gangsters gained undue influence at city hall. Gang leader John Lazia rose to command the Democratic organization in Kansas City's First Ward, heading the North Side Democratic Club from 1928 until his assassination by machine-gun-wielding rivals in 1934. According to United States District Attorney Maurice Milligan, Lazia was a "gum-chewing, weak-eyed egomaniac who had the First Ward and the whole Kansas City Police Department in his fingers" and whose "annual take on slot machines ran into seven figures." A grand jury discovered that the gang leader made appointments to the police department, and a federal agent reported that when he called the office of the city police chief John Lazia answered the telephone. By 1932 a local rabbi was leading a crusade against municipal corruption, backed by Protestant clergy seeking to save Kansas City from "its present demoralization and prevent the growth of racketeering, vice, and general law violation." Few municipal administrations could claim such an unsavory reputation as the city manager government of Kansas City, and during the 1930s a leader of the International City Managers Association admitted that "the members of this association have been apologizing for Kansas City for the last five years." Kansas City, like Cleveland, was a skeleton in the reform closet.

In some major cities, the manager plan seemed to provide honest, efficient administration, largely realizing the dreams of its proponents. For example, in 1924 Cincinnati voters adopted manager rule, and that city was a showcase for reformers during the following decade. Supporters of the reform scheme captured control of the city council, appointed as manager an army colonel dedicated to spit-and-polish administration, and forced the deposed Republican party organization to nominate more reputable candidates for local office or face political oblivion. Cincinnati soon gained renown as one of the best-governed cities in the United States, and by the late 1930s no political figure in the Ohio city would publicly attack the manager plan.

But the history of manager rule in Kansas City and Cleveland demonstrated that a change in the formal municipal structure would not necessarily revolutionize city government nor introduce a new reign of civic purity and achievement. An increasing number of skeptics questioned the Progressive faith in structural reform, but they did not offer an alternate solution to the perceived problems of urban rule. At the close of the 1920s, "Big Bill" Thompson presided over the municipal bachanalia of Chicago, Tammany's debonair Jimmy Walker was seemingly devoting more time to trans-Atlantic travel, chorus girls, and haberdashery than to the government of New York City, Tom Pendergast was giving orders to Kansas City's city manager, and Cleveland reformers were muddling through their experiment with good government. This was hardly an encouraging state of affairs for devotees of nonpartisan, honest, efficient administration.

THE IMPERFECT MOSAIC

In 1900 the city consisted of an array of ethnic blocs that interlocked imperfectly in a pattern of often clashing cultures and discordant social goals. During the next three decades settlement workers like Jane Addams tried to ease the transition of foreign-born newcomers to the city and housing reformers like Lawrence Veiller sought to ensure them decent living conditions. But in 1930 the ethnic divisions in urban America persisted. At the close of the 1920s the social and ethnic mosaic of the city was not a harmonious blend of peoples but remained an imperfect pattern of stark social and economic contrasts. Some children of late-nineteenth-century immigrants from Southern and Eastern Europe were shedding their ethnic identities and merging into the mass of undifferentiated Americans. Yet old grievances and hostilities died slowly. New migrants from the rural South and from Latin America added to the complexity of the ethnic mix. Just as moral and political reformers had failed to create an urban commonwealth of uniform standards and shared ideals, so Progressive social reformers had made only limited headway in fashioning a socially harmonious city.

Indicative of the persistent ethnic hostilities during the years following World War I were the urban race riots of the summer of 1919. Thousands of southern blacks had migrated to northern cities during World War I, and in Chicago alone more than fifty thousand black migrants sought a greater degree of prosperity and freedom than was available in the cotton fields of Alabama or Mississippi. With the newly arrived blacks threatening white jobs and the ethnic purity of white neighborhoods, racial hostility and fears increased. In July 1919 this tension bred violence when a black teenager drowned at Chicago's Twenty-ninth Street beach after whites had reportedly stoned him. Fighting ensued among blacks and whites on the beach, and exploded into six days of rioting. White Chicagoans attacked blacks who passed through white neighborhoods, dragging them from streetcars and beating them. Aggressive white gangs also drove through black districts and fired shots into residences. Blacks retaliated by assaulting whites who dared to enter the city's black zone. Finally, rain and the state militia dampened the fury of the mob, ending the carnage that left 38 dead and 520 injured. That same month race riots convulsed Washington, D.C. Reacting to inflammatory newspaper coverage of supposed attacks by black men on white women, white soldiers and sailors went on a rampage along Pennsylvania Avenue and throughout the downtown area, pursuing and attacking unwary blacks. As in Chicago the melee escalated. Blacks loaded into automobiles for shooting raids of white neighborhoods, and whites jumped into their Model T Fords for a blitzkreig of the black districts. Again, only rain and troops were able to quell the disorder.

Throughout the nation there were over twenty serious racial incidents or riots recorded during the summer and fall of 1919. In the minds of many whites, this outbreak of violence simply proved that blacks and whites could not live together and that any hopes of racial integration were unrealistic. Responding to Chicago's riots, a local newspaper editorialized: "Despite the possible justice of Negro demands, the fact is that the races are not living in harmony. . . . How long will it be before segregation will be the only means of preventing murders?" A white clergyman expressed the view of many Chicagoans when he said: "I believe in segregating the blacks for their own good as well as the good of the whites." Moreover, a white neighborhood association dedicated to the residential segregation of blacks testified forcefully to the ethnic fragmentation of the city when it declared: "There is nothing in the make-up of a Negro, physically or mentally, which should induce anyone to welcome him as a neighbor. . . . Niggers are undesirable neighbors and entirely irresponsible and vicious."

With such attitudes prevailing, the black population was forced to remain segregated within the city. Black businessmen and professionals catered to a black clientele that lived in black neighborhoods and attended all-black churches and belonged to all-black lodges. But this concentration of the black population in segregated neighborhoods also led to enhanced political power for Afro-Americans. By the 1920s there were black majorities in an increasing number of wards and assembly districts, and these majorities ensured that more blacks would hold political office. In 1917 the Harlem district of New York City elected its first black representative to the state assembly and three years later Harlem voters chose the first black alderman in the city. From 1883 through 1913 the Chicago delegation to the Illinois House of Representatives included one black. In 1914 Chicago blacks captured a second seat, in 1918 they won a third seat, and by 1929 the black caucus in Springfield consisted of five representatives and one state senator.

Moreover, in 1928 Chicago's South Side elected the first black congressman from a northern city. Chicago's "Big Bill" Thompson recognized the growing importance of the black vote and awarded blacks an unprecedented share of city appointments. During his third term, six assistant corporation counsels, five assistant city prosecutors, and one assistant city attorney were black. Though only 6 percent of Chicago's population was black, Afro-Americans held 14 percent of the positions in the city law department. In response, grateful black leaders lauded Al Capone's favorite mayor as a "second Lincoln," whereas white critics nicknamed Thompson's city hall "Uncle Tom's Cabin."

In most cities, however, white public officials remained either indifferent or hostile to the growing black community, and black victories at the polls only gradually produced begrudging change in municipal policies. Only after blacks won three of the twenty-five council seats in Cleveland did the white city manager finally admit blacks to internships at the municipal hospital or to the hospital's nurse training program. Likewise, New York City's first black alderman broke the color line in that municipality's public hospitals, convincing white officials to hire black nurses and admit black physicians. Some racial barriers were falling, but occasional victories in city council elections did not ignite a revolution in race relations.

Meanwhile, other new migrants were arriving in American cities, adding to the ethnic fragmentation of the metropolis. For example, the lure of higher wages attracted thousands of Mexican migrants to the city, and during the 1920s sizable Mexican-American communities appeared in a number of urban areas. In 1923 the founding of the Mexican Our Lady of Guadelupe Church added one more ethnic parish to the polyglot religious map of Detroit, and five years later the Motor City was home to an estimated fifteen thousand Mexicans. Many Mexican migrants to Chicago clustered around Jane Addams's Hull House on the near west side, moving into tenements formerly occupied by Italians and Greeks. Whereas the automobile factories drew Mexicans to Detroit, packing plants, railroads, and steel mills were the magnets attracting Hispanic immigrants to Chicago.

In no city did the Mexican immigrants represent as large a proportion of the population as in San Antonio. Ninety thousand of the city's 265,000 residents were Mexican at the close of the 1920s. According to sociologist Max Handman, every evening in the heart of the Mexican district "men with big sombreros, mellow eyes and gentle expressions and . . . women with their heads wrapped in dark shawls" promenaded along streets lined with theaters, stores, and restaurants catering to immigrants from south of the Rio Grande. Although Mexican San Antonio may have been colorful to outsiders, in many ways it represented a grim contrast to the non-Hispanic neighborhoods. Handman reported that according to one survey of 1,500 Mexican families in San Antonio, 1,264 families had to go outdoors for their water supply and only 159 had inside toilets. The survey also found that twenty-eight families with seven children each had only one bed for the entire family and that eighty-two families with seven children had only two beds. The Mexican immigrants not only lacked physical comforts and conveniences but also educational advantages. In 1929 records show that 56 percent of the children in San Antonio's elementary schools had Spanish names, but only 9 percent of those in high school came from Hispanic families. Only a privileged few among the Mexican-Americans could afford the luxury of keeping their children out of the labor force long enough to graduate from high school.

By the 1920s, however, the largest Mexican-American community was not in San Antonio but in the booming city of Los Angeles. In 1930 there were 167,000 Mexicans living in Los Angeles County, and the growing barrio on the east side of the city was developing into the Hispanic capital of the Southwest. In fact, the east side was becoming the Mexican Harlem, a segregated residential zone housing a minority despised by many in the non-Hispanic majority. According to a Los Angeles social worker, by the late 1920s Mexican-Americans had "become accustomed to segregation and [referred to] Americans as white people." Restricted largely to menial, unskilled jobs, the Mexican residents of Los Angeles, like those of San Antonio, were at the bottom of the social heap with little money and few comforts. Some, however, were planting roots in Southern California and investing in businesses. As early as 1922 there were about 239 Mexican-owned businesses in the Los Angeles barrio; one-fourth of these establishments were grocery stores whereas many of the rest were restaurants and cleaning operations. But these businesses catered solely to Mexicans, and both owners and customers lived in a society apart from non-Hispanic Los Angeles.

Even immigrants who had lived in the United States for two or more decades remained dedicated to preserving their separate identity within the city. For example, the Poles of Chicago continued to attend Polish churches, reside in Polish neighborhoods, rally behind Polish political candidates and crusade for symbols of ethnic recognition such as changing the name of Crawford Avenue to Pulaski Road. With increasing prosperity many moved out of immigrant tenements, but distinctive Polish sectors survived in Chicago, and in Detroit and Buffalo as well.

Chicago's Roman Catholic Archbishop, George William Munde-lein, soon discovered the strength of Polish separatism when he attempted to impose "Americanizing" reforms aimed at lessening the ethnic divisions within the church. He refused to create additional national churches, churches for a single nationality, insisting on territorial parishes, neighborhood congregations including Catholics of all nationalities residing within the district. He attempted to assign Polish priests to Irish parishes in the hope of creating an American clergy rather than a clergy tied to the old country, and in addition required that all classes in the parochial schools other than catechism be taught in the English language. In 1924 the prelate told Chicago's Catholics that it was their duty "to keep [the American] people one and undivided; to keep it far from alien influences . . . to repel from our midst those who would split up in parts." And he claimed that the future Catholic clergy should be the "real leaders of Americanization in this city, youths . . . in whose heart burns ardently, and undyingly, the love of but one country, the land of their birth, the land of the Star Spangled Flag."

Most Polish clerics viewed this melting-pot church with little enthusiasm. Whereas Mundelein sought to eradicate the ethnic divisions within his urban domain, many Polish-Americans argued that their Polish identity must be preserved. The editor of a Polish-language periodical responded to the archbishop by declaring that "all violent, intolerant attempts upon the religio-nationalistic schools . . . upon the souls and traditions of those who were born elsewhere, will only spoil the really noble work of Americanization and we will stand as one man against them." In 1920 the General Union of the Polish Clergy in America, led by Chicago and Milwaukee priests, appealed directly to the Vatican, urging that under no circumstances was the "Catholic Church through its bishops to become the instrument of Americanization among the Polish immigrants." And other petitions followed. Eventually there was an accommodation between the Americanizing archbishop and his Polish clergy and parishioners. Mundelein did not create new Polish national parishes, but since Poles remained clustered in certain neighborhoods the territorial parishes in those areas were almost wholly Polish. Moreover, the archbishop obligingly appointed Polish clergy to Polish congregations, and relented from his policy of integrating Polish priests into Irish or German parishes. By their own choice, Chicago Poles were to remain segregated, and older Polish pastors often forbade the younger Polish clerics from attending seminary reunions with non-Poles or going on vacation with Irish clergy.

Thus the Poles were to remain a distinct ethnic fragment of metropolitan America as were the Mexican newcomers and the blacks. Many offspring of immigrant families were turning their backs on their ethnic origins, dropping the "skis" and "witzes" from their surnames and forgetting whatever Polish, Czech, or Italian phrases or customs they had once known. But ethnic divisions remained evident in the American city, especially for dark-complexioned newcomers from Latin America or the South. The antagonisms and animosities survived.

Indicative of the continuing ethnic divisions of the 1920s was the popularity of the Ku Klux Klan. Dedicated to pure white, native-born Protestant Americanism, the Klan was a bulwark against the cultures and religions of immigrant newcomers to the city. Especially troubled by the crime and immorality associated with foreigners, Klan members equated ethnic purity and moral purity. In such cities as Indianapolis and Denver, where native-born white Protestants were the predominant ethnic group, the Klan took control of municipal government and attempted to impose its version of pure American Protestantism on the populace. For example, in 1925 Indianapolis voters elected the Klan candidate for mayor as well as five men running on the Klan-backed United Protestant School Board ticket. In accord with Klan principles, this ticket emphasized the importance of the Bible and the American flag in the public school curriculum.

But the Klan's empire in Indiana soon crumbled, for on a train trip to Chicago the order's Grand Dragon, David Stephenson, repeatedly assaulted an Indianapolis secretary and "chewed" on her body. Distraught at the loss of her chastity, the secretary took poison but Stephenson secured no medical assistance and she died. Stephenson was found guilty of second-degree murder, and from his prison cell he revealed the skullduggery of his Klan associates in public office. The mayor of Indianapolis, the city controller, the municipal purchasing agent, the county sheriff, a local congressman, and numerous other officials joined Stephenson in prison, and their convictions sealed the fate of the Klan.

In other cities where native, white Protestants were a minority, the Klan not only failed to win office but was hounded out of existence by angry opponents. Fighting intolerance with intolerance, foes of the Klan stole the order's membership lists, boycotted the businesses of Klansmen, and in Buffalo roving gangs painted or defaced the property of purported members. Boston's Catholic Mayor Curley barred Klan meetings in his city, even on private property, and New York City's Catholic mayor ordered his police commissioner to "ferret out these despicable disloyal persons who are attempting to organize a society, the aims and purposes of which are of such a character that were they to prevail, the foundations of our country would be destroyed." Similarly, in 1921 the Chicago city council declared the "traditions and odium attached to the Ku Klux Klan . . . a menace to a city like Chicago, having a heterogeneous population and different religious creeds" and pledged "its services to the proper authorities to rid the community of this organization." Chicago councilmen also voted to fire city employees who joined the Klan. Exposed to such pressure, the Klan faltered and gradually faded from prominence.

Yet the spirit of the Klan persisted. Native-born white Protestants continued to fear and distrust the immigrant, the Jew, the Catholic, and the black. And the ethnic mosaic of the American city continued to form a jarring pattern of clashing contrasts. Klan prejudice, Polish particularism, and widespread discrimination against blacks and Mexicans characterized the metropolis of the 1920s. Ethnic separatism and divisions persisted, and urban America remained a collection of disparate social and cultural fragments.

AUTOMOBILES AND THE PROMISE OF SUBURBIA

Although metropolitan Americans failed to realize dreams of moral purity, political efficiency, and social harmony, the advent of the automobile did seem to promise a solution to the problem of urban congestion. The automobile offered urban dwellers a new mobility, freeing them from the centripetal streetcar lines and allowing them to travel more quickly from the urban core to the suburban fringe. Fords and Chevrolets liberated urban Americans from the tyranny of the trolley, running along fixed tracks, loaded with its tightly-packed human baggage. With an automobile urbanites could travel wherever the avenues and boulevards led and could even escape to the mountains or seashore on weekends. This new mode of transportation seemed to promise a more open, expansive city, a city of greater mobility and individual autonomy.

Automobile manufacturers and dealers never failed to emphasize the new freedom and pleasure to be derived from their product, and they found many ready customers in American cities during the 1920s. In 1915 there was one automobile in Chicago for every sixty-one residents; by 1920 the number had risen to one for every thirty; five years later it was one for every eleven Chicagoans; and in 1930 there was one car in the Windy City for every eight persons. Elsewhere automobiles were even more prevalent. By 1930 in Detroit and Seattle there was one car for every four residents, and in that hotbed of motoring madness, Los Angeles, the ratio was one to three. Most commuters and shoppers in the largest cities still relied on public transportation; according to a traffic survey, in 1926 only one-third of those entering and leaving

Chicago's loop did so by private automobile. This figure, however, was rising, and in some urban areas the automobile surpassed the streetcar as a means for traveling downtown. In 1931, for example, 435,000 persons entered downtown Los Angeles each day by automobile whereas only 262,000 entered by public transportation.

Though many praised the automobile, as the number of motor vehicles mounted its shortcomings became increasingly evident. Narrow downtown streets proved incapable of handling both the long line of trolleys and the new mass of motor vehicles. Thus rush-hour traffic jams became increasingly common. "From the moment your car hits the edge of Peachtree," one frustrated Atlantan wrote in 1929, "it is touch and go, jostle and jump, 'horn in' fast and then throw your wife abruptly through the windshield by suddenly braking down. Finally you find yourself in a huddle of harassed drivers tooting horns, looking blackly at each other and swearing softly." Because of such traffic snares, in many cities the automobile did not greatly reduce the travel time of commuters. In 1929 the average automobile journey between Chicago's Loop and suburban Evanston was only five minutes shorter than the scheduled trip on the elevated railroad fifteen years earlier. In other words, traffic jams were eroding the advantages of the new technology.

To ease the flow of vehicles and facilitate automobile travel, municipal officials imposed traffic controls and attempted to adapt city thoroughfares to the motor age. A new corps of traffic engineers experimented with sequentially timed traffic lights in order to ensure an even and efficient flow of automobiles. Moreover, city governments widened and repaved major streets. For example, between 1915 and 1930 the city of Chicago widened and opened 112 miles of streets at a cost of $114 million. Chicago's most notable achievement was the double-decked Wacker Drive along the Chicago River. With one deck underground and another on the surface, Wacker Drive could carry twice as much traffic as the conventional street. But some visionaries proposed more drastic solutions. One planner seriously suggested paving over the entire Chicago River, transforming the waterway into a highway. A leading municipal engineer in New York City advocated a three-level elevated expressway along the Hudson River, and others conceived of four or even six-layer projects. The age of superhighways had not yet arrived, but America's planners were already dreaming of grand schemes to serve the growing number of motorists.

Yet street widenings and sequentially timed signals did not solve the traffic problem. The smoother pavements, the wider streets, and the efficient flow of traffic simply encouraged more urban residents to invest in an automobile and forsake public transportation. Improvements thus bred more traffic which in turn bred more improvements. Municipalities could barely keep pace with motorist demands, and the strain on city budgets was serious. In 1930 an Atlanta editor expressed the attitude of a growing number of civic leaders: "When Mr. Henry Ford, his successors and predecessors . . . put some kind of automobile within easy reach of almost everybody, they inadvertently created a monster that has caused more trouble in the larger cities than bootleggers, speakeasies, and alley bandits."

Once motorists navigated through the traffic snares and reached their downtown destination, they confronted the additional problem of parking. Streetcars simply passed through the central business district and were housed overnight in suburban depots. Consequently city authorities previously had not needed to deal with the storage of vehicles downtown. With the growing popularity of the automobile, however, the problem became serious, especially since curb parking reduced the space available for the flow of through traffic and thus exacerbated vehicle congestion. In the early 1920s the *Literary Digest* printed the observation that "the American public is thinking more about where to park its cars than about the League of Nations," and by the close of the decade a Memphis resident was complaining that "finding an unoccupied space large enough to park a car in the business district is like sighting an oasis in the desert." Business leaders recognized the economic consequences of a parking shortage, and in 1925 a planning expert with the US Chamber of Commerce warned readers of the *Saturday Evening Post* that if a business district was "virtually inaccessible by automobile transportation," then "real estate there will soon feel the stifling effect of that restriction." This planner concluded that "automobile day-storage is real-estate insurance in congested centers."

By the late 1920s scores of downtown parking garages and lots offered this necessary insurance. Perhaps the most innovative garage was in the Pure Oil Building in Chicago. Opened in 1926, the Pure Oil Garage provided twenty-two stories of fully mechanized parking. Three elevators carried the cars from the entrance on the lower level of Wacker Drive to the floors above. When the elevator reached the level designated by a switchboard operator at the garage entrance, the elevator floor tipped forward allowing the automobile to roll onto a conveyor belt which deposited the vehicle into the appropriate berth. It was a marvel of mechanical ingenuity and an innovative though expensive answer to the problem of storing automobiles. Elsewhere less ingenious facilities catered to the motorist. By 1925 private investors had constructed three garages in downtown Detroit which provided parking for 1,500 cars at a rate of 75¢ a day and also offered car washing and polishing services. That same year Cleveland could boast of garages holding 7,000 automobiles, plus a newly completed lakefront lot for 1,000 vehicles. Meanwhile, New York City's deputy police commissioner in charge of traffic submitted a plan for a garage beneath Central Park to accommodate 30,000 cars.

At the same time new garages and lots opened to eager motorists, city officials sought to guarantee adequate space for the flow of traffic by banning curb parking along major thoroughfares. In one city after another, however, downtown merchants and shoppers rebelled at the restrictions. For example, in 1920 the Los Angeles city council adopted a no-parking ordinance, setting off an outcry among retailers and motorists. The *Los Angeles Times* editorialized that the council had "deprived motorists of the rights of citizens and taxpayers" and had inferred "that they are also outcasts, not entitled to the reasonable privileges accorded human beings." Two weeks after the ban went into effect, the film star Clara Kimball Young led a protest caravan of automobiles through the downtown streets, and shortly thereafter the council repealed its ban. In Chicago similar protests kept the city council from imposing a curb parking ban until 1927, and the story was the same throughout the nation. Merchants recognized that auto-borne customers were more devoted to their automobiles than to the downtown stores. Therefore, if cars were excluded from the central business district, then some customers would stay away. By 1930 the problem of parking was beginning to threaten traditional patterns of retailing, and the rising popularity of the automobile seemed to cloud the future of the downtown merchant.

In automobile-dominated Los Angeles the motor vehicle was already taking its toll on downtown business. Of every one hundred persons residing within a ten-mile radius of downtown Los Angeles in 1923, sixty-eight entered the central business district daily. By 1931 this figure had fallen to fifty-two, a drop of 24 percent. In 1929 Bullock's Department Store opened a giant branch on Wilshire Boulevard, far to the west of the central business district but convenient to such affluent suburbs as Beverly Hills and Westwood. Among its attractions was ample off-street parking. Other retailers joined Bullock's westward migration along Wilshire, and development of the boulevard's "Miracle Mile" shopping area contributed further to the relative decline of the central business district.

Not only did the automobile bode ill for some downtown merchants, it also was beginning to pose problems for public transit lines. Millions of Americans still commuted to work by streetcars and underground or elevated lines, and many downtown department stores still prospered from the mass of shoppers who relied on public transportation. But by the mid-1920s the number of streetcar fares was leveling off, and in the last years of the decade use of the public transit lines was declining. Combined patronage on streetcar and bus lines in the United States peaked at 17.2 billion riders in 1926, but fell to 15.6 billion by 1930. In 1932 *Transit Journal* offered city-by-city statistics on the drop in transit patronage and found it was especially severe in moderate-sized communities having a population between 100,000 and 250,000. For example, in 1918 in San Diego the number of fare-paying rides per capita was 299, whereas in 1931 the typical San Diego resident averaged only 124 transit rides annually; in Fort Worth the figure for per capita rides dropped from 312 in 1918 to 87 thirteen years later. In these cities traffic jams were less frequent and parking spaces more abundant than in larger urban areas, and thus residents more readily abandoned the streetcar. But even in metropolises of over 500,000 the drop in patronage was notable. In Baltimore per capita rides plummeted from 296 to 180, in Saint Louis from 300 to 203, and in Los Angeles from 292 to 169. Only New Yorkers defied the trend and increased their per capita use of public transit facilities from an annual average of 354 rides to 447 rides. Congested Manhattan was especially ill-suited for motor vehicles and no American city could claim such a rapid and inexpensive means of transportation as the New York subway. Consequently, New Yorkers alone resisted the lure of commuting and shopping by automobile.

As urban Americans forsook the streetcar, transit revenues plummeted and operating deficits became commonplace. Although fares in most cities rose from five cents to seven or eight cents during the decade following World War I, revenues generally remained static or declined. In Los Angeles the combined revenues for the two street railway companies dropped 14 percent between 1923 and 1930: one company stayed out of the hands of receivers only because it was a subsidiary of the profitable Southern Pacific Railroad, whereas the other transit corporation earned a modest profit by failing to invest in improvements or expand service. In 1927 the company operating Chicago's surface trolleys was forced into receivership, and elsewhere the financial picture was almost as gloomy. As early as 1923 eleven of the twenty-three transit lines within the city of Atlanta failed to earn enough to meet operating expenses. In Atlanta as in Chicago and Los Angeles, fewer urban residents were dropping their coins into the fare boxes, and streetcar franchises no longer ensured their owners a place in the plutocracy.

Although the automobile may have bred traffic jams, created parking woes, and deprived transit companies of needed revenues, it represented the hope of the future for many urban Americans. With enhanced mobility, more Americans could move to the suburbs, and for profit-hungry speculators and idealistic planners alike decentralization was a much desired goal. So long as urban Americans relied solely on fixed rail transportation, population would cluster along the rail routes and business crowd together at the junction of transit lines. In the minds of many Americans, fixed rail lines predestined urban dwellers to congested living in ill-lit, ill-ventilated cubicles far removed from the benefits of nature. The new mobility offered by motor vehicles, however, broke the bond of dependence on the fixed rail lines and opened new opportunities for restructuring urban settlement. The suburban fringes now beckoned an ever increasing number of Americans, and for many suburbia seemed a land of promise.

Among those who looked to the suburban periphery for an answer to urban woes were a number of professional planners seeking to create an alternative to the drab rows of houses and apartments in the central city. In 1927 the distinguished planner John Nolen wrote that the automobile and "good roads, extending nearly everywhere, are opening up millions of acres hitherto inaccessible," and "these facilities come opportunely as a relief to the congestion of population in the large cities, now becoming more and more intolerable because of high rents and the tendencies to crowding in the slums." According to Nolen, the worker now had the opportunity "to escape the oppressive urban surroundings that have been keeping him under, body and soul," and together with his wealthy patron Mary Emery, Nolen attempted to realize the dream of an ideal community for urban refugees. In the town of Mariemont on the outskirts of Cincinnati, Nolen and Emery hoped to provide "an extensive housing of industrial workers of various economic grades under conditions that fairly deserve the term ideal." Georgian and Tudor rowhouses lined the handsomely landscaped avenues which converged on a quaint village green. More than 20 percent of the land area was reserved for parks and playgrounds that offered public tennis courts, a golf course, and a lagoon for boating and skating. Moreover, utility lines were buried underground, sparing residents the overhead web of wires that marred the appearance of so many urban streets. Such improvements, however, were costly, and neither Emery nor the executor of her estate intended to take a loss on the development. Thus they fixed the level of rents so high that wage earners could not afford to live in the community, and by the 1930s Mariemont had become an unusually attractive upper-middle-class residential retreat.

In New York City an idealistic band of planners and architects led by Clarence Stein and Henry Wright also hoped to create a utopia in the suburbs. Their efforts resulted in the model community of Radburn, laid out in 1928–29 in suburban northeastern New Jersey. Advertised as the "Town for the Motor Age," Radburn was an attempt to fashion a community where automobiles and human beings could coexist in safety and happiness. The development was divided into superblocks of thirty or forty acres penetrated by a ring of dead-end lanes. Along these cul-de-sacs were rows of houses with their fronts facing on a common park in the interior of the superblock and their backs or motor entrances leading to the lane. Since each of the houses was on a dead-end lane, residents did not need to worry about through traffic roaring by their homes and massacring their children. Moreover, pedestrian underpasses linked the various superblocks in the community so that a resident could stroll throughout the development without ever stepping from a curb and dashing between threatening motor vehicles. Rejecting the gridiron plan of small rectangular blocks inherited from the horse-and-buggy era, the planners of Radburn attempted to segregate housing and traffic, isolating their happy homes from the noxious fumes, honking horns, and speeding bedlam of the thoroughfare.

But the promoters of Radburn could not protect suburbanites from the insecurities of the economy. Five months after the first residents moved into the community, the stock market crashed and home construction slowed. In 1934 the company that had developed Radburn went bankrupt, bringing a close to the innovative project. Yet during the late 1920s Radburn was a significant experiment in suburban development. Although only a portion of the community was completed according to original plans, the scheme excited many professional planners and influenced their work. Moreover, the Radburn project was indicative of the growing concern for minimizing the discomforts and dangers posed by the automobile.

Most suburban developers were not so idealistic or innovative as John Nolen, Clarence Stein, and Henry Wright. But throughout the nation other figures were making their mark on suburban landscape. During the 1920s vast tracts of rural America succumbed to the bulldozer, and Tudor estates, Georgian manors, and Spanish haciendas rose in former cow pastures, orange groves, and swamps. One of the most successful developers was J. C. Nichols of Kansas City, Missouri. Purchasing thousands of acres to the southwest of the city, Nichols laid out block after block of generous building lots for the well-to-do and named his development the Country Club District. Before property owners could build on the lots, the Nichols Realty Company had to approve the proposed floor plan, a sketch of the facade, and the external color scheme. In this way Nichols ensured that aesthetically offensive structures would not tarnish the good name of his development. The centerpiece of Nichols's layout, however, was the shopping center, Country Club Plaza. Built in a Mediterranean motif, complete with a replica of the famous Giralda tower of Seville, Country Club Plaza was one of the first and most attractive auto-oriented shopping centers. Wide streets permitted diagonal parking at the curbs, and ample parking lots were available for additional motorists. Just as Radburn attempted to adapt residential patterns to the motor age, Country Club Plaza sought to create a suburban shopping district suitable for autoborne Americans.

Nichols's development proved very profitable, and elsewhere in the nation speculators hoped to be just as successful. In booming Los Angeles promoters advertised the hillside Beverly Wood subdivision as the "Switzerland of Los Angeles," a cool haven when "heat blankets Los Angeles." The developers of suburban Palos Verdes Estates did not rely simply on claims of a perfect climate; they attracted prospective suburbanites with free coffee and lunch accompanied by programs of music, Spanish dancing, aquaplaning, yacht racing, and stunt flying. Few suburban real estate promoters, however, could match the excesses of George Merrick, developer of Coral Gables on the outskirts of Miami. Merrick equipped the drainage canals crisscrossing the former swampland with gondolas and advertised his sunny, suburban tract as a new Venice. A recycled gravel pit became the Venetian Pool, a glamorous public swimming hole, and the leading dance bands in the nation played melodic strains along these sunlit waters. In order to attract even more prospective buyers, Merrick hired the perennial presidential candidate and Bible-thumping fundamentalist William Jennings Bryan to conduct "the largest outdoor Bible class in the world." Between his poolside rhetorical flourishes on Old Testament prophets and New Testament morality, Bryan obligingly inserted occasional tributes to the beauty of Coral Gables and the profitability of owning land in the Florida paradise.

Most Americans, however, needed little encouragement to purchase a suburban home. A bungalow, garage, and well-manicured lawn in suburbia was the dream of millions, a dream that came true for many. In suburban Cleveland, the population of Shaker Heights increased 1,000 percent between 1920 and 1930 and the number of inhabitants in Garfield Heights increased 500 percent; the population of Chicago's suburb of Elmwood Park rose over 700 percent; and in Southern California the population of Glendale rose over 360 percent, and the number of persons residing in Beverly Hills skyrocketed almost 2,500 percent. By 1930 row after row of suburban homes testified to the dispersion of America's urban population.

Yet the benefits and joys of suburbia were balanced by its short-comings. Although some enthusiasts viewed the suburban trend as "an evangel of hope," the emergence of additional outlying communities exacerbated many urban problems and most notably furthered the social and economic segregation of metropolitan America. Coral Gables, the Country Club District, and even Radburn were not open to all. These communities were retreats for the white middle class, and they were off-limits to "undesirables." Of the more than 350 families living in Radburn in the early 1930s, only 2 were Jewish (and one of these was actually of mixed heritage, practicing both Catholicism and Judaism). Although white Protestants were a minority in the New York City area, in Radburn they constituted 77 percent of the population. No unskilled workers lived in the model community, and an extraordinary 87 percent of the male heads of households had attended college. The motor age permitted white, middle-class Americans not only to escape from the congestion, soot, and clatter of the central city, it allowed them to isolate themselves from those ethnic and economic groups deemed incompatible with their way of life. Thanks to the ingenuity of Henry Ford and J. C. Nichols, the distance between the ethnic and economic fragments of metropolitan America was increasing.

Thus for the automobile-oriented suburbanite the likelihood of mixing with persons of different social and economic classes was diminishing. By commuting to work in a private automobile, the middle-class office worker no longer needed to jostle for space with Italian-Americans, Poles, or blacks on the streetcar. Country Club Plaza was for the motorist of comfortable circumstances, and few outside this class traveled to the suburban shopping center. Likewise, the middle-class residential neighborhood remained a bastion against social and economic diversity.

Moreover, building restrictions and zoning ordinances bolstered divisions within metropolitan America. During the 1920s developers added to the list of protective restrictions in the deeds to subdivision lots, and among these restrictions were covenants forbidding sale or rental of the property to blacks, Jews, or others who might destroy the ethnic homogeneity of the suburban enclave. Architectural controls of the type imposed by J. C. Nichols were also an increasingly common feature of developments, so middle-class purchasers could rest assured that only structures of "good taste" would grace their community. And the introduction of zoning ordinances meant that the homeowner need not fear that a gas station or meat market would open on the next lot. In 1916 New York City had adopted the first comprehensive zoning ordinance, dividing the metropolis into zones for business, manufacturing, and residences. By 1923 there were 183 communities, containing 40 percent of the nation's urban population, that had enacted zoning ordinances, and the number of zoned municipalities was to increase rapidly through the remainder of the decade. These legal strictures added one more barrier to aesthetic and economic offense and further safeguarded property holdings in America's model suburbs.

One protected community of the 1920s was the suburb of Westchester, outside of Chicago. Writing in the *National Real Estate Journal,* a Westchester promoter boasted that the community's homes were "without exception charming examples of the modified English type" and their owners did not need to fear "that at some future time a misguided owner will erect on adjoining property a 'Moorish Castle' done in the Spanish manner and finished in bright red or blue stucco." Moreover, "no factory building may be built within the corporate limits," and "the unsightly and unnecessary fence is forever tabooed." Through such restrictions and zoning the "well-intentioned home builder" was protected from "the thoughtless and unsympathetic owner," and early investors in the subdivision would "know in advance the kind of community Westchester would be and the class of people that would inhabit it." In other words, the developers of Westchester and other suburban communities like it were leaving little to chance. These suburbs were intended to be white, gentile preserves of good taste removed from unpleasant commerce. A wall of zoning and restrictions kept out unwanted persons, architectural styles, and businesses, ensuring a neighborly compatibility within the community that precluded the need for fences.

Not only did suburbanization exacerbate the social and economic fragmentation of metropolitan America, it also encouraged the fragmentation of urban government. Along the fringes of the central cities suburban municipalities burgeoned, developing public services equal if not superior to those of the central cities. The multitude of "Heights," "Woods," and "Gardens" that were proliferating in suburbia adopted zoning ordinances tailored to the class aspirations of residents and financed "good schools" to inculcate middle-class values in their offspring and prepare them for college. The governments of the socially segregated suburbs thus provided services expressly suited to their narrow populations, something that the governments of the polyglot central cities could not do. Moreover, many suburbs also provided adequate water, sewerage, police, and fire protection. With all this, there was little reason for suburbanites to favor consolidation with the central city, and throughout much of the nation the largest cities were no longer able to annex new territories. Instead, bands of suburban municipalities ringed many central cities, and in a single metropolitan area scores of municipalities shared governing power. The consequence was overlapping authority, conflicting policies, and yet another barrier to the unity of the metropolitan population.

Throughout the 1920s many suburbanites strongly resisted consolidation with the central city. As early as 1920 Cleveland's Cuyahoga County contained thirty-five separate municipalities, each governing a fragment of the metropolitan area. But when Cleveland attempted to annex the middle-class suburb of Lakewood in 1922, suburban voters decisively rejected the proposal. By the close of the 1920s, suburban Saint Louis County could claim twenty-one independent municipalities, yet among Missouri suburbanites there also was little desire to succumb to central-city rule. In 1926 a scheme for consolidating the city and county of Saint Louis appeared on the ballot, a scheme that a newspaper in suburban Maplewood denounced as "so preposterous . . . that we cannot see how any fair-minded citizen could conscientiously support it." Likewise, in Webster Groves a local editor claimed that the suburbs "would stand to gain absolutely nothing from such a plan" but only suffer big-city corruption in the form of immoral "saloons, soft drink parlors, pool rooms, dance halls and this type of undesirable so-called amusements." Such sentiments expressed the views of many outlying residents, and the Saint Louis consolidation proposal suffered a humiliating defeat in the suburban county. Even in the more permissive, star-studded society of Beverly Hills, the notion of annexation to the central city was anathema to many. When in 1923 some land developers proposed the consolidation of the plush suburb with Los Angeles, such movie celestials as Douglas Fairbanks, Mary Pickford, Tom Mix, and Rudolph Valentino dashed to the rescue and saved their beloved community from the higher taxes of the big city. During the 1920s some major municipalities were able to annex additional territory, but generally the richest chunks of suburbia remained aloof and separate.

Faced with this resistance, metropolitan reformers of the 1920s turned to a federative alternative for metropolitan rule. They proposed a two-tier system of government which preserved the individual municipalities but allocated those services demanding areawide coordination to an overarching metropolitan government. For example, the metropolitan government might have charge of regional planning, major thoroughfares, an integrated sewerage system, and a countywide park system, whereas the member municipalities would retain control of their fire and police departments, the local playgrounds and streets, and garbage collection. This compromise appealed to many business leaders and white-collar suburban commuters who were boosters of the central city and wished to see it grow but who also sought the protection and security of the independent suburb. Yet others living along the suburban fringe remained suspicious and in the late 1920s and the 1930s voters defeated two-tier federative plans in the Pittsburgh, Saint Louis, and Cleveland metropolitan areas.

In each of these cities and elsewhere as well, those concerned about the regional coordination and planning of government services made little headway. The split between the central city and suburbs reflected social and economic divisions that ran deep in metropolitan life, and during the 1920s the bonds among the fragments of urban society seemed to loosen. The automobile gave urban Americans unprecedented mobility, and they used this new freedom of movement to isolate themselves in homogeneous suburban cells.

Thus the number of automobiles soared, and suburban tracts proliferated. Decentralization definitely seemed to be the wave of the future. In most cities the dispersion of population had not yet proved detrimental to the prosperity of the downtown business district. During the 1920s a new wave of ever-taller skyscrapers accentuated the urban skyline, and at the close of the decade work had begun on the Chrysler and Empire State buildings, structures that soared over a thousand feet. Moreover, downtown hotels became larger and grander, and most downtown department stores suffered no dearth of shoppers. Yet the automobile and the suburb were beginning to pose a threat to the still booming business district, a threat that could prove lethal to the existing structure of the city.

An Interlude in Urban Development, 1930–1945

In many ways the 1930s and early 1940s were years of arrested urban development. A tourist visiting New York City, Chicago, Philadelphia, or Boston in 1931 who returned fourteen years later would find few changes in the cityscape. Virtually no new skyscrapers soared overhead; instead, the same office blocks dominated the skyline in 1945 as in 1931, the same hotels catered to travelers, and the leading department stores had changed little but their window displays. The tourist might note a post office building or municipal auditorium that had not existed earlier, but the buildings and institutions in the downtown business district of 1945 were essentially the same as those of 1931.

Along the outskirts of the major cities, the tourist might note greater change. Developers, however, had invested in few new suburban housing tracts between 1931 and 1945, and only a scattering of neocolonial manses built in the 1930s supplemented the miles of bungalows from the 1920s. Near defense plants and military bases, especially in the burgeoning cities of the West, the tourist would discover acres of temporary housing that certainly was indicative of change. And along the shores of Miami Beach many new hotels cast their shadows across the sandy expanses. But in the older metropolises of the Northeast and Midwest the permanent building stock of the city remained remarkably unchanged. For decades American cities had experienced rapid development, with two-story frame structures quickly succumbing to four-story brick buildings which in turn made way for the steel frameworks of twenty-story skyscrapers. This pattern of constant physical change had prevailed throughout the first three decades of the century. But economic depression in the 1930s and war in the early 1940s produced an unusual interlude in the physical development of the American metropolis.

The period of the 1930s and early 1940s is not, however, a blank page in the history of the American city, an era when nothing worth mentioning occurred. While the physical appearance of many cities did not change radically, the relationship between the municipality and the federal government did. In no previous period did the federal government play such a significant role in American urban development as during the depression and World War II. For over a century the national authorities had invested in the development of rivers and harbors essential to urban commercial development, but the federal role in the cities expanded greatly after 1930 as city governments turned increasingly to Washington for financial aid. And with the outbreak of war federal defense spending became the mainstay of many urban areas. When measured in terms of skyscraper construction, the years from 1930 to 1945 may have been unimportant, but in terms of the federal-city relationship it was a revolutionary era.

THE DEPRESSION

In October 1929 stock market prices plummeted, ushering in a decade of economic woes. From 1929 to 1933 economic indicators headed steadily downward; they moved slowly upward between 1933 and 1937, fell again in 1937–38, and then turned up in 1939. But throughout the period the economic picture remained grim, and America's cities did not escape the suffering. Construction came to a virtual standstill, unemployment soared, local relief payments mounted, tax delinquencies rose, and discontent among the working class seemed to threaten the capitalist system.

No segment of the economy was so hard hit as the construction industry. During the year 1926, when the 1920s building boom was at its peak, almost 43,000 residential units were erected in the city of Chicago. Seven years later, in the depths of the depression, Chicago builders produced only 137 dwelling units. In fact, during the entire period from 1931 through 1938 only 8,000 new units rose in the Illinois metropolis. By December 1931 Chicago's forty-six excavating firms were so desperate that they jointly pledged to do work at cost in order to "start things going." Yet few took advantage of their offer and the building industry continued to spiral downward. During the Christmas season of 1932 underemployed architectural draftsmen turned their unused talents to the building of doll houses, and Chicago architects paid jobless draftsmen to construct canvas-and-paint street scenes as backdrops for a charity ball. Even in the formerly booming oil town of Houston, construction figures plummeted and few were willing to finance anything more ambitious than doll houses or party scenery. In 1929 the total value of building permits in Houston was over $35 million; in 1932 the figure had dropped to $2.9 million. Only the

Rockefeller family, with their depression-proof fortune, defied the trend and invested heavily in urban construction during the 1930s. From 1932 to 1940 the Rockefeller Center complex rose in midtown Manhattan, a monumental exception to the general halt in skyscraper construction. Thus many job-hungry New York construction workers earned paychecks owing to Rockefeller daring and enterprise. But elsewhere the construction industry languished.

Not only did building starts nose dive during the 1930s, so did automobile sales. Throughout the 1920s automobile production continued to rise, and it seemed that in the near future every household would boast of at least one car in the garage. After 1929, however, the onslaught of the automobile slowed as fewer Americans were able to afford their dream machine. Between 1929 and 1933 the number of registered automobiles dropped 11 percent, from 23,121,000 to 20,657,000, and auto sales plummeted 75 percent, from the 1929 high to the low in 1932. The Stearns, Locomobile, Jordan, and Marmon automobiles disappeared from showrooms as their manufacturers permanently ceased production, and red ink even filled the ledgers of that model of manufacturing success, Henry Ford. In his left-wing diatribe, *The Flivver King,* Upton Sinclair expressed the hostility of many depression-era Americans when he attacked the great automaker who had "made a million people dependent upon him for their daily bread, and [had] left them to rot in garrets and cellars and empty warehouses, in shacks made of tin and tar-paper." When auto sales inched upward after 1933, some of these displaced thousands again found work in the Ford plants, but not until 1936 did automobile registrations reach 1929 levels, and as late as 1945 there were only 25,800,000 cars in the United States. Thus the flow of traffic stabilized, and throughout the 1930s and early 1940s urban America experienced a temporary reprieve from the transforming impact of motor vehicles.

Yet the momentary setback in the automobile industry during the early 1930s did not benefit public transit lines. Streetcars and buses also felt the impact of the depression. The number of transit passengers dropped from 15.6 billion in 1930 to 11.3 billion in 1933 and had rebounded to only 13.1 billion in 1940. During the early 1930s it was clear that many Americans were abandoning both the automobile and the streetcar for the oldest and cheapest form of transportation, the feet.

By 1933 many urban Americans no longer needed transportation to work or to the stores, for millions were unemployed with little or no money to spend. At the depth of the depression in early 1933, an estimated 25 percent of the work force was jobless, and in some cities, such as Chicago, Saint Louis, and Detroit, unemployment figures topped 30 percent. Those who kept their jobs had thinner pay envelopes, for payrolls dropped even more drastically than employment. Between 1929 and 1933 employment in Chicago's manufacturing industries tumbled 50 percent but the total payroll for manufacturing concerns in the city fell 75 percent. In other words, in 1933 those Chicagoans still employed in factories were earning only half as much as four years earlier.

Moreover, many urban Americans lost not only their jobs and incomes but also their savings and the equity invested in their homes. Hard times destroyed thousands of banks and building and loan associations, wiping out the deposits of millions of thrifty city dwellers. In Chicago 163 small neighborhood banks folded during the first four years of the depression. From 1930 through 1933 fifty Philadelphia banks closed their doors, including the Bankers Trust Company with over 100,000 depositors. Rumors of impending collapse stampeded frenzied customers who rushed the teller's windows with withdrawal slips clenched in their nervous hands. In 1932 a Los Angeles bank vice-president counseled the readers of *Bankers Magazine* on how to restore the confidence of frightened depositors, advising bank officers to take panicky customers behind the counter away from prying eyes and to calmly present the institution's reassuring financial figures. That same year the seventy-year-old president of one of Chicago's largest banks was forced to climb atop a marble pedestal in the savings department and deliver an eloquent, confidence-building harangue to an army of frightened depositors that had invaded his august institution. Yet for thousands of banks and savings and loans calming words proved insufficient to stave off collapse. Meanwhile, hard-pressed financial institutions began foreclosure proceedings against the multitude of homeowners unable to meet their mortgage payments. In Chicago the number of foreclosures rose from 3,148 in 1928 to 15,201 four years later, and in Philadelphia there were 19,000 foreclosures in 1932. The dream of a suburban home that had become a reality for so many during the 1920s was now shattered by the economic depression.

Many who lost their homes moved in with more fortunate relatives. Others, unable to pay rent, settled in the numerous Hoovervilles or shack communities that sprang up in vacant lots across the country. Abandoned packing crates became home for many destitute Americans during the worst years of the depression, and some took refuge on park benches or under bridges. In August 1931 the Chicago branch of the Urban League reported that "every available dry spot of ground and every bench on the west side of Washington Park between 51st and 61st Streets is covered by sleepers." Another observer contrasted the glamour of the Chicago skyline with the harsh economic conditions when he wrote: "You can ride across the lovely Michigan Avenue bridge at midnight," with "the lights all about making a dream city of incomparable beauty, while twenty feet below you, on the lower level of the same bridge, are 2,000 homeless, decrepit, shivering and starving men, wrapping themselves in old newspapers to keep from freezing, and lying down in the manure dust to sleep." The destitute lacked food as well as shelter, and Edmund Wilson reported to the readers of the *New Republic* that "there is not a garbage-dump in Chicago which is not diligently haunted by the hungry." "Last summer," Wilson noted, "when the smell was sickening and the flies were thick, there were a hundred people a day coming to one of the dumps, falling on the heap of refuse as soon as the truck had pulled out" and devouring "all the pulp that was left on the old slices of watermelon and cantaloupe till the rinds were thin as paper." They salvaged meat as well, but before one impoverished widow would pick up the discarded meat, "she would always take off her glasses so that she couldn't see the maggots."

Black newcomers to the northern cities often suffered the most severe economic hardships. These migrants from the South were usually the last hired and the first fired; thus, the black unemployment rate surpassed the white. As early as February 1930 the *New York Herald Tribune* reported that the stock market crash had "produced five times as much unemployment in Harlem as in other parts of the city." In 1931 in Saint Louis 21.5 percent of the white work force was unemployed, but 42.8 percent of Saint Louis blacks were out of work. By the spring of 1933, unemployment figures for Saint Louis as a whole jumped to over 30 percent, yet an estimated 80 percent of the city's black work force was either underemployed or unemployed. In November 1933, when new federal regulations forced a raise in wages, a paint and varnish company in Saint Louis laid off all eighteen black women in the filling and labelling department, replacing them with white females. The company explained that it would not pay such high wages to blacks. Many whites believed that blacks should not retain good jobs so long as whites were unemployed. Thus blacks moved from the assembly line to the soup line, victims of both economic depression and racial discrimination.

Hispanics were also among the first to lose their jobs. Regarded by many native-born Americans as supplemental labor to fill in during boom periods, Mexican-Americans became a redundant burden on the American city during the 1930s. Consequently, in a number of urban areas civic leaders in cooperation with the Mexican consul organized repatriation programs for the return of the migrants to their native land. The Mexican consul in Detroit estimated that five-sixths of the

Mexicans from the Michigan area had departed by the end of 1932. Unable to find work, many Mexicans also abandoned the Los Angeles barrio, and Los Angeles officials encouraged their departure, making arrangements with the Southern Pacific Railroad to ship the unemployed Hispanics back to Mexico at a wholesale rate of $14.70 per head. Overall, almost 500,000 Mexicans migrated southward across the border during the 1930s. Those Mexican-Americans who failed to leave the country may have regretted their decision, because American employers, native-born workers, and welfare agencies often showed them little sympathy. In 1932 a lack of funds forced the Houston city commissary to refuse any further relief applications from Hispanics and blacks except in the most dire circumstances. Native-born whites had prior claim on the little money and few jobs available. Mexican-Americans had to wait in line for whatever was left over.

The depression not only struck certain ethnic groups more harshly than others, it also had a more devastating impact on certain urban areas. No city in the United States escaped economic hardship, and many boom towns of the 1920s found themselves in desperate straits in 1933. But generally the older metropolises of the Northeast and Midwest recovered more slowly from the slump and suffered the greatest permanent setbacks. In 1939 when national industrial production was 84 percent of the 1929 level, production in Kansas City was at 65 percent of the predepression mark, in Saint Louis it was at 70 percent, in Pittsburgh at 75 percent, and in Chicago at 77 percent. In 1929 the Chicago district produced 8.2 percent of the nation's manufacturing output; in 1939 its share was down to 7.15 percent. The share for the Saint Louis district dropped from 2.26 percent to 1.91 percent. In contrast, Los Angeles's proportion of American manufacturing output rose from 1.9 percent in 1929 to 2.1 percent in 1939. As early as the 1930s the migration of business from Frostbelt to Sunbelt was already evident. Los Angeles was advancing at the expense of her eastern sister cities, and cities in the warmer climes seemed more resilient than those hugging the Atlantic coast north of Chesapeake Bay or lining the shores of the Great Lakes. There were abundant vacancies in Miami hotels during the winter of 1932–33. Yet by 1935 construction had resumed in Miami Beach, with ten new hotels rising that year and nearly forty additional buildings in 1936. Meanwhile, shoe factories were leaving Boston and Saint Louis, and textile manufacturers were closing their mills in Philadelphia.

During the early 1930s, however, city officials everywhere faced a financial pinch. As the economy withered so did sources of municipal revenue. Property taxes had traditionally been the mainstay of local government, yet between 1930 and 1935 the assessed valuation of property in American cities with 100,000 or more inhabitants dropped 21 percent. In some cities the drop in assessed valuations was more precipitous, plunging 45 percent in Los Angeles and 42 percent in Cleveland. Exacerbating the problem of a declining municipal tax base was the rise in tax delinquencies. As an increasing number of property owners lost their bank deposits and exhausted their cash reserves, they also failed to pay their taxes. In 1930 the median year-end tax delinquency for 150 cities with population over 50,000 was 10 percent; by 1933 this figure had risen to 26 percent. Thus more than one-quarter of the property taxes owed municipalities were not being collected. With valuations declining and delinquencies rising, many cities felt the financial pressure.

At the same time local revenues were declining, relief expenditures were soaring. Local government had traditionally been responsible for aiding the needy, and with the onset of depression this task severely burdened the beleaguered city treasuries. Between 1929 and 1931 annual relief payments in New York City tripled from $7.4 million to $22.1 million, in Philadelphia they rose sixfold from $580,000 to $3.46 million, and in Detroit the increase was more than sixfold from $2.4 million to $14.9 million. Moreover, some cities instituted limited makework projects. For example, Philadelphia's sanitation and health departments hired 1,200 men to remove rubbish from vacant lots, clean alleys, post signs, and board up slum buildings. Some state legislatures made emergency appropriations to hard-pressed local relief agencies, and churches, business organizations, and charitable groups supplemented municipal efforts by distributing food and small sums of cash. In 1931 and 1932 private charitable drives raised millions of dollars for relief. Yet funds were quickly exhausted. No matter how much money was raised the relief burden seemed too great for the local community.

With their tax bases shrinking and their relief expenditures rising, some cities found themselves on the brink of bankruptcy. At the beginning of 1933 40 percent of Detroit's taxes for the previous year remained unpaid, and 70 percent of the municipal budget was committed to service charges on the inordinately large city debt contracted during the booming 1920s. The previous spring Detroit's mayor had slashed municipal payrolls by 50 percent, and still the city remained in serious financial straits. About thirty cities with a population of more than 50,000 were in default on their debt payments at some time during the first half of the 1930s, and others barely escaped the humiliation through eleventh-hour schemes of refinancing. Most major cities, however, were able to honor their debt obligations, although everywhere during the early 1930s it was necessary to cut salaries and abandon plans for expensive public improvements.

No crisis in local government financing received so much national attention as the school funding woes of Chicago. From 1931 to 1934 the Chicago school board only occasionally was able to meet its payrolls. For five months at a time, teachers went without paychecks, and when they received any remuneration it was often in the form of tax anticipation warrants, I.O.U.s from the city which usually could not be redeemed at face value but only at a substantial discount. At one school students' mothers organized cake sales to raise money for destitute teachers unable to pay the streetcar fare to work each morning. In April 1933 approximately ten thousand pupils went on strike to protest the school board's failure to pay their teachers, and twenty thousand instructors and students organized a protest parade complete with high school bands and placards. One disgruntled teacher led a decrepit old mule and carried a sign reading, "I haven't been paid since Nellie was a colt." In July the Chicago school board adopted an economy measure abolishing junior high schools, closing the city's junior college, eliminating manual training and home economics in grade schools, and raising the daily teaching load for high school instructors from five to seven classes. This only aroused further furor, and not until a year later did the tension ease when Chicago negotiated a loan from the federal government and paid the teachers' back salaries.

The protests of Chicago's teachers and students were mild, however, compared to other examples of growing insurgency in the city. In one city after another violent strikes and militant rallies fueled the fears of many middle-class Americans who believed that the depression was nurturing working-class radicalism. For example, in March 1932 American Communist leaders organized the Ford Hunger March, a protest parade to the Ford plant in the Detroit suburb of Dearborn. When the marchers moved from Detroit into Dearborn, the Dearborn police demanded that they disperse. The protesters persisted, the police responded with tear gas, and shots were fired on both sides, leaving four dead and a hundred injured. In 1934 a member of the Trotskyite wing of the Communist party led a truckers' strike in Minneapolis. This, too, left many dead or wounded, and Minnesota's governor sent in the national guard and declared martial law. A leading Minneapolis newspaper claimed that "the real objective of the Communists is to enlist Minnesota in the revolution they hope to start in this country for the overthrow of the constitution and the laws of the land." The following year a streetcar strike in Omaha ignited three nights of rioting as mobs roamed the streets and set fire to trolleys. In Omaha as in Minneapolis the state governor sent in the national guard to quell what seemed to be incipient revolution.

Riot and rebellion in Omaha, Minneapolis, and Dearborn, chaos in Chicago's schools, near bankruptcy in Detroit, and unemployment and hardship throughout the nation — all this added up to a grim total that was unacceptable to the American public. America's cities seemed to be collapsing under the weight of economic depression, unable to deal with growing class conflict, worsening financial woes, and the task of feeding and clothing the populace. From 1929 to 1933 President Herbert Hoover had repeatedly emphasized local and private initiatives in dealing with the nation's economic troubles. By 1932 city officials and most American voters were tired of Hoover's rhetoric. At a conference of mayors, Detroit's chief executive expressed the view of many present when he said: "We have done everything humanly possible to do, and it has not been enough. The hour is at hand for the Federal Government to cooperate." Local initiative had not been sufficient; federal intervention was necessary. A new era in American urban history had arrived.

THE FEDERAL RESPONSE

On March 4, 1933, Franklin D. Roosevelt took the oath of office as president of the United States and ushered in the New Deal. Roosevelt's New Deal was dedicated to alleviating the hardships of economic depression by virtually any possible means. Thus the new president and his Democratic Congress experimented with an array of agencies and schemes aimed at priming the economic pump and restoring national prosperity. Among the programs adopted were several that had a significant impact on the nation's hard-pressed cities. By the mid-1930s city governments that had traditionally fended for themselves were becoming entangled in a web of relationships with the booming federal bureaucracy.

Of primary importance was the feeding and clothing of those who were destitute. In many areas local government relief funds were exhausted and private charities could not cope with the enormity of the task. Consequently, in May 1933 Congress established the Federal Emergency Relief Administration (FERA) and authorized it to grant $500 million to state and local agencies charged with distributing handouts to the poor. This appropriation and others that followed not only alleviated the worst miseries of the poor, they were also a welcome boon to beleaguered municipal and county officials who came to rely increasingly on federal aid. For example, in 1934 in Detroit and surrounding

Wayne County, an average of 210,000 people received relief each month, and $52 million of the $64 million in relief funds distributed in the Michigan metropolis that year came from FERA. No longer were the destitute solely a local responsibility. They were wards of the nation as well as the city, and the national government could now be counted on to help fund the dole.

The idea of giving unearned handouts to the poor was offensive, however, to many Americans who believed that such charity undermined individual dignity and self-respect. In response to such views, the Roosevelt administration embarked on a work relief program supervised by the Civil Works Administration (CWA). A temporary program intended to help the poor survive the winter of 1933–34, the CWA employed more than four million Americans at an impressive array of tasks. The agency built and patched streets and roads, modernized school buildings, laid or repaired 12 million feet of sewer pipe, and renovated streetcar systems. It employed artists and musicians and conducted real estate surveys and archaeological digs. New York City's autocratic park commissioner Robert Moses had charge of 68,000 CWA workers, and within six months every structure in the municipal parks was repainted, every lawn reseeded, every tennis court and playground resurfaced, and thousands of trees were removed, replanted, and pruned. Elsewhere the public improvements may have been less impressive, but everywhere money was passing into the hands of millions who had been unemployed and they were spending that money, bringing profits to others. No matter what else the CWA achieved, its director, Harry Hopkins, was correct when he observed that it "had brightened the retailers' tills."

Although the CWA passed out of existence at the end of March 1934, other federal agencies were also investing in urban construction projects. The Public Works Administration (PWA) spent $4.5 billion, much of it in cities. For example, it financed New York City's monumental Triborough bridge, the world's largest sewage treatment plant in Chicago, a handsome municipal auditorium in Kansas City, Oklahoma City's new civic center, and a 360-room building at the Municipal University of Omaha. The Works Progress Administration (WPA) did even more, spending $11 billion and employing 8.5 million people during its eight-year existence. It built, repaired, or improved 650,000 miles of streets and highways, 125,000 public buildings, and 8,000 parks. Moreover, it financed the Federal Theatre, which presented comedies and drama throughout the country, and it employed artists to paint post office murals and writers to compile travel guides. If a project promised to put people to work, then the WPA would finance it. America's cities benefited from this largesse in a wide variety of ways. After a freak snowstorm struck Denver in September 1936, the WPA came to the rescue, disposing of 23,000 truckloads of trees and limbs toppled by the destructive blizzard. In Chicago the WPA dumped 700,000 cubic yards of black dirt on new lawn areas in the city parks. Meanwhile, the agency constructed a dozen public wading pools for the children of Indianapolis. During the second half of the 1930s, the helping hand of the WPA was seen everywhere in the city.

The WPA was not without its critics, however. Many claimed, with some justice, that the program invested in meaningless boondoggles and financed slackers. Completion of a project meant renewed unemployment for WPA workers, so it often seemed in the interest of these federally-funded artists, writers, and construction crews to procrastinate. Some wits claimed that the agency's initials stood for "We Plod Along." Others circulated the story about a WPA foreman who sent in a requisition for additional shovels. "No more shovels available," replied the headquarters, "Let the men lean on each other."

Most mayors saw little humor in these attacks. They depended on the PWA and WPA, and throughout Roosevelt's first two terms the United States Conference of Mayors clamored for more public works money from the federal government and less restrictions on the existing agencies. Denver's mayor knew that his city alone could not have financed the blizzard clean-up. Chicago's chief executive knew that without federal aid his city would have failed to complete its vital sewage treatment project. And there would have been no new civic center in Oklahoma City without federal funding. Federal aid seemed essential, and most mayors wanted their share of Washington's beneficence. Some mayors, like New York City's feisty Fiorello La Guardia, became masters at milking money from the federal government. From 1934 through 1938 New York City received more than $1.15 billion for public works through the generosity of the CWA, PWA, and WPA. Without these funds, La Guardia's New York could have done little to improve its parks, bridges, and schools. In 1934 one mayor ably summed up the new dependence on the federal government when he observed: "Mayors are a familiar sight in Washington these days. Whether we like it or not, the destinies of our cities are clearly tied in with national politics."

Beleaguered homeowners, real estate agents, building contractors, and savings and loan associations also became increasingly dependent on the federal authorities during the troubled 1930s. In 1933 Congress created the Home Owners Loan Corporation (HOLC), a federal agency that exchanged its own bonds for delinquent mortgages and then refinanced the homeowner's debt on liberal terms. Between 1933 and 1936 it refunded a million mortgages, saving homeowners from foreclosure and bolstering financial institutions that had made bad loans. In 1934 Congress established the Federal Housing Administration (FHA), another agency that proved a godsend to lending institutions and homeowners, especially middle-income suburbanites. The FHA insured low-interest, long-term mortgages, guaranteeing to pay the lender if the homeowner defaulted. With its unusually low interest rate and lengthy amortization, the FHA enabled middle-income Americans to again consider migration to a new suburban dwelling. Moreover, it provided the nation's distressed savings and loan associations with a guaranteed income. By the late 1930s lenders and borrowers alike recognized the advantages of the scheme, and between 1938 and 1941 34 percent of new home mortgages were FHA-insured.

The HOLC and FHA, however, were simply means for remedying the ills in the existing capitalist system of home financing and home ownership. They aided middle-class Americans to keep their mortgaged dwellings or to buy new houses in the suburbs, but they were not intended to provide better living conditions for the poor or to create a new system for allocating shelter within the city. As such they failed to satisfy the mounting demands of idealistic housing reformers who believed private lenders and private builders alone could not solve the problem of providing decent homes for all Americans. Such housing reformers as Edith Wood and Catherine Bauer, together with their colleagues in the National Housing Conference, believed that the federal government should intervene more forcefully and finance the destruction of urban slums and the construction of new homes for the nation's disadvantaged. Like Lawrence Veiller and Jane Addams thirty years earlier, they hoped to raise the living conditions of the poor to a minimum standard of decency. Rather than perpetuate the sharp contrast between wealth and poverty in the city, they sought to eradicate the slum and narrow the environmental gap that separated working-class Americans from their more fortunate middle-class compatriots.

During the 1930s these housing reformers repeatedly decried the evils of the urban slum. According to the crusaders, slum housing undermined the physical health of residents and increased the incidence of rickets, tuberculosis, infant mortality, and a long list of communicable diseases. In the words of one proponent of improved housing, "when you plant an infant in sickening surroundings you make it harder for him to grow up strong." Moreover, bad housing destroyed the moral fiber of millions of Americans and nurtured juvenile delinquency and crime. Edith Wood granted that "neither old plumbing nor broken plaster has a directly demoralizing effect on human behavior," but she claimed that "there is none the less a very real sense in which bad housing is directly — one might almost say mechanically — a cause of juvenile delinquency." Sexual immorality also flourished in slum conditions, corrupting children as well as adults. According to Wood, "Sexual matters are thrust on the attention of children at an abnormally early age by the impossibility of privacy within a 1- or 2- or even a 3-room dwelling," and "lack of space within the home forces the sharing of bedrooms and sometimes of beds by adolescent boys and girls." More seriously, the slum environment bred "class hatred, social unrest, and revolutionary propaganda." Thus blighted, inadequate housing seemed to undermine good health, respect for the law, sexual morality, and devotion to the political and economic system, all virtues highly valued by the middle class and regarded as basic to a decent society.

Not only did the slum undercut all that the middle class viewed as good and decent, it was supposedly very costly. Housing reformers marshaled a long list of figures to prove that slum neighborhoods produced little tax revenue but were disproportionate burdens on the municipal treasury. For example, one slum district in Cleveland contained 2.47 percent of the city's population and its assessed property value was only 0.75 percent of the total for the city. But housing reformers noted that 4.47 percent of the city's police budget was expended in this district, 7.3 percent of the public health funds, and 14.44 percent of the fire department expenditures. In other words, slums cost the taxpayers money, and it made good business sense to tear down blighted neighborhoods and build decent housing. Investment in improved housing would supposedly reap future dividends in the form of reduced municipal expenditures.

According to housing reformers, however, only federal funding of massive construction projects could realize this goal of improved shelter. Tougher municipal housing codes could not remedy the problem. Despite Lawrence Veiller's model codes of the turn of the century, slum conditions had persisted. Moreover, private builders could not handle the task, for low-cost housing earned little or no profit and therefore failed to attract private capital. To the extent that anyone was building homes in the 1930s, they were building them for the wealthy. In Detroit only 980 dwellings built from 1929 to 1935 were in the price range of the 123,000 families having a yearly income of less than $1,500. Likewise, in 1941 it was estimated that only 1 percent of the new urban housing constructed by private contractors was built for the one-third of American families earning less than $1,200 annually, and 76 percent was only within the means of the upper third earning $2,100 or more per year. Federally-funded housing projects thus seemed the correct answer to the problem of sheltering the lower classes. European nations had embarked on public housing programs while the United States was still tinkering with building codes. Now the federal government needed to copy the Old World model and guarantee a satisfactory living environment for all urban Americans.

The PWA pioneered federal construction of low-cost housing. But employment was its chief concern; providing decent housing was of secondary importance. Once the private building industry rebounded, the PWA would supposedly disappear, having served its purpose of providing jobs during the temporary economic downturn. Lacking a permanent commitment to low-cost housing, the PWA program thus failed to satisfy housing reformers who believed that federal construction of adequate shelter for the lower classes should persist during good times and bad. Moreover, from 1933 to 1937, the PWA constructed less than 22,000 dwelling units, a negligible achievement considering the magnitude of the problem. President Roosevelt claimed that one-third of the nation's population was ill-housed, and a Senate committee estimated that even before the depression over ten million families "were subjected to housing conditions that did not adequately protect their health and safety." If the nation was to do something about this problem, it needed a more ambitious housing program than that of the PWA.

In order to expand the public housing program and ensure its permanency, in 1937 Congress passed the Wagner-Steagall Act, creating the United States Housing Authority (USHA). The USHA was not empowered to build public projects but was authorized to extend long-term, low-interest loans to local housing agencies for the purpose of financing slum clearance and the construction of low-rent housing. Moreover, the federal authority was to aid local agencies through annual cash contributions. To assuage the fears of those members of Congress who despised the growing centralization of power in Washington, D.C., the Wagner-Steagall Act thus made public housing a joint responsibility of the federal government and the locality. Federal authorities could not force public housing on the nation's cities. Instead, the locality had to take the initiative and apply for federal aid.

Across the nation city officials quickly responded to the federal offer of money. In November 1937 there were only 46 local housing authorities, but one year later the number had risen to 214 and by 1941 there were 622 local agencies. At the outbreak of World War II twenty-five of the nation's thirty largest cities had housing authorities ready to avail themselves of USHA funds. In one city after another, the local agencies broke ground for new projects amid much fanfare expressing the exalted hopes for a better urban environment. Yet construction still fell far short of perceived needs. By the close of 1941 the local authorities had completed only 100,000 dwelling units in USHA-aided projects, and only 76,000 more were under construction or in the planning stage. Public housing was beginning to make its mark on the urban landscape, but few of America's ill-housed third had ever set foot in a USHA apartment.

The completed PWA and USHA projects generally consisted of a monotonous collection of low-rise brick apartment buildings or rowhouses. A sterile grimness advertised the fact that they were low-rent developments, and the prevailing architectural style was functional plain. But in many ways public housing was superior to the structures that it replaced. Whereas slum dwellings often lacked hot running water and contained one toilet shared by several households, the PWA and USHA units boasted the latest plumbing and appliances and a fully-equipped private bathroom for each family. Many cleared slum areas had consisted of rotting frame shacks which were highly flammable and infested with vermin; the new brick structures were fireproof and originally free of unwanted pests. Moreover, in public housing every room had a window admitting light and air, and extensive landscaped grounds and play areas offered the former slum dweller an escape from the urban congestion of the blighted neighborhood. For example, in the 1,027-unit Jane Addams Houses, the first PWA project completed in Chicago, the buildings covered only 28 percent of the land area, leaving an abundance of open space. And because the USHA subsidized construction costs, the rents in public housing projects were generally less than those charged for slum tenements or dilapidated shacks. Public housing may not have been notably attractive or luxurious in its appointments, but it was safer and more sanitary than slum dwellings and less expensive for the hard-pressed tenant.

Recognizing these advantages, lower-income Americans vied for apartments in the new urban projects. In Chicago there was an average of ten applicants for every unit of public housing. Consequently, public housing administrators could be selective in accepting tenants, and they generally preferred stable families of good repute with an employed male breadwinner. The Chicago Housing Authority accepted no families on direct relief as tenants in the city's three PWA projects, although in Chicago's first USHA project 17 percent of the early tenants were on relief. Early public housing was primarily for the working class and not for the welfare class. It was for those who conformed to middle-class standards of morality, cleanliness, and character but who were not wealthy enough to pay the market price for middle-class housing.

In selecting tenants, housing officials also considered the race of the applicant. It was the policy of the PWA and USHA not to disturb the racial composition of the neighborhood in which a project was built. If a neighborhood were all white, then only whites would be eligible for the public housing units. If it were a black district, then the project would be for blacks. If the neighborhood was mixed racially, then the public housing project would be mixed in the same proportion, with blacks assigned to one section of the project and whites to another. Although housing officials may have been trying to narrow the gap in living conditions between the middle class and lower classes, they were not attempting to close the abyss that separated blacks and whites in the American city. In the 1930s the federal government did not intervene in support of racial mixing. Instead, racial apartheid remained accepted public policy.

During the late 1930s and early 1940s the segregated brick compounds of decent but disadvantaged Americans elicited euphoric praise from delighted housing reformers. According to the first chief of USHA, Nathan Straus, "life in a well-designed and well-managed public housing project is no more like life in a slum than an automobile is like an ox-cart or a fluorescent tube is like a tallow candle." In the slum neighborhood children aimlessly roamed the streets and no community spirit united their parents. But Straus claimed that in public housing projects, "social clubs flourish . . . , children play in safety, [and] mothers sew and gossip as neighborliness is awakened and civic pride grows apace." The chairman of the Phoenix Housing Authority seconded Straus's views and testified that "one of the great thrills of my life was to walk through our project . . . when the families had settled down for their first night in their new homes. . . . A dream had come true." When he asked one of the new tenants how he liked the project, the tenant replied: "When I woke up this morning, I pinched myself to make sure that I was still in Phoenix and not in Heaven." At the onset of World War II, then, the promise of public housing still stirred many souls. The National Association of Real Estate Boards together with some conservative Republicans grumbled about socialistic housing and naive reformers, but for many Americans public housing seemed a viable means for ensuring all urban dwellers a decent living environment and for minimizing the differences in lifestyle between social classes in the city.

But PWA and USHA housing were not the only New Deal alternatives for a better life. Some within the Roosevelt administration also dreamed of relocating the urban masses in suburban utopias, and the chief of the federal government's Resettlement Administration, Rexford Tugwell, attempted to realize this dream. In a trio of federally-constructed suburban developments nicknamed the greenbelt communities, Tugwell sought to create working-class towns protected from the encroachments of urban sprawl by surrounding greenbelts of forests and farms. Because of unexpectedly high development costs, the federal government had to charge rents beyond the price range of most working-class Americans. Moreover, the three greenbelt communities contained only a few thousand dwelling units. Thus few low-income urban dwellers benefited from the scheme. Like public housing in the central city, however, the greenbelt communities offered new hope for those dissatisfied with urban America. Some ridiculed the developments, labeling them as communistic and attacking Tugwell as "the Sweetheart of the Regimenters." Yet the greenbelt communities testified to the possibilities of federal intervention in the suburban housing field.

For some Americans, FERA, CWA, PWA, WPA, HOLC, FHA, and USHA were a threatening agglomeration of letters that spelled regimentation and socialism, but for many they spelled security and promise. During the 1930s the federal government set a precedent for intervention in local affairs, and henceforth America's cities turned to Washington in time of need. Mayors haunted the lobbies of Congress, housing officials testified before Senate committees, and idealists with schemes for a better, more equitable city looked to the federal treasury for the realization of their plans. Each believed in the potential of the federal government to set matters right in urban America; each believed that the federal government's billions might succeed where local reformers had failed in the past. Urban America was emerging as a national problem for which the national government had to take responsibility. And those millions of Americans who had converted to the New Deal faith believed that Franklin Roosevelt and his ilk could meet the challenge of the city.

THE WARTIME CITY

The emerging federal authority of the 1930s paled beside the awesome power of the federal government during World War II. From 1941 to 1945 the United States government mobilized the nation for defense, recruiting and conscripting millions of persons for the armed forces, rationing essential materials, and spending billions for tanks, airplanes, uniforms, rifles, and warships. The national government was dedicated to the defeat of Germany and Japan, and it sought to ensure that every city and town, every factory and office, and every employee and boss were working toward this single end. Thus the nation was expected to march in lockstep behind the federal government, accepting loyally whatever sacrifice was necessary for victory.

The impact on the city was notable. Gasoline and tire rationing kept automobiles off the streets and put more Americans back on the trolleys and buses. Public transit enjoyed a temporary boom, transporting more Americans than ever before. Private construction for nondefense purposes halted, and other than defense plants and defense housing there were few new additions to the urban building inventory. Factory production, however, soared as the federal government ordered billions of dollars of war matériel. The economic depression was over, but Americans could not yet spend their money on new cars or on the construction of suburban dream houses.

Throughout the nation cities felt the economic effects of the war. At suburban Willow Run outside of Detroit, the Ford Motor Company built an enormous bomber plant employing more than 42,000 workers. In Philadelphia, where industry had been declining even before 1929, war brought new life to the city's manufacturing sector with 3,500 businesses producing everything from armor plate to mosquito netting for troops in the tropics. Manufacturing employment in Omaha had dropped from 16,000 in 1929 to 11,000 in 1939. But in 1941 the Glenn L. Martin aircraft company opened a plant south of the city which employed 14,500 at peak production to assemble thousands of planes, including the B-29s that dropped the atomic bombs on Hiroshima and Nagasaki.

The war gave an especially potent economic boost to cities in the Southwest and along the Pacific coast. Prior to World War II communities like Phoenix, Tucson, and Albuquerque were minor desert trading centers, with populations of 65,000, 37,000, and 35,000 respectively. But their sunny desert climate proved a boon when the federal government began selecting sites for pilot training bases. In these cities the sun shone 85 percent of all daylight hours, and rain, fog, clouds, or blizzards would not close down airfields or limit valuable flying time. Thus three air corps training installations located in the Tucson area, Phoenix could boast of six air bases and three army camps, and the opening of Kirtland air base in 1941 brought new life to Albuquerque's economy.

Not only did the Southwest attract military bases, it also experienced unprecedented industrialization. Fearful that the concentration of industry in a few eastern centers left the nation particularly vulnerable in case of enemy air strikes, military planners urged the dispersion of manufacturing facilities throughout the nation, including the undeveloped Southwest. Moreover, the sunny Arizona climate appealed to aircraft manufacturers who needed good flying conditions in order to test their products. Thus a giant aircraft plant opened in Tucson, employing 6,000 residents of the formerly sleepy town. In Phoenix Goodyear Aircraft began production of airplane parts and balloons, and Alcoa opened an aluminum plant to supply metal to the aircraft industry. During the war Phoenix, Tucson, and Albuquerque all swelled with newcomers to staff these factories and the nearby bases, and for the first time the Southwest got a taste of big-city life.

Along the Pacific coast the federal government invested even greater sums in new bases and defense plants. San Diego became a boom town when the navy expanded its operations in the area and the Consolidated Vultee (Convair) aircraft plant won fat defense contracts. Douglas, North American, Lockheed, Hughes, and Northrop all erected huge aircraft plants in the Los Angeles area, making Southern California the aircraft capital of the world. One-fifth of all planes built in the United States during the war were assembled in California. Farther north, in the San Francisco Bay region and in Portland, Oregon, Henry Kaiser employed hundreds of thousands of men and women in his shipyards, and at peak production he was launching one new freighter every ten hours. In the Portland area 92,000 persons worked at the Kaiser yards, and in four years the metropolitan population soared 32 percent. To house this influx of workers Kaiser quickly erected Vanport, the nation's largest defense housing project, with 10,000 units and 40,000 residents. Although some praised this instant community as "one of the marvels of the war effort," historian Carl Abbott described it as "dull gray buildings awash in a sea of gray Oregon mud." Meanwhile, in Seattle the Boeing Aircraft Company increased the number of persons on its payroll from 4,000 in 1939 to 50,000 in 1944, thus attracting hordes of newcomers to Washington's chief metropolis. War brought an industrial boom to the previously underdeveloped West and introduced many members of the armed forces and the civilian labor force to the sunny climate and natural beauty of the Southwest or to the damper but equally beautiful Northwest. Once the war was over, soldiers would not forget the advantages of western living, and large numbers would return to San Diego, Los Angeles, Phoenix, or Seattle to take up permanent residence, joining the many civilian workers who had opted to remain in their new western homes.

Nowhere was the war's impact more strongly felt, however, than in the navy town of Norfolk, Virginia, and nowhere were the problems of the wartime city more evident. With the outbreak of World War II a deluge of sailors and shipyard workers swamped Norfolk and surrounding communities, and the population of the Norfolk-Portsmouth-Newport News metropolitan area more than doubled, from 367,000 in 1940 to 778,000 in 1943. By 1943 there were 40,000 civilian employees at the Navy Yard as compared to 12,000 in normal times, and the number of workers at the Newport News shipyard rose from 4,000 to 24,000. Daily water consumption jumped from 13 million gallons to 30 million, and the influx of new residents so taxed the municipal waterworks that Norfolk was forced to ration water and prohibit the washing of automobiles and the sprinkling of lawns. The understaffed municipal health department could not meet the demands of the expanded city, nor could the police handle the thousands of men on shore leave. Although Norfolk's conservative city fathers were suspicious of Washington bureaucrats, local officials looked to the federal government for aid, and one was quoted in *American Mercury* as saying, "We need more government help, and still more government help."

Housing proved an especially troublesome problem for the beleaguered port city. Mobilization began in 1940, and from April of that year to November 1941 rents in Norfolk rose on the average almost 14 percent. They continued to climb until June 1942 when the federal government finally imposed rent controls on the area. This action, however, did not increase the supply of housing, and for some the situation was desperate. Home-seekers advertised for information about apartments or houses and offered rewards to those who could aid them in locating decent shelter. Some landlords rented beds in shifts, each lessee having use of the bed for only half a day; at the close of one shift, another occupant crept under the covers for a restful sleep. An estimated 3,000 to 5,000 families moved into cramped trailers. Owners of vacant lots rented out space for the primitive metal boxes on wheels, charging three or four dollars a week. Recognizing the plight of Norfolk's defense workers, the federal government did respond to the housing problem and construct 10,000 dwelling units. But the housing market remained tight.

The burgeoning market for immoral pleasures also was a problem that both Norfolk officials and navy bigwigs had to confront. In order to curb the spread of venereal disease, the navy demanded that Norfolk's police close down the city's red-light district. The prostitutes dispersed, but sailors demanded something more than tea and sponge cake served by respectable matrons at USO canteens. According to reporter J. Blan Van Urk, Norfolk's East Main Street "must be the largest, most solid block of beer joints in the world." The typical joint had "a big bar in the center, with vast hamburger facilities along both walls"; behind the bar stretched a "dimly-lit space devoted to tables, stalls and coin-operated 'shooting' devices," and "hovering everywhere are 'waitresses' of all sizes, shapes and dispositions." Some "waitresses" set up shop in trailers at the edge of town, emblazoning their trailer doors with such suggestive movie titles as "It Happened One Night" and "All That Money Can Buy." Again local officials sought federal aid; the city's chief of police unsuccessfully petitioned the federal government for a concentration camp in which to imprison Norfolk's prostitutes for the duration of the war. But this would not have solved the gambling problem in the Norfolk district where slot machines and the roll of dice deprived many defense workers and servicemen of their paychecks.

Gambling, prostitution, housing shortages, and inadequate municipal services were commonplace complaints in the urban arsenals of wartime America. Norfolk represented an extreme case, but in every city with a major military base or booming defense industries these problems occurred. Even more serious, however, was the growing social tension between newcomers and established residents. Thousands of strangers were pouring into cities, disturbing the status quo. Their arrival was especially disruptive if they represented an ethnic or cultural minority abhorrent or threatening to the existing majority. Thus the massive migration of blacks, Mexicans, and Appalachian whites to America's urban areas during World War II sparked new tension and exposed the fissures in the wartime facade of national unity.

In one city after another newcomers with dark complexions or strange ways of speech and unfamiliar lifestyles filled the labor shortage created by the recruitment and conscription of soldiers and the unprecedented demand for war matériel. From Georgia and Alabama thousands of blacks moved to Chicago, Detroit, and Philadelphia, crowding into urban ghettos and threatening to spill over into white neighborhoods. Reversing the depression-era policy of repatriation, the wartime government of the United States welcomed hundreds of thousands of Mexican workers to harvest crops in the Southwest and to labor on the railroads. Many gravitated toward Los Angeles and El Paso, but more than 15,000 Mexican railroad workers were relocated as far away as Chicago. Meanwhile, displaced coal miners and marginal farmers from the hills of West Virginia and Kentucky sought the opportunity to earn a decent wage in the booming war industries of Detroit, Cleveland, Columbus, and Cincinnati.

Though urban employers welcomed their labor, these newcomers moved into communities that regarded them with coldness and hostility. Most Southern Appalachians were whites whose ancestors had settled in America two hundred years earlier, yet their "hillbilly" manners and customs made them the butt of jokes and often the objects of contempt. One longtime resident of the Willow Run area complained of the migration of these newcomers, saying: "Before the bomber plant was built, everything was perfect here. . . . Then came . . . this influx of riffraff, mostly Southerners. You can't be sure of these people." Most residents of Detroit, Chicago, and Los Angeles had no more respect for the thousands of "greasers" moving northward from Mexico. And many blacks who moved to the city confronted verbal abuse and racial violence. In 1943 at Detroit's Packard plant 25,000 workers went on strike because of the upgrading of 3 black employees; according to the Bureau of Labor statistics, from March through May 1943 over 100,000 man-days of war production were lost owing to strikes protesting the employment or promotion of blacks. Likewise, in Cincinnati 10,000 white workers at the Wright aircraft engine plant commemorated D-Day, June 6, 1944, with a wildcat strike protesting the integration of the machine shop.

Meanwhile, the newcomers grew more bitter and hostile. Black street gangs fought their white counterparts, promising to take care of the "Hunkies." Rejected by non-Hispanic society, some Mexican-American youth expressed their rage through their attire. In defiance of conventional codes of dress, they sported pointed shoes, ducktail haircuts, and flashy, broad-shouldered zoot-suits, complete with thigh-length jackets and trousers that were full at the top and narrow at the cuffs. These "zoot-suiters" frequented pool and dance halls, roamed the streets, and occasionally brawled with "Anglo" gangs.

In some cities the festering antagonism burst into full-scale riots. For example, ethnic tension mounted in California when zoot-suiters allegedly began to attack sailors dating young Mexican-American women. In May and June 1943 soldiers and sailors retaliated first in Oakland and then in Los Angeles by cruising through Mexican-American neighborhoods, waylaying zoot-suiters, stripping them of their clothes, and beating them. After a few days of mob action by servicemen, commanding officers at local bases ordered areas frequented by the zoot-suiters off-limits to the military. The Los Angeles city council responded by enacting an ordinance that outlawed the wearing of a zoot-suit.

A few weeks later rioting between blacks and whites broke out in Detroit. On Sunday June 20, Belle Isle Park was crowded with over 100,000 Detroiters seeking relief from the summer heat. In the course of the day a number of incidents erupted between blacks and whites at the park, and by eleven o'clock that night 5,000 people were fighting on the bridge linking Belle Isle with the remainder of the city. Rumors that whites had murdered a black woman and child swept black neighborhoods while tales of blacks raping white women circulated in white districts. Such stories fueled race hatreds, and the next day black mobs vandalized white property and whites attacked blacks who ventured outside the ghetto. In all 34 persons were killed and more than 700 injured.

In August 1943 blacks went on a rampage in New York City. The riot began with a confrontation between a white policeman and a black soldier that left both men wounded. Rumors of the attack on the black serviceman spread through Harlem, and black residents responded with an orgy of looting and vandalism. Mobs smashed plate glass windows along major Harlem thoroughfares, and, according to civil rights leader Walter White, a "blind, unreasoning fury swept the community with the speed of lightening." When the violence subsided, 5 persons were dead, 500 were injured, and property damage amounted to $5 million.

The rioting in Los Angeles, Detroit, and Harlem demonstrated that urban Americans were not only at war with Germany and Japan, they were also at war with each other. Between 1941 and 1945 Americans were expected to close ranks and unite in a common effort to destroy the enemy abroad. They were called upon to sacrifice peacetime pleasures and conveniences, and they did momentarily abandon their automobiles for crowded streetcars and double up in substandard housing. But beneath the surface commitment to a united front old divisions and animosities persisted. The fragmentation of the city remained a vivid reality.

Suburbia Triumphant, 1945–1964

On August 14, 1945, Japan surrendered and World War II came to an end. Two million people packed New York City's Times Square tossing confetti, blowing horns, kissing one another, and screaming with delight and relief. Every ethnic fragment of the city shared in the exhilarating moment. According to the *New York Times,* in Harlem "couples jived in the streets and the crowd was so large that traffic was halted and sprinkler trucks were used . . . to disperse pedestrians." In New York's Chinatown four dragons moved through the narrow, crowded lanes, trampling over an effigy of the Japanese emperor, and "strings of firecrackers exploded, accompanied by a splitting cacophony of horns." In the Italian-American sections of Brooklyn "tables were brought to the streets and food, wine and liquor were offered to passers-by." Elsewhere in the United States the story was much the same. In downtown Saint Louis office workers dumped waste paper and paper bags filled with water from their windows, high school youths snakedanced through the streets, and automobiles dragged tin cans over the pavements. San Franciscans ignited huge bonfires shooting flames thirty feet in the air, pulled trolleys from their wires, and spun the city's cable cars around on their turntables. The war was over, and all urban Americans shared a common joy.

Meanwhile, officials in Washington announced that rationing of gasoline would soon cease and that automobile production would resume by December. Wartime shortages were to become only a memory. The nation was ready to resume a peacetime footing, and again prosperity would prevail. Defense workers used their wartime savings and indulged in a consumer binge, buying what they had dreamed of for sixteen long years of depression and war. Thus America's metropolitan areas took up where they had left off in 1929. With the return of peace and prosperity Americans could resume the task of renovating and rebuilding their cities.

During the next two decades the transformation of the American city was startling. Motor mania gripped the nation, and metropolises, like everything else, had to adapt to the automobile. Moreover, construction boomed, population soared, and decentralization of residences and businesses proceeded at a remarkable pace. By the early 1960s the American city was something quite different from what it had been in 1945. Suburbia was gradually becoming the predominant element of metropolitan America, and the central city was declining. Schemes for central-city revival were commonplace, yet year after year both commerce and population migrated outward from the urban core, escaping from the anachronistic downtown and the decaying neighborhoods. Some newcomers did arrive in the central city, but they were mostly poor migrants seeking their fortunes in the declining core. Thus the metropolis remained a mixture of success and failure, of problems and promises, a troubling dilemma for the American nation.

SUBURBAN BOOM

The postwar era was a boomtime for suburbia. America's birth rate rose, and millions of young families with children abandoned the crowded central cities and invested in suburban homes with yards large enough to accommodate a sandbox and swingset. In 1950 in the twenty largest metropolitan areas 58 percent of the population lived in central cities, whereas in 1960 those same cities together accounted for only 49 percent of their combined metropolitan population. During the 1950s the aggregate population of these central cities inched upward only 0.1 percent, while the suburban population in their metropolitan areas soared 45 percent. Suburban communities everywhere were growing at rates that brought fantastic profits to real estate agents and builders. In 1950 the Detroit suburb of Warren had 727 inhabitants; in 1960 it had over 89,000. During the 1950s the Saint Louis suburb of Florissant grew from a village of 3,700 to a city of 38,000. In Southern California the population of Anaheim soared from 15,000 to 104,000, while that of nearby Garden Grove jumped from 4,000 to 84,000. The suburban municipalities of Bloomington, Minnesota, and Lakewood, California, had not even existed in 1950, but by 1960 they each housed more than 50,000 residents. Everywhere suburban land was sprouting a new crop of housing, shopping centers, and motels, drawing millions of dollars and luring people from the older central cities.

Underlying this dispersion of America's urban population were changing transportation patterns. In the postwar era auto sales soared, and two-car families became commonplace. Although the nation's population increased only 35 percent between 1945 and 1965, automobile registrations climbed almost 180 percent, from 26 million to 72 million. By 1963, the proportion of American families owning an automobile was up to 80 percent, and few adults went anywhere without their Ford or Chevrolet. In the early 1950s Los Angeles residents relied on their automobile for 95 percent of their journeys to the store, to work, or to places of amusement. Other southwestern cities could almost match this figure; for example, in postwar Albuquerque residents used the private automobile for 86 percent of their trips and in Phoenix the figure was 82 percent. In the older, congested cities of the Midwest and East, urbanites relied less on the automobile; at the close of the first half of the century only 43 percent of travel in Baltimore was by car, and in Philadelphia private motor vehicles accounted for only 31 percent of all trips. But in every city reliance on the automobile was increasing, and public transit patronage was declining. Freed from the slow-moving, centripetal transit lines and devoted to the greater flexibility of the automobile, Americans now migrated farther from the urban core and often chose their residence without regard to bus routes or streetcar lines. As in the 1920s, the automobile was expanding the residential options of metropolitan Americans and opening the suburban fringes to millions of urbanites.

Without adequate highways, however, the automobile might well have proved a slower and more irritating means of travel than the public transit lines. By the late 1940s and early 1950s it was evident that limited-access expressways were needed to facilitate the flow of automobiles, unsnarl traffic jams, and ensure a safe journey to the suburbs. Los Angeles pioneered the construction of urban expressways, opening the Arroyo Seco freeway shortly before the outbreak of World War II. After the war the California metropolis resumed its ambitious superhighway program, and other cities followed its example. During the first half of the 1950s New York City laid out the Cross-Bronx Expressway, Detroit began construction of the John Lodge and Edsel Ford superhighways, and Chicago built the Congress Street (later Eisenhower) Expressway. By 1956 there were an estimated 376 miles of urban freeways in the nation's twenty-five largest cities, with at least 104 additional miles under construction. Yet many public officials and motoring enthusiasts regarded this as insufficient and lobbied for a federal system of limited-access highways. Congress responded to these demands by passing the Federal-Aid Highway Act of 1956, which authorized the construction of 41,000 miles of interstate freeways including 5,000 miles in urban areas. Washington would pay 90 percent of the cost of the expressways from a special trust fund financed by federal taxes on gasoline, tires, and heavy trucks. Thus the federal government embarked on an interstate highway scheme that increased the competitive edge of the automobile over public transit and facilitated travel to and from suburbia.

Some scoffed at the new urban freeways, claiming that rush hour traffic continued to crawl along at a snail's pace while gasoline fumes corrupted the air. But traffic did move faster and more efficiently on the freeways than on the city streets, and few Americans in the 1950s or early 1960s forsook the automobile for the bus or left their homes on the suburban fringe for apartments in the urban core. In the late 1930s it took twenty minutes to travel along Los Angeles's Sunset Boulevard from the Civic Center to the corner of Hollywood and Vine; in the late 1950s this same journey on the parallel Hollywood Freeway took an average of only seven minutes thirty-five seconds. According to traffic surveys, the completion of Chicago's Dan Ryan Expressway in 1962 cut as much as fifteen minutes from a seven-mile journey, and a study conducted in 1959 found that Chicago's freeways moved 3.5 times as many vehicles per hour as the city's arterial streets. Without the freeways, then, suburbia would have been more remote and less accessible to places of employment, shopping, and amusement in the central city. Freeway driving may not have been a pleasure, but the mammoth ribbons of concrete and asphalt did cut travel times between the increasingly dispersed fragments of the metropolis.

The automobile and freeway encouraged suburbanization, yet it was the postwar housing developer who transformed suburban fields and groves into row after row of homes. In 1945 America's veterans returned to a nation suffering from a serious housing shortage. Sixteen years of depression and war had discouraged residential construction, and consequently young families were forced to squeeze into whatever vacant apartments they could find. But private builders soon responded to the demand, and the nation embarked on the greatest residential construction boom in its history. In 1944 only 142,000 housing units were started in the United States, by 1946 this figure had shot up to 1,023,000, climbing to a peak of 1,952,000 units in 1950. During the 1950s and 1960s builders would not surpass this record, but in every year from 1947 through 1964 the number of housing starts topped the 1,200,000 mark. The majority of these new homes were single-family, owner-occupied suburban houses with their own yards, rather than midtown apartments. American families desired a house and yard that they could call their own along suburbia's fringe, and this was what the nation's builders offered.

Perhaps the most enterprising of the postwar builders were the

Levitt brothers of Long Island. The Levitt family had developed some high-priced subdivisions in the 1930s, and during World War II had built 2,350 units of low-cost defense housing in Norfolk. In the late 1940s, however, the Levitts won national renown with their famous community of Levittown, New York. Buying thousands of acres of potato fields in Hempstead, Long Island, twenty-nine miles from Manhattan, they began erecting at a breakneck pace thousands of four-room Cape-Cod cottages selling for $7,990. Not satisfied with prewar construction methods, the Levitts produced their houses in an assembly line method. First, the Levitt workers laid a standard 25-by-30-foot concrete slab on which each of the cellarless houses rested. Next, truckloads of precut rafters, studding, and roof sheathing arrived. Then it was a simple matter for construction workers to fit the parts together with a hammer and nails before proceeding to the next house. All the houses had identical measurements and floor plans, so little time was wasted on individuality. Only some differences in exterior trim distinguished one house from another. Thus workers could move from house to house without consulting blueprints or changing their routine. One Levitt employee did nothing but walk from one house to the next caulking windows at a rate of three hundred windows a day. Another crew did nothing but install bathtubs, whereas others spent all day nailing shingles on one house after another. In this manner the Levitts built as many as 150 houses a week, grinding them out at the rate of one every sixteen minutes.

Although the Levitt houses may not have been luxurious, thousands of young families yearned for a home in the Long Island development. The FHA, together with the Veterans Administration (VA), guaranteed long-term low-interest mortgages, and with this backing from the federal government an ex-serviceman could become the owner of a Levitt cottage for only $90 down and payments of $58 a month for twenty-five years. Veterans camped in front of the Levitt office all weekend so that they could submit their applications for housing ahead of others on Monday morning. Within one week in 1949 the Levitts sold 707 houses to eager young couples. When the Hempstead Town Board hesitated about revising the building code to permit the Levitts to construct cellarless houses, over 800 veterans crowded into an open meeting at the town hall to express their support for the builders. One ex-serviceman stated the views of many when he shouted: "No cellar beats one room in an attic where you freeze to death." And *Fortune* quoted a veteran's wife who commented in a local newspaper: "Too bad there aren't more men like Levitt & Sons. . . . I hope they make a whopper of a profit."

The woman's hope was realized, for on each Levittown cottage the brothers cleared a $1,000 profit. With the intention of making still more money, the Levitts reinvested their profits in a second community, Levittown, Pennsylvania, outside of Philadelphia. Built in the early 1950s, the Pennsylvania subdivision covered 5,000 acres and was to house 60,000 residents. It was a complete community, with an area reserved for light industry, a central shopping center with parking for 5,000 cars, a professional building, and sites for ten elementary schools, two high schools, and about eighteen churches. Moreover, there were 250 acres of forest preserves, and the Levitts landscaped the development lavishly, planting 48,000 blooming fruit trees. To encourage some sense of community among the thousands of residents in the vast housing tract, the builders divided their new project into eight "master blocks," each centering on a school, a recreation area and a swimming pool. And each master block contained three or four neighborhoods easily identified as such because all the streets in a neighborhood began with the same letter; thus the Stonybrook neighborhood included Sunset Lane, Summer Lane, Shadetree Lane, Strawberry Lane, and Sweetbriar Lane, the adjacent Farmbrook neighborhood Friendly Lane, Fireside Lane, Freedom Lane, and Fortune Lane. Arterial streets surrounded the master blocks dividing them from one another, but within the blocks there were only curving lanes free of fast-moving through traffic. As in the pioneer motor-age community of Radburn, the planners attempted to create an automobile-oriented community in which the dangers of the automobile were reduced to a minimum.

While the Levitts were planning suburban communities on the outskirts of the great eastern cities, in the Chicago area American Community Builders was laying out Park Forest. Located twenty miles south of the Loop, Park Forest was a planned city of 30,000 that included housing, industry, shopping centers, schools, and churches. Unlike the Levitt communities, however, it also contained a large number of apartments. By 1952 there were 682 two-story garden apartment buildings in the community as well as 1,300 completed houses. Park Forest owed more to the planners of Radburn and the federal greenbelt communities than did the Levitt developments. The president of American Community Builders had been a federal public housing commissioner during World War II and the community's chief planner had worked on the design of the greenbelt projects in the 1930s. In a manner reminiscent of Radburn and the greenbelt towns, the Park Forest garden apartments were located on superblocks with their fronts facing on common parkland and their backs opening onto cul-de-sacs. An adjacent 1,000-acre forest preserve formed at least a partial green buffer between the community and the encroachments of urban sprawl. Moreover, the project attempted to house a wider range of income groups than the Levitt developments with their uniform little houses. Park Forest was, then, a venture in innovative community building, but it was also a private, profitmaking enterprise. It was intended to demonstrate that the private sector could build model communities just as well as the public sector. As the building journal *House & Home* observed, the developers of Park Forest proved that "big-scale town building is possible *and* profitable *without* government subsidy."

By the early 1950s, however, the private sector did not need to fear competition from the public sector in the field of suburban housing, for the federal government had no intention of constructing additional greenbelt towns, and the three existing communities were for sale. Between 1950 and 1954, after protracted negotiations, the federal government finally disposed of the communities and withdrew from the business of managing suburban real estate. Although Washington provided indirect subsidies to home buyers through its FHA-VA mortgage guarantees, during the 1950s private builders were responsible for housing America's burgeoning suburban families.

Throughout the country every metropolitan area had its own version of the Levitts building scores of houses along the suburban fringes. Some were erecting inexpensive prefabricated dwellings, quickly nailing together finished panels fresh from the factory. This was cheap and easy and seemed to answer the need for low-cost houses. Between 1946 and 1952 there were 250,000 prefabricated housing units erected, prefabricated dwellings accounting for 8 percent of the nation's housing starts by 1952. Wealthier home buyers shunned the mass production of the Levitts and the prefabricators, opting for architect-designed ranch houses in suburbia. In posh subdivisions four-bedroom mammoths sprawled across acre lots with generous picture windows staring out on nursery-bred saplings. Housing tracts for moderate-income families and subdivisions for the wealthy consumed outlying acres, and everyone with at least $90 down seemed to be buying their share of the suburban dream.

The new suburban tracts, however, were not necessarily open to everyone with the requisite cash. Postwar suburbia was largely white territory with few black enclaves. In New York's Levittown each homeowner's contract included a clause stating that "no dwelling shall be used or occupied by members of other than the Caucasian race." A few black families did move into the development in the 1950s, but blacks remained a rarity in the community. Real estate agents likewise steered blacks away from Levittown, Pennsylvania, and until 1957 the giant development was 100 percent white. In August 1957, however, the black William Myers family moved into a house on Darkleaf Lane in the Dogwood Hollow neighborhood. The night after their arrival a crowd of 200 gathered and began stoning the Myers house, shattering the picture window. Pennsylvania's governor ordered the state police to cordon off the embattled dwelling, but harassment continued. The Dogwood Hollow Social Club met in an adjoining house, which flew a spotlit Confederate flag from its rooftop, and disturbed the Myers family with blaring phonograph music and cacophonous renditions of "Old Black Joe." Others drove by the house tooting bugles and shouting catcalls. Many white Levittowners supported the Myers's right to live in the community, but they too were the objects of attack. One white neighbor who befriended the black family found KKK painted across one wall of his home, and others were taunted as "nigger lovers."

Protestants, Catholics, and Jews all lived harmoniously in the Levitt development, and thousands of persons of foreign birth or parentage shared the community with neighbors whose ancestors had fought in the American Revolution. Thus families of Italian ancestry lived next door to the offspring of Polish immigrants and around the corner from Protestants raised in small-town Pennsylvania. For white residents Levittown seemed finally to realize the dream of the melting pot, creating a homogeneous amalgam of persons with diverse roots. But it was clear from the Myers controversy that Levittown was not the place for blacks who wanted to live in peace and security. And the Levittown experience was representative of attitudes in many suburban communities. Suburbia was a white haven, perpetuating the racial fragmentation of the metropolis. It was a place where one could escape from the social, economic, and racial heterogeneity of the central city. In Levittown and other such developments one could live among those of similar income, lifestyle, and complexion, enjoying the neighborliness of persons who thought, acted, and looked alike.

Suburbia, however, did not appeal to everyone. While many moved willingly to the outlying fringes, others applied their acid pens to bitter critiques of Levittown and its ilk. Authors lambasted the uniformity of suburbia, depicting it as a homogeneous land where one "buys the right car, keeps his lawn like his neighbor's, eats crunchy breakfast cereal, and votes Republican." Architecture critic Peter Blake referred to "the massive, monotonous ugliness of most of our Suburbia" and attacked the "stratified, anesthetized and standardized society being bred" in the nation's new housing tracts. Author John Keats, in his best-selling *The Crack in the Picture Window,* likewise blasted the monotonous landscape of suburbia where "identical boxes spreading like gangrene" corrupted the virgin countryside. By the late 1950s it had become fashionable to decry the ticky-tacky little houses that were defacing God's handiwork and seemingly destroying the American character.

Yet Americans continued to migrate to the suburbs, for in spite of all its flaws suburbia provided what people wanted. Blake and Keats to the contrary, even standardized Levittown offered greater opportunities for individual creativity than life in dreary urban apartment blocks. Within a few years after the completion of their uniform suburban dwellings, homeowners were enclosing their carports, knocking out walls, adding shutters and removing trim, planting new shrubs and trees, and laying out patios. After a decade of occupancy, the individual tastes of the homeowners had tempered the monotony of the streetscape and had produced rows of distinguishable homes. Yet the homogeneity of the community survived, for the advantage of suburbia was that it permitted a degree of individuality while preserving the security of a homogeneous environment. Planned suburban tracts excluded unwanted ethnic, economic, or aesthetic influences, but each family could develop its own private plot in any way so long as it did not violate broad zoning ordinances and subdivision restrictions. Suburbia offered most middle-class Americans the freedom to create their dream homes, but it tempered this freedom with enough restraint so that a neighbor's bizarre dream would not become the community's nightmare.

As more and more Americans responded to the advantages of suburban life, retailers joined the outward migration in hot pursuit of the suburban dollar. But retailing had to adapt to the suburbanite's devotion to the automobile, and thus the shopping center was born. In the 1920s Kansas City's Country Club Plaza was a pioneer retailing complex for the motorist, yet the real boom in suburban shopping centers did not occur until the 1950s. By 1955 there were 1,000 shopping centers; a year later the number had jumped to 1,600 and 2,500 more were in planning or construction phases. *Business Week* quoted a leading economic analyst who estimated that more new store space opened in large regional shopping centers during September and October 1956 than had opened during the entire period from 1948 to September 1956. Among the giant new centers completed in 1956 was the 110-store complex at Roosevelt Field in suburban Long Island. Located conveniently at an expressway exit, the new center could boast of 11,000 parking spaces. That October the most innovative of the new complexes opened, the Southdale Center in suburban Edina, Minnesota, seven miles southwest of downtown Minneapolis. The seventy-two store complex was the first completely enclosed center, heated in the bitterly cold Minnesota winters and air conditioned in the summer. Thus no matter the weather, shoppers could stroll comfortably around the two-level mall amid the decorative sculpture or linger at a sidewalk cafe in the block-long, three-story garden court admiring the tropical plants, the fountains, and the giant cage holding eighty colored canaries. Like Chicago's Marshall Field Store and Philadelphia's Wanamaker's in the early twentieth century, Southdale in the late 1950s was not only a place to shop, it was a tourist attraction. On a Sunday soon after its opening, when the stores were closed for the Sabbath, 75,000 people drove to Southdale just to walk around the new complex and window shop.

Throughout the nation shopping malls were becoming the centerpieces of suburban America where suburbanites communed and amused themselves as well as purchased shoes, clothes, and gifts. At the seventy-two store Hillsdale Center in San Mateo, California, south of San Francisco, a series of promotional events enlivened the suburban calendar in 1956. According to *Chain Store Age,* a blossom festival opened the spring season in early March; a "Most Outstanding Mother of San Mateo County" contest marked Mother's Day; Hillsdale celebrated Father's Day with a children's operetta; in August there was a children's art exhibit; then came the fall flower festival; in November there was an auto show attracting 300,000 people; and in December giant animated figures, a fifty-foot lighted tree, and a Santa's workshop delighted Christmas shoppers. With all this and ample parking as well, suburbanites no longer felt the need or desire to make such frequent trips to downtown department stores. During the Christmas season in 1954, suburban shopping centers accounted for only 10 percent of all shopping trips in Pittsburgh's Allegheny County, whereas 41 percent of the shopping trips were to Pittsburgh's central business district. By the 1960 Christmas season the suburban centers accounted for 38 percent of all shopping trips, and the downtown figure had dropped to 35 percent. In other words, by the close of the 1950s, residents in metropolitan Pittsburgh were traveling more often to suburban centers for Christmas season shopping than to downtown stores. And the same was true throughout the United States. Within a single decade the shopping habits of a nation had changed radically as the outlying shopping mall won the loyalty of the growing body of motoring suburbanites.

Meanwhile, manufacturing, warehouse, and wholesale firms were joining the retailer and the resident in the migration to suburbia. Just as the automobile encouraged the suburbanization of retailing, the growing significance of truck traffic encouraged the development of manufacturing plants and wholesaling facilities on the outskirts. Whereas in 1940 trucks accounted for only 10 percent of the total ton-miles in intercity freight traffic and the railroad's share was 61 percent, by 1959 the figure for trucks had more than doubled to 22 percent while the rails moved only 45 percent of the nation's goods. As business became increasingly dependent on the truck, congested inner-city locations with clogged streets and little space for parking or loading facilities became increasingly undesirable and the open spaces of suburbia more appealing. Moreover, sprawling, one-story plants were better adapted to modern assembly-line production than multistory mill buildings. Manufacturers needed large, undeveloped tracts of land for their new plants, and they could find such land in suburbia.

By the early 1960s new factories lined suburban highways, providing thousands of jobs and millions of dollars in tax revenue for outlying municipalities. From 1954 through 1956 roughly 90 percent of the capital committed to the construction of new factories in the New York metropolitan region was invested in suburban areas beyond the boundaries of New York City. Between 1947 and 1954 the number of manufacturing plants in Chicago's suburbs doubled, and in suburban Detroit there was a 220 percent rise in the number of factories. Meanwhile, manufacturing plants proliferated along California's freeways, forming ribbons of industry emanating from Los Angeles, San Francisco, and Oakland. But the magnetic attraction of the suburban superhighway was especially powerful in the Boston metropolitan region. Between 1951 and 1957 the state of Massachusetts completed Route 128, a freeway along the circumference of the metropolitan area about ten miles from downtown Boston. By the end of 1957 manufacturers had already invested $94 million in ninety-nine industrial plants adjacent to the superhighway, and these new suburban factories employed 17,000 persons. During the late 1950s and early 1960s more plants joined the migration to Route 128, and the freeway soon was the center of New England's burgeoning high technology industries. In the popular imagination suburbia may have connoted row after row of split-level homes and manicured lawns. By the early 1960s, however, Route 128 and its counterparts in metropolitan areas across the country were as much a part of the suburban scene as Levittown or Park Forest.

But suburbia was not only giving birth to new factories, shopping centers, and housing tracts, it was also nurturing an abundance of new governmental units. Between 1945 and 1964 the governmental fragmentation of metropolitan America continued apace, reinforcing the ethnic, economic, and social divisions between the central city and the suburb and between the suburbs themselves. In 1940 there were forty-one municipalities in suburban Saint Louis County, Missouri, whereas by 1950 there were eighty-three. In 1950 forty-five municipalities clustered within Los Angeles County; ten years later the number had risen to sixty-eight. Some of these new municipalities were organized in order to protect special interests located in that fragment of the metropolis. For example, in Los Angeles County Rolling Hills and Rolling Hills Estates were wealthy residential enclaves that incorporated in order to protect themselves from commercial and industrial encroachments as well as low-cost housing tracts. In contrast, the Los Angeles suburbs of Industry and Commerce were industrial areas that opted for independent municipal rule in order to exclude residential developments and to prevent adjoining municipalities from annexing the tax-rich manufacturing properties. And nearby Dairy Valley incorporated to protect dairy operations from both residential and commercial encroachment. Through the exercise of municipal zoning powers, each of these newly-incorporated communities could exclude whatever seemed obnoxious or threatening. Rolling Hills Estates could zone its territory for single-family residential development with a minimum lot size of two acres, thus excluding factories, apartments, Levitt-built boxes, and unwanted trailer parks. Industry could zone itself industrial, excluding homeowners who might demand expensive services and higher taxes on business properties. Dairy Valley could permit only low-density development, thereby preserving the agricultural economy of the community. In each area, suburbanites could use the law to carve up the metropolis into mutually exclusive zones.

According to many postwar reformers, however, Americans needed to look beyond the special interests of the suburban fragment and consider the good of the metropolitan community as a whole. As in the 1920s numerous civic leaders and political scientists believed that some form of overarching metropolitan government was necessary to ensure efficient rule and areawide planning. Thus the two-tiered, federative plan again appeared on the ballot in the 1950s. Toronto, Canada, adopted such a scheme in 1953, and inspired by this Canadian triumph, metropolitan reformers in Saint Louis, Cleveland, and Miami conducted vigorous campaigns on behalf of federative rule. Yet in Cleveland and Saint Louis the scheme met defeat just as it had a quarter of a century earlier. Only in Miami did voters adopt the two-tiered plan, allocating certain metropolitan functions to Dade County yet preserving the area's separate municipal governments. Elsewhere Americans willingly abdicated municipal powers to special-function metropolitan agencies — metropolitan park boards, metropolitan sewerage commissions, regional port authorities. But beyond this piecemeal cooperation there was little progress toward metropolitan union.

Some cities were able to limit governmental fragmentation through vigorous annexation campaigns. This was especially true in the South-west where the area of Phoenix increased from 17 square miles in 1950 to 187 square miles in 1960 and Albuquerque ballooned from 16 square miles in 1946 to 61 square miles in 1960. Similarly, Texas's lenient annexation laws allowed Houston to expand from 76 square miles at the beginning of 1948 to almost 447 square miles nineteen years later and San Antonio to absorb 115 square miles of new territory between 1950 and 1970. Independent suburban municipalities did not ring these booming Sunbelt cities; in fact as late as the 1970s there were only two incorporated places in the entire Albuquerque metropolitan area. But in the older urban areas of the Midwest and Northeast a pattern of governmental fragmentation was firmly established and the chances of Chicago or Cleveland annexing adjacent cities and villages were nil. For most large American cities annexation was no longer an alternative and metropolitan federation remained only a defeated dream.

Thus political boundaries, as well as social, economic, and ethnic frontiers, divided metropolitan America. The federal census bureau identified a region as the Chicago metropolitan area, but in fact it was a loose grouping of political fragments, the people linked by a common allegiance to the White Sox or the Cubs but not united under a single government. During the 1950s suburbia was booming, but this boom was deepening the fissures in metropolitan America, dividing central-city blacks from suburban whites, plebeian Levittowners from the country club set of Rolling Hills Estates, and farmers in Dairy Valley from manufacturers in Industry.

CENTRAL-CITY BUST

During the postwar era, suburbia's gain was the central-city's loss. As millions of Americans migrated to the suburbs, the population of major central cities in the Northeast and Midwest plummeted. Of the twelve cities that ranked as most populous in 1950, eleven lost population during the following decade. Boston's population dropped 13 percent, the total for Saint Louis was down almost 13 percent, and the number of inhabitants in Pittsburgh fell 11 percent. Among the largest cities only Los Angeles, with its vast undeveloped tracts, gained residents. During the 1960s this trend persisted as the old giants continued to slip in rank (see Table 1). Every major metropolitan area (with the exception of Pittsburgh in the 1960s) increased in population, but the gains were all in the suburbs. A baby boom filled America's nurseries and schools and prosperity put a car in every garage and a television in every living room, but the old giants like Philadelphia,

Chicago, and Saint Louis were out of step with this new era of growth and good fortune. They were falling behind the expanding suburbs and losing their preeminent position within metropolitan America.

The venerable central business district tried to adapt to this changing world, but by the early 1960s its location at the convergence of public transit lines no longer guaranteed it a dominant role in the life of the metropolis. Between 1945 and 1965 transit patronage dropped 64 percent, from 23 billion passengers to 8 billion passengers, and public transit's share of all the passenger-miles logged in urban America plummeted from 35 percent to 5 percent. In the 1960s only a small percentage of Americans rode the buses, elevated trains, or subways, and thus accessibility to transit lines no longer was a great advantage for retailers or theater owners. Ample parking space was more important than a convenient bus stop at the shop door. Yet available space was the very thing congested business districts lacked. There never seemed to be enough parking places downtown, and the parking facilities that existed charged too much or were not as conveniently located as the giant shopping center lots.

Thus the downtown was ill-suited to be the focus of commerce, retailing, and amusement in the auto-borne postwar era, and a number of origin-destination studies demonstrated that fewer people were travel-

TABLE 1. Population of Central Cities 1950–1970

City	1950 Population	Rank	1960 Population	Rank	1970 Population	Rank
New York City	7,891,957	1	7,781,984	1	7,894,862	1
Chicago	3,620,962	2	3,550,404	2	3,366,957	2
Philadelphia	2,071,605	3	2,002,512	4	1,948,609	4
Los Angeles	1,970,358	4	2,479,015	3	2,816,061	3
Detroit	1,849,568	5	1,670,144	5	1,511,482	5
Baltimore	949,708	6	939,024	6	905,759	7
Cleveland	914,808	7	876,050	8	750,903	10
Saint Louis	856,796	8	750,026	10	622,236	18
Washington	802,178	9	763,956	9	756,510	9
Boston	801,444	10	697,197	13	641,071	16
San Francisco	775,357	11	740,316	12	715,674	13
Pittsburgh	676,806	12	604,332	16	520,117	24

SOURCE: U.S. Department of Commerce, Bureau of the Census, 1950–1970 *Censuses of Population.*

ing to the aging urban core. For example, between 1953 and 1965 the number of trips to or from Detroit's central business district dropped 22 percent, and downtown trips as a percentage of all metropolitan trips fell from 6 percent to 3 percent. Likewise, from 1956 to 1970 trips to and from Chicago's Loop plummeted 25 percent, and in the latter year only 5 percent of all trips were to or from downtown as opposed to 1956 when 12 percent began or ended in the Windy City's central business district. All these figures simply proved what was obvious to everyone. More people were driving automobiles, yet the downtown was ill-adapted to motor vehicles. Therefore Americans were transacting their business elsewhere and avoiding the urban core.

Changing transportation patterns were especially detrimental to downtown retailers. Before World War II, when few families had more than one car and the husband was usually behind the steering wheel, middle-class housewives still rode the streetcar to downtown department stores. By the 1950s, however, a second car in the family freed the wife from this journey and enabled her to frequent the newest suburban shopping centers. The result was declining sales figures for downtown retailers. Between 1948 and 1958 retail sales in downtown Pittsburgh dropped 9 percent while suburban sales soared 51 percent. Likewise, there was a 5 percent decline in sales in downtown Philadelphia but a 64 percent rise in suburban merchandising, and in Boston downtown sales dipped 1 percent while suburban trade soared 70 percent. In 1948 the Philadelphia central business district accounted for 21 percent of all retail sales in the metropolitan area and 83 percent of all department store business; ten years later Philadelphians made only 13 percent of their purchases downtown and downtown outlets accounted for only 57 percent of the department store trade. When adjusted for inflation, the level of department store sales in downtown Boston in 1960 equaled that of 1933, the worst year of the depression. In other words, the postwar boom did not hit downtown retailers. Instead, all the statistics for downtown sales testified to the stagnation of the urban core.

The largest department stores continued to flourish, though an increasing portion of their profits was from suburban branches. But marginal downtown retailers collapsed under the pressure of changing times. Between 1958 and 1960 three major department stores in Pittsburgh folded, reducing downtown department store facilities by a million square feet. From 1947 to 1957 the number of employees in downtown Boston's apparel and accessory stores fell 32 percent, and between 1948 and 1954 retail employment in downtown Chicago also dropped by a third. For rent signs appeared in windows along once-fashionable shopping streets, and cut-rate stores and novelty shops moved into buildings that had formerly housed the finest retailers. This shabbiness only further repelled middle-class shoppers and strengthened their loyalty to the suburban mall. But transportation was the decisive factor undermining downtown retailers. In the early 1960s urban expert George Sternlieb summed up the problem: "We are asking the customer to pay a penalty to visit the downtown store — either to use the mass transit system which she has voted against or an automobile in an environment which cannot comfortably accommodate it." A retailing center created for the streetcar city simply did not meet the needs of the motoring age.

Another downtown landmark that suffered from changing tastes in transportation was the railroad depot. Fewer Americans were passing through these once-magnificent portals to the city, for the passenger train was falling victim not only to the automobile but to the airplane as well. When measured in terms of passenger-miles, patronage of noncommuter passenger trains dropped 84 percent from 1945 to 1964, whereas airline traffic soared more than 1,400 percent. Outlying airports were the centers of intercity travel by the early 1960s; downtown rail depots were monumental white elephants. Resigned to inevitable doom, the railroads spent little for the maintenance of passenger terminals, and deprived of any cosmetic repairs, the great waiting rooms grew ugly with age.

Indicative of the plight of downtown depots was the fate of New York City's two great stations. In 1961 the owners of Grand Central Station asked New York City's zoning board for permission to lower the waiting room ceiling from 58 feet to only 15 feet and add three tiers of bowling alleys in the space thus created. The idea of transforming the great waiting room into a bowling alley incensed many leading architects and prominent New Yorkers who together squelched the scheme. Yet the owners were able to sell the air space over the terminal, and by 1963 the fifty-five-story Pan Am Building loomed above the depot, its ugly enormity dwarfing the grandeur of the terminal. Pan Am's overpowering presence was, however, an appropriate symbol of the changing times, for airlines were now supreme, overshadowing railroads as carriers of intercity passenger traffic.

New York City's Pennsylvania Station suffered a sadder fate. In 1963 developers won approval to tear down the great vaulted concourse of the terminal and replace it with an office building, sports arena, and a cramped commuter station. Those dedicated to preserving the landmark picketed and protested but to no avail. Wreckers pulled down the station's mighty columns and destroyed the finest architectural monument to the railroad age. The decor of the new scaled-down station was described by critic Carl Condit as "men's room modern." Yet the new facility was suited to the function it now served, for by the 1960s Pennsylvania Station was a stop for commuter trains and not a principal gateway to the nation's greatest city.

Another central-city institution affected by the triumph of the automobile and the airlines was the downtown hotel. Hotels in the central business district had once dominated the hostelry business for they offered lodging convenient to both the railroad station and the city's stores and offices. But as railroads declined and business dispersed, competition developed in the form of motels, motor inns, and airport hotels. These outlying establishments were more convenient to persons traveling by car or airplane, and during the 1950s and early 1960s they attracted a larger share of the lodging trade. In 1948 hotels accounted for 92 percent of combined hotel/motel revenues; in 1964 this figure had fallen to 64 percent. Between 1948 and 1964 the number of hotel rooms in the United States dropped from 1,550,000 to 1,450,000, whereas the number of rooms in motels and motor hotels soared from 304,000 to 1,020,000. Neon signs lined the peripheral highways flashing the names of the latest motels, but in the heart of the city few new hotels were built during the first fifteen years after World War II.

Oversupply of hotel rooms was one factor discouraging new construction. In the 1920s there had been a hotel building boom, and consequently the number of first-class hotels tripled. During the depression this excess of lodging brought bankruptcy to four out of five hotels, and even after World War II there was little desire to build new establishments. Instead, the Hilton and Sheraton chains bought existing hotels, changed the names, imposed the chain logo, and pocketed the profits. Not until the early 1960s did a new wave of hotel construction begin. For example, when the 800-room Summit Hotel opened in 1961, it was New York City's first new hotel since the completion of the Waldorf-Astoria thirty years earlier. After this drought of three decades, a torrent of building followed. Loew's Americana in midtown Manhattan opened in 1962, and the New York Hilton welcomed its first visitors in 1963. Elsewhere the story was the same. The old prewar hotels were wearing out and finally needed replacing. The supply of downtown hotel rooms was not expanding markedly; the new was simply replacing the outdated and obsolete. So long as there were conventions and commercial travelers, the downtown hotel would survive. But for every new downtown hotel, there were ten Holiday Inns opening along the interstate highways in suburbia.

Not only did overbuilding in the 1920s discourage postwar hotel construction, it also cut the production of new office towers. During the first decade following World War II, in most cities construction of downtown office buildings was at a standstill. The skyscraper legacy of the 1920s still satisfied the demand for office space, and developers invested in suburban housing tracts or shopping centers rather than downtown structures. Chicago's Prudential Building, completed in 1955, was the first new office building in the Loop since 1934. Likewise San Francisco's Equitable Building, also completed in 1955, was the first major addition to downtown office space in that city in more than two decades. Construction of the CEI Building in Cleveland in 1956 ended a quarter-century lull, and in 1956 a new office structure also opened in downtown Philadelphia, the first since World War II. Only in New York City, Pittsburgh, and Dallas was there major office construction during the late 1940s and early 1950s. As the preeminent headquarters city in the nation, New York had a seemingly insatiable appetite for new skyscrapers, and Manhattan acquired fifty-five additional office structures from 1947 through 1955.

The rate of office construction picked up gradually during the late 1950s and accelerated rapidly during the early 1960s. In the three-year period from 1957 through 1959, an extraordinary fifty-one new office towers opened in Manhattan, a feat that *Fortune* described as "a terrific visible demonstration of the vitality of purely private enterprise." Though the automobile and suburbia had taken their toll on downtown retailing, the office sector flourished to a degree that warmed the capitalist heart. Financial institutions, business services such as advertising agencies and accounting firms, law offices, and corporate headquarters all remained downtown and all demanded more office space. There may have been fewer shoppers on the downtown streets by the early 1960s, but there were more employees in the shining glass high-rise structures. Physicians and dentists did tend to abandon the central business district and move their offices closer to hospitals or nearer to their patients' suburban homes. But others remained downtown, ensuring that the central business district would remain a major center of employment if not the preeminent one.

Thus the role of the downtown was narrowing. At the turn of the century, the downtown had been the center of urban transportation, business, industry, amusement, and government. It was the unchallenged focus of economic endeavor and public policymaking in the metropolitan area. By the 1960s, however, the American metropolis no longer had a single dominant nucleus. Instead, retailing was increasingly dispersed, outlying airports dominated intercity transportation, industry was spread out along the superhighways and rail lines, each home was equipped with a color television and stereo that provided a center of entertainment equal to the old vaudeville theaters, and government authority was distributed among the multitude of municipalities that made up the metropolitan area. Yet the central business district was still the headquarters of all the major banks, law firms, and brokerage offices. The diversity of the early-twentieth-century downtown was yielding to rows of glass-sheathed towers and armies of gray-flanneled office workers.

Meanwhile, the residential neighborhoods of the central city were also changing. Most notably, white residents were leaving for the suburbs and black newcomers were arriving. From 1945 to 1964 millions of blacks migrated northward to the central cities of the Northeast and Midwest, attracted by high-paying factory jobs and opportunities for greater personal advancement. Whereas the white population of New York City declined 7 percent between 1950 and 1960, the black population soared 46 percent. In Chicago the white total dropped 13 percent while the number of blacks rose 65 percent, and in Philadelphia there were also 13 percent fewer whites in 1960 than in 1950 but 41 percent more blacks. Overall, the black population in central cities having over 50,000 inhabitants rose 50 percent, climbing from 6,456,000 in 1950 to 9,705,000 ten years later.

This combined outflow of whites and influx of blacks resulted in a marked change in the composition of the central-city population. Whereas in 1950 only one-sixth of the populations of Detroit, Cleveland, and Saint Louis were black, by 1960 each of these cities was 29 percent black. In 1950 Washington, D.C., was approximately one-third black; in 1960, 54 percent of its inhabitants were black. And during the following decade the trend persisted (see Table 2). Washington was the first major American city with a black majority, but by the early 1960s it was clear that blacks would soon outnumber whites elsewhere as well. Such cities as Detroit and Newark were changing from overwhelmingly white to predominantly black in a single generation. Postwar Americans were a mobile group, moving frequently from one address to another. Nowhere was this mobility more striking than in the census figures recording the racial composition of America's central cities.

The rapid change transformed neighborhoods in a few short years. Before 1950 Euclid Avenue had been the boundary between blacks and whites on Cleveland's east side. During the following decade, however, blacks broke through this traditional barrier and flooded into the Hough neighborhood north of the avenue. In one twenty-one-block area of Hough blacks had occupied only 7 of the 1,350 dwellings in 1950; by 1960 there were over 1,000 black households in the district. Block after block lost old residents and gained new ones as blacks pushed to the city's eastern limits and whites migrated to the independent suburbs of Cleveland Heights, Euclid, and Lyndhurst. By the early 1960s Cleveland was a polarized city consisting of a predominantly black east side and a west side inhabited by white ethnics from southern and eastern Europe. Black expansion and racial polarization also characterized other postwar cities. Chicago's traditional south-side ghetto continued to expand, its southern boundary shifting from Seventy-first Street in 1950 to Ninety-fifth Street in 1960. Meanwhile, the west-side Afro-American district spread rapidly toward suburban Cicero and Oak Park. Yet existing north-side black enclaves did not grow markedly, for the northern half of Chicago remained white territory. In New York City also blacks won new territory, especially in Brooklyn and the Bronx. Harlem no longer housed the majority of New York City's

TABLE 2. Percentage of Black Population of Major Cities

City	1950	1960	1970
New York City	9.5	14.0	21.2
Chicago	13.6	22.9	32.7
Philadelphia	18.2	26.4	33.6
Los Angeles	8.7	13.5	17.9
Detroit	16.2	28.9	43.7
Baltimore	23.7	34.7	46.4
Cleveland	16.2	28.6	38.3
Saint Louis	17.9	28.6	40.9
Washington	35.0	53.9	71.1
Boston	5.0	9.1	16.3
San Francisco	5.6	10.0	13.4
Pittsburgh	12.2	16.7	20.2
Milwaukee	3.4	8.4	14.7
Houston	20.9	22.9	25.7
Buffalo	6.3	13.3	20.4
New Orleans	31.9	37.2	45.0
Minneapolis	1.3	2.4	4.4
Cincinnati	15.5	21.6	27.6
Seattle	3.4	4.8	7.1
Kansas City	12.2	17.5	22.1
Newark	17.1	34.1	54.2

NOTE: Cities are listed according to their population rank in 1950.

SOURCE: U.S. Department of Commerce, Bureau of the Census, 1950–1970 *Censuses of Population.*

blacks, and the dispersion of population from Harlem actually resulted in a net outmigration of 40,000 nonwhites from Manhattan during the 1950s. But as in Cleveland and Chicago, dispersion did not mean residential integration. Instead, white housing and black housing remained segregated, even though blacks were bursting out of the confines of the traditional ghetto.

As blacks expanded into new neighborhoods, some whites reacted with violence. Between 1945 and 1954 at least nine race-oriented riots occurred in Chicago, and from 1948 to 1951 racial antagonism in the Windy City resulted in 217 reported attacks against property. For example, in 1949 rioting exploded along Peoria Street in the Englewood neighborhood when a white union organizer invited some blacks to his home for a labor meeting. Rumors circulated that the visiting blacks were about to move into the neighborhood, and fears of this imminent black peril ignited five days of violence. Mobs of 2,000 people roamed the streets attacking blacks, Jews, and strangers, especially University of Chicago students. Four years later Chicago's largest and costliest racial disturbance of the 1950s broke out when a black family moved into the previously all-white Trumbull Park Homes, a low-cost public housing project constructed by the PWA. A campaign of terror and intimidation ensued, and after nine months of harassment the black family departed. Other blacks moved in, however, and window smashing, rock tossing, and incidents of arson persisted for two years. In other cities violence also greeted blacks who moved into new neighborhoods. Occasionally homes of black "invaders" were stoned and smeared with paint, and in some cases bombing incidents welcomed newcomers to the neighborhood. But blacks persisted and gradually claimed a larger portion of the city as their turf.

Other newcomers, however, were also moving into the city, arousing additional ethnic and cultural tensions. During the postwar era, New York City became the mecca for many Puerto Ricans who sought to escape the poverty of their native island. In 1940 there were only 61,000 persons of Puerto Rican birth in New York City, but by 1960 this figure had risen to 430,000. At the beginning of the 1960s persons of Puerto Rican birth or parentage constituted 8 percent of New York City's population. Midwestern cities received few Puerto Ricans, but newcomers from Southern Appalachia continued to move northward, adding to the cultural diversity of these urban areas. During the 1950s the Southern Appalachian region had a net outmigration of almost 1,600,000 and nearly one-third of the population of eastern Kentucky abandoned their native land of profitless coal mines and eroded farms. Thousands of these migrants settled in "hillbilly" ghettos such as Cincinnati's Over-the-Rhine neighborhood and Chicago's Uptown district. Meanwhile, in southwestern cities Mexican immigrants filled the slum barrios and provided a ready pool of cheap labor. By 1960 there were over 600,000 Spanish-surnamed persons in the Los Angeles metropolitan area and more than 250,000 in greater San Antonio.

Mexicans, Appalachians, Puerto Ricans, and blacks all moved to America's cities during the postwar era. Although of different races, religions, and cultures, they shared a background of rural poverty. And all faced hardships in their new urban homes. Life in New York City, Chicago, and Los Angeles was generally an improvement over hunger and deprivation in some Latin village, Mississippi shack, or West Virginia hollow. But unemployment rates for the newcomers exceeded the national average, and crime rates in black, Appalachian, and Hispanic neighborhoods were also high. Just as many earlier immigrants had found the city to be a cold home, postwar newcomers had to cope with a harsh alien environment in which they often faced antagonism and prejudice.

Thus the central-city population changed rapidly during the dynamic two decades following World War II. Middle-class urbanites left for suburbia, and refugees from rural poverty took their place. The net result was the impoverishment of the central city. Social, economic, and racial segregation continued to characterize metropolitan residential patterns. But increasingly the social and ethnic boundary between rich and poor, white and black, seemed to conform to the municipal boundary between central city and suburb. Such a pattern did not bode well for the future of New York City, Detroit, and Chicago.

REVIVING THE CENTRAL CITY

As urban blight spread and central business districts decayed, a growing number of Americans demanded action to halt the deterioration. Business leaders, city officials, and members of Congress all placed urban revival near the top of their public policy agendas, for all perceived the telltale signs of decline in the cities, and believed that something could be done to renovate and renew the urban core. Thus at both the local and the national levels, policymakers embarked on programs for lifting the sagging face of the city and rejuvenating aging urban areas.

Leading the revival campaign in each city was an alliance of business chiefs and municipal officials. Wealthy downtown property owners had much to lose if the business district slipped into hopeless decay, for blight threatened the sales figures at their downtown department stores and the profits from their office buildings. Likewise, big-city mayors had no intention of presiding over doomed cities or watching property tax revenues plummet as assessed values dropped. By the late 1940s and early 1950s both the chieftains of commerce and the leaders of local government agreed that the central cities needed new revenue-producing businesses.

Responding to this need, businessmen throughout the country cooperated with dynamic mayors dedicated to accelerating the economic pace of the languishing central cities. In Pennsylvania's largest city the business-dominated Greater Philadelphia Movement joined with reform mayors Joseph Clark, Jr., and Richardson Dilworth and sponsored a scheme for eliminating downtown eyesores. Through the combined efforts of local business and the Clark-Dilworth administrations, a shining new high-rise office complex known as Penn Center replaced an aging terminal and unsightly railroad viaduct. This government-business alliance also was responsible for the destruction of the city's decaying waterfront wholesale market and the construction of luxury apartments on the cleared site. In Chicago Mayor Richard Daley won some plaudits from the business community with his construction projects, including the creation of a giant convention center along Lake Michigan. Detroit's Mayor Albert Cobo, too, sought to bolster the fortunes of the central city through the building of a new civic center and mammoth convention hall. In New Orleans Mayor DeLesseps S. Morrison earned the loyalty of the business community with his construction schemes, most notably his plan to clear downtown slums and erect a civic center complex and railroad terminal. The civic centers of Detroit and New Orleans did not directly enrich the city through the payment of property taxes, but these gleaming new complexes would supposedly reverse the negative image of the central business district and attract private investment to the urban core.

In Saint Louis business and government conducted an especially vigorous crusade to lift their city from the economic doldrums. In 1955 a group of business troubleshooters known as Civic Progress, Incorporated, joined with Mayor Raymond Tucker to win voter approval for a $110.6 million civic improvement bond issue which would spark the city's revival. Advocates of the spending measure organized a fifteen-mile parade consisting of twenty-three floats, one for each category of proposed improvements, sixty-two other vehicles, and five blaring bands. The measure won endorsement from 950 labor unions, religious groups, civic clubs, and miscellaneous organizations, and the Ministerial Alliance of Greater St. Louis resolved that "every vote against the bond issue . . . is a vote for physical and moral decay and degradation."

The *St. Louis Post-Dispatch* referred to the election as "D-Day Against Decay" and warned ominously that "physical decline of a community is accompanied by a decline of community morale, a laxness, an indifference which gives disease, crime and the other scourges of a city their chance." The hard-sell campaign paid off, for Saint Louis voters overwhelmingly approved all twenty-three parts of the bond issue scheme. In the minds of business leaders and city officials, massive spending for expressways, slum clearance, street improvements, bridges, and hospitals seemed the answer to urban ills. And builder-mayors like Tucker, together with growth advocates like Civic Progress, were able to convince voters in the stagnant city to embrace this spending panacea.

Saint Louis leaders also attempted to reverse central-city decline by offering property tax abatements to those investing in downtown redevelopment projects. In 1945 Missouri's legislature enacted Chapter 353, the Urban Redevelopment Corporations Law. Under Chapter 353 private investors could organize corporations for the purpose of redeveloping blighted sites and, subject to the city's approval, could force slumlords to sell their property by exercising the municipality's power of eminent domain. Moreover, for ten years after purchase of a blighted site the corporation would only have to pay property tax on the assessed valuation of the raw land, exclusive of buildings or improvements, as determined during the year preceding purchase. For an additional fifteen years the city would assess the corporation's property at only one-half its full value. By the 1960s private developers were taking advantage of these tax breaks and investing in the Plaza Square and Mansion House Center redevelopment schemes. During the next two decades the city tax collector would demand little from these projects, for in Saint Louis public officials were willing to sacrifice needed municipal revenues in order to bolster the sagging economy.

No city won more publicity for its revival campaign, however, than the dingy industrial metropolis of Pittsburgh. Probably no city so desperately needed a refurbishing. Blankets of smoke shrouded the steel capital much of the year, floods were commonplace, and raw sewage choked the rivers. Between 1936 and 1947 the total assessed valuation of property in Pittsburgh dropped from $1,212 million to only $961 million, and at the close of World War II some corporate headquarters were planning to flee the benighted city. When asked his views on improving Pittsburgh, the great architect Frank Lloyd Wright replied, "It'd be cheaper to abandon it!"

Yet the fabulously wealthy Mellon family had both a financial and sentimental stake in the city, and together with Mayor David Lawrence the Mellons spearheaded a revival effort known as the Pittsburgh Renaissance. Through the Allegheny Conference on Community Development Richard King Mellon successfully won adoption of smoke abatement, flood control, and stream pollution programs. The mayor and business community also embarked on a massive redevelopment program of Pittsburgh's central business district or Golden Triangle. In 1945 Pittsburgh's leaders convinced the state to clear the land at the juncture of the Allegheny and Monongahela rivers of the existing railroad yards and create a park commemorating two historic forts that once stood on the site. The following year Mellon and his associates persuaded the Equitable Life Assurance Society to redevelop an adjacent area of commercial slums and transform it into a complex of offices. Using its power of eminent domain, the municipal redevelopment authority purchased the decaying properties and then sold them to the insurance company. In 1952–53 three twenty- to twenty-four-story office buildings opened in the redevelopment area, and by 1960 the complex could boast of three additional office structures together with a hotel and a 750-car underground parking garage. At the close of the 1950s an article in the travel magazine *Holiday* described Pittsburgh as "the city that quick-changed from unbelievable ugliness to shining beauty in less than half a generation."

In its initial stages the Pittsburgh redevelopment program relied on the funding and authority of the state, the city, and private business. To duplicate the Pittsburgh experience in other cities, however, many developers, planners, and public officials believed that federal action was necessary. With the passage of the Housing Act of 1949, Congress did finally commit the federal treasury to urban redevelopment. Under Title I of the Housing Act, local redevelopment authorities were to plan the renewal projects, purchase, assemble, and clear the blighted properties, and sell the bulldozed land to private developers. Since the purchase cost of slum property with standing buildings would presumably exceed the sale price of vacant, raw land, the local redevelopment agency would lose money on each renewal project. To aid these agencies and encourage slum clearance, the federal government was to pay two-thirds of the difference between the purchase and sale prices and two-thirds of the cost of demolition. Thus under Title I, cities received federal money to subsidize the clearance of blighted areas, and the local redevelopment agency and federal government jointly spared private investors the expense of purchasing slum buildings and demolishing them.

During the next fifteen years, cities throughout the nation were to avail themselves of federal largesse and initiate well-publicized urban renewal projects. By the close of 1964 the federal and local authorities had approved funding for 970 urban renewal projects covering 36,400 acres. Redevelopment agencies had demolished 158,000 buildings and many more would soon succumb to the wrecking ball. Urban universities like Fordham and Saint Louis University exploited the renewal process to expand their campuses, and the University of Chicago relied on urban renewal money to preserve the middle-class status of the surrounding Hyde Park–Kenwood neighborhood. New York City's Lincoln Center of the Performing Arts was a renewal project, as was its mammoth coliseum on Columbus Circle. For the ambitious builder-mayors who led the nation's cities in the 1950s and early 1960s the federal program seemed to promise a rebirth of the central cities. With federal money the resurrection of the urban core seemed possible if not imminent.

By the 1960s urban renewal czars throughout the country were battling the forces of decay, and the role model for many of these pugnacious administrators was Edward J. Logue. First as redevelopment administrator in New Haven, Connecticut, and later as urban renewal chief in Boston, Logue aggressively wrenched millions of dollars from the federal treasury, leveled hundreds of buildings, built scores of structures and won national renown. When Logue assumed his Boston post in 1960, the Massachusetts capital suffered from a classic case of urban decrepitude. During the previous decade, 14,000 downtown jobs had vanished, and $78 million of taxable property had disappeared from the central business district. In cooperation with Mayor John Collins and a business committee of Boston Brahmins, Logue quickly won federal funding for the construction of a government center, the redevelopment of the waterfront complete with high-rise luxury apartments, and the renovation of run-down residential neighborhoods. The ambitious government center was to rise on the site of Boston's skid row. In place of honky-tonk bars, Logue planned a red-brick pedestrian plaza ringed by a monumental new city hall and a group of towers to house federal and state agencies as well as private business concerns. It was to be a civic showcase, and planners estimated that it would draw 50,000 persons into the area each day, thereby bringing new vitality to the urban core. Within a few years of Logue's arrival in the New England metropolis, national magazines were writing of Boston's "comeback" and describing it as a metropolis "on the move." In 1964 one old-time Boston resident summed up the views of many when he told a reporter for *U.S. News and World Report*: "A few years ago, the feeling here was one of pessimism. Boston seemed to be proceeding calmly to its own strangulation. Now people are working together and getting us off dead center."

Despite all the rhetoric of hope, criticism of urban renewal programs was mounting by the early 1960s. In fact, a credibility gap was developing as promises far exceeded accomplishments. Throughout the nation renewal seemed to generate more destruction than construction and produce more vacant lots than corporate headquarters. In Saint Louis redevelopment of the Mill Creek Valley site proceeded slowly at first, earning the area the nickname "Hiroshima Flats." Likewise, Detroit residents labeled an empty site in their city "ragweed acres." Thirteen years after approval of redevelopment plans, according to the *New York Times,* the bulk of a 160-acre tract in Buffalo remained "an overgrown lot with a few junked cars, piles of garbage and rat nests. Trees that were saplings when the land was cleared have grown tall." Eventually urban renewal sites sprouted new buildings, but in cities where there was little demand for cleared property the lag between destruction and construction could be lengthy. Although 124 projects were in the planning or execution stage in 1950, only 41 were completed in 1960. In the minds of many citizens, the gestation period of the city's rebirth seemed inordinately long.

A more serious complaint was that the program burdened the poor for the benefit of the rich. Redevelopment authorities destroyed low-rent housing and small, marginal businesses and built in their place luxury apartments, civic centers, office complexes, and university campuses. Thousands of low-income residents were displaced from their neighborhoods because middle-class planners and officials deemed those neighborhoods blighted. One of the most criticized renewal schemes was Boston's West End project, which demolished the homes of 7,500 working-class Italian-Americans to make way for a sterile grouping of high-rise luxury apartments. According to a survey of the displaced persons, their median rent just before eviction from the West End in 1958-59 was forty-one dollars a month, but after relocation in new neighborhoods the median monthly rent was seventy-one dollars. Their living conditions had not improved markedly, yet owing to urban renewal their housing costs soared 75 percent. Moreover, clinical psychologist Marc Fried reported that 46 percent of West End women and 38 percent of the neighborhood's men gave "evidence of a fairly severe grief reaction or worse" when answering questions about their eviction from the tight-knit ethnic community. Thus the poor bore the financial and psychological brunt of change so that renewal authorities could house the rich.

City officials, however, were not ignoring the problem of sheltering the poor. Instead, their agenda of urban revitalization included the construction of additional public housing. In the Housing Act of 1949 Congress recommitted itself to public housing and authorized the construction of 810,000 units over the next six years. Opponents of the program successfully cut annual appropriations, and between 1949 and 1955 barely 200,000 dwelling units were actually completed. Yet each year local authorities added thousands of new apartments to the public housing stock, and by the close of 1964 there were 575,000 units housing 2,100,000 persons.

By the postwar era, however, the clientele of public housing projects was changing, Whereas in the late 1930s public housing tenants were primarily working-class families with an employed male head, during the 1950s and early 1960s the projects admitted an increasing number of fatherless welfare families. By 1963, 50 percent of the families moving into Saint Louis's projects were on welfare, and in Detroit 63 percent of the newcomers were welfare recipients. That same year 51 percent of Chicago's public housing units were occupied by families with both a husband and wife present, yet by 1968 this figure had fallen to 38 percent. Moreover, in many cities public housing projects were becoming all-black reservations, segregated enclaves for unwanted migrants from the South. In 1955 about two-thirds of Chicago's public housing tenants were black, and four years later blacks occupied 85 percent of the public housing units in the Illinois metropolis.

Postwar public housing not only served a different clientele than the prewar projects, it also was markedly different in design. Seeking to cut costs, postwar housing planners rejected the low-rise designs of the 1930s and opted instead for high-rise construction. In high-rise projects local authorities could house more people for less money and still preserve open areas for play and recreation. Thus in New York City, Chicago, Philadelphia, and Boston housing agencies built grim rows of high-rise structures, giant brick honeycombs sheltering swarms of the poor. For example, in 1960 the Chicago Housing Authority began construction of the Robert Taylor Homes, the largest public housing project in the world. Consisting of 4,415 units in twenty-eight identical sixteen-story buildings, the project originally contained 27,000 poor, black residents. In 1965 the *Chicago Daily News* attacked it as Chicago's "leading civic monument to misery, bungling, and a hellish way of life" and claimed that the tenants themselves referred to the project as "a 'death trap,' a concentration camp, and even, with sardonic self-derision, 'the Congo Hilton.'" Teenage crime and vandalism were rampant; unable to wait for an elevator to take them to their apartments, children urinated in the hallways and stairwells; and within a few years of completion a chronic state of disrepair prevailed. According to one resident, "We live stacked on top of one another with no elbow room. Danger is all around. There's little privacy or peace and no quiet. And the world looks on all of us as project rats, living on a reservation like untouchables."

Although the Robert Taylor Homes may have suffered many shortcomings, the favorite whipping boy of public housing critics was the Pruitt-Igoe project in Saint Louis. In the early 1950s, while still in the blueprint stages, this project had attracted nationwide attention as a model that other cities could emulate. It incorporated open galleries, eleven feet deep and eighty-five feet long, on every third floor, which the adjacent tenants were to share as communal porches, laundries, and play spaces. According to an admiring report in *Architectural Forum,* these galleries would be the focus of "vertical neighborhoods" in the thirty-three eleven-story apartment buildings. Winding between the buildings there was to be "a river of trees," a long narrow park offering tenants ample open space for recreation. Altogether it seemed an ideal plan, and the project opened amid high hopes. Ten years later it was a renowned disaster. In the mid-1960s *Architectural Forum* reported contritely that Pruitt-Igoe's buildings loomed "formidably over broad expanses of scrubby grass, broken glass and litter," and "the galleries are anything but cheerful social enclaves." The crime rate exceeded that of other public projects, and the elevators provided convenient settings for muggings and rapes. Some claimed that the housing authority's cost-cutting measures had ruined the project, and others argued that with 2,800 units it was simply too big. Looking back on his battered handiwork, the architect could only lament, "I never thought people were that destructive. . . . It's a job I wish I hadn't done." A $7 million renovation in 1965 did not salvage the faltering apartment complex, and by 1971 only seventeen of the thirty-three buildings were occupied. Finally in 1975 the housing authority began demolition of the entire project.

The slow death of Pruitt-Igoe attracted the scavenger press, and it became a symbol of public housing's failure. Few projects, however, suffered such a sad fate, and there were waiting lists for apartments at many public housing complexes. Yet by the early 1960s even the best of the projects inspired little enthusiasm. The great expectations of the housing reformers of the 1930s seemed naive in retrospect, and the schemes and proposals of Edith Wood and Catherine Bauer were joining those of Lawrence Veiller on the ash heap of urban promises.

The most trenchant critic of the whole range of public housing and urban renewal programs was Jane Jacobs. A resident of the Greenwich Village section of New York City, Jacobs had successfully waged war on the local renewal agency when it threatened her neighborhood with destructive "revitalization." But her crusade was not limited to the few blocks surrounding her home. Instead, in the 1961 volume *The Death and Life of Great American Cities* she carried her campaign to a nation-wide audience and expressed her contempt for the accepted dogmas of urban renewal. In this work, she attacked the "wistful myth that if only we had enough money to spend . . . we could wipe out all our slums in ten years" and "anchor the wandering middle class and its wandering tax money." According to Jacobs, billions of federal dollars had only bought "low-income projects that become worse centers of delinquency, vandalism and general social hopelessness than the slums they were supposed to replace," and "luxury housing projects that mitigate their inanity, or try to, with a vapid vulgarity." In her opinion urban renewal and housing authorities were not rebuilding the city but sacking it. As an alternative she proposed the preservation of old buildings rather than their destruction, the concentration of population rather than its dispersion, and a healthy mix of retailers, residences, manufacturing lofts, and restaurants rather than the segregation of these establishments through enforcement of zoning ordinances. Mixed economic functions, dense population, and continued use of old buildings would bring vitality to the dying cities and again make the urban core a center of excitement and activity. Thus she eschewed the policy of massive retaliation against blight and emphasized the value of small-scale private investment in older, densely-populated districts as a means for gradually restoring life to America's declining metropolises.

During the following decade Jacobs's views were to win many adherents, for anyone visiting the urban core could see the shortcomings of monumental renewal schemes. In fact, by the 1960s all the rhetoric of urban revival was wearing thin. Cities were rebuilding their central business districts, and Pittsburgh was free of the smoke and sewage of the past. Yet everywhere there were signs of decay and decline. Despite all the Mellon money and the massive investments from government and business, not only the city of Pittsburgh but the entire Pittsburgh metropolitan area lost population during the 1960s. No matter how many millions of dollars Saint Louis raised through bond issues that city was still sliding rapidly downward. Even though Edward Logue was applying a fresh face to old Boston, residents were moving out and suburban municipalities were capturing a larger share of the area's commerce. The postwar era was a period of suburban ascendancy, and central-city mayors and redevelopment agencies could not reverse the outward flow of people and money. In the 1960s the older central cities of the Northeast and Midwest were still alive but hardly vital.

An Age of "Urban Crisis," 1964–1979

On the morning of July 16, 1964, Thomas Gilligan, a white police lieutenant, was in a New York City television shop, when he saw a nearby disturbance between a white building superintendent and some black teenagers. He rushed from the shop to the site of the conflict; then, according to Gilligan, a fifteen-year-old black, James Powell, darted at him with a knife and in defense the lieutenant fatally shot the teenager. A crowd quickly gathered at the scene of the Powell killing, and one onlooker cried in rage, "Come on, shoot another nigger!" At that moment rocks, bottles, and garbage-can lids began to fly, the opening barrage in the first battle of the riot ridden 1960s. Black mobs roamed the streets of Harlem and Brooklyn's Bedford-Stuyvesant district for the next six nights, attacking police and looting stores. When peace finally returned to the black ghetto, 1 rioter was dead, 118 were injured, and 465 had been arrested.

Gilligan's shots sounded the start of an era of violence and conflict, of "long hot summers" disturbed by rioting and rampages. During the following summers of the 1960s such incidents ignited riots in cities throughout the country. Each year, with the return of hot weather black mobs took to the streets expressing their rage through acts of violence. Moreover, the once-passive poor of all races began venting their anger at urban authorities through sit-ins, pickets, and verbal tirades rich with four-letter words. Crime also seemed on the rise with muggers and rapists making their ugly contribution to the chaos of the city. Journalists, politicians, and scholars all spoke of an "urban crisis" gripping the nation. To many Americans, it appeared that the nation's cities were disintegrating as residents indulged in an orgy of anger and violence.

Adding to the miseries of beleaguered public officials was the persistent decline in the central-city economy. The older central cities were continuing to lose business, and although new downtown office buildings offered some hope of renewal, in the central cities' residential neighborhoods there was little to inspire confidence. With middle-class whites, retailers, and manufacturers moving to suburbia at a quickening pace, the central-city tax base was contracting, and by the early 1970s some of America's largest cities were on the brink of bankruptcy. Violence, anger, crime, and fiscal distress — the catalog of urban ills was growing at a disturbing rate.

Meanwhile, the federal government intervened to salvage the faltering central cities and in the process markedly expanded its commitment to urban America. Yet at times the task seemed too great for even the national chieftains in Washington. The loose threads linking the social and ethnic fragments of metropolitan America were finally unraveling. Throughout the first six decades of the twentieth century the American city had somehow coped with the rents in the metropolitan fabric, patching, mending, and making do. But by the late 1960s and early 1970s, the city no longer seemed to work. The governmental divisions between central city and suburb resulted in a maldistribution of tax resources that was especially detrimental to the urban core. The racial segregation of blacks and whites had nurtured violent hatreds that no longer could be suppressed. And the economic gap between rich and poor was similarly a source of heightened overt bitterness.

When Thomas Gilligan gunned down James Powell, he exposed these raw divisions in metropolitan America, and it was not a pretty sight. Television crews now transmitted visual proof of the fragmentation of the city into living rooms across America as the evening news brought the latest communiqués from the urban battlefield. Some may have downplayed the crisis in the city, claiming that the problems were not so serious as they appeared. But for those who remembered the Progressive promise of a unifying civic ideal and the work of Jane Addams, Tom Johnson, and the others who believed in a better urban future, the television reports were the death knell of a dream.

REBELLION AND CRIME

The New York City riots of 1964 were minor league compared to the outbreaks of the following summers. But there were certain traits that linked the riots of 1964 with those of 1965, 1966, and 1967. In most cases, the violence began with a police incident, an arrest on the street within the earshot of others. And police prejudice and brutality were the grievances most commonly cited among rioters. The police represented the white governing authority that for so many years had deprived blacks of their rights, and, as in the case of James Powell, had occasionally deprived them of their lives. Despite the rising number of blacks in the central cities, the police forces remained overwhelmingly white and seemingly insensitive to the feelings of the black community. In 1967 more than 30 percent of the population of Detroit and Cleveland was black, but only 5 percent of Detroit's police force was black and only 7 percent of Cleveland's. To many blacks the white cop patrolling the ghetto was a symbol of subjugation that they were no longer willing to tolerate.

Black resentment was tragically evident in the Watts riot of 1965. It began with a routine arrest by Los Angeles police in that city's black neighborhood of Watts. At 7 P.M. on August 11, a twenty-one-year-old black man, Marquette Frye, was driving home with his brother, both having just consumed several "screwdrivers." Weaving in and out of traffic at an excessive speed, Frye attracted the attention of a white police officer who pulled him over and arrested him for drunk driving and speeding. At the scene of the arrest a crowd gathered and the Frye brothers became increasingly belligerent. The policeman radioed for help, and the newly arrived officers subdued the Fryes with blows on the head, stomach, and ribs. Just as the police were about to leave one officer felt someone in the now seething crowd spit on him. The police seized the suspected culprit, a young woman in a loose-fitting smock resembling a maternity dress, and dragged her into a police car. On seeing this outrage against a seemingly pregnant woman, the crowd erupted, letting loose a barrage of bricks, stones, and bottles. Six days of violence ensued.

So as not to provoke further violence, the police withdrew from the Watts area the first night of the riot. But the next afternoon they returned in full force, and their invasion set off a rampage of looting and burning among Watts residents. From a "war room" downtown the Los Angeles police coordinated their maneuvers but to little avail. An estimated 31,000 to 35,000 adults participated in the rioting, which was scattered over a forty-six-square-mile area encompassing all of south-central Los Angeles. Sixteen hundred police and sheriff's deputies together with 13,900 National Guard troops finally imposed some order on the district but only after 34 persons were killed, at least 1,032 injured seriously enough to require treatment, and 3,952 arrested. Property damage was estimated at $40 million with almost 1,000 buildings burned, looted, damaged, or destroyed.

White Americans were shocked by the violence, but few whites, other than police and national guardsmen, had any personal contact with the rioting. In Los Angeles whites lived in their own fragments of the sprawling city, apart from the "troublesome" blacks. The San Fernando Valley and the west side was white territory, Mexican-Americans populated the east side, and blacks were confined to the south-central area. At the close of the 1960s a survey of white residents of Westlake Village in the San Fernando Valley revealed that two-thirds of them had never or only once been to the south-central Los Angeles ghetto. Thus blacks rioted on their own turf, and whites in the Southern California neighborhoods of Westlake Village or Encino, like residents in New York or Pennsylvania, knew about the violence primarily from newspaper and television reports.

Whites were to hear more about rioting from their television commentators, for in 1966 there were twenty-one major riots and civil disorders. In July Cleveland's Hough area was the scene of rioting after the police intervened in a dispute between a white bartender and a black man at a neighborhood tavern. The first night of violence thirty-eight fires broke out, twelve policemen were injured, and a young black mother standing at an apartment window was killed by a stray bullet. And two more nights of sniping and firebombing followed. In September the Hunter's Point neighborhood of San Francisco erupted when a white policeman shot and killed a fleeing black teenager whom he had ordered to halt. The Hunter's Point disturbance was less violent than the outbursts in Hough, Watts, or Harlem, but there was enough brick throwing, looting, and breaking of store windows to earn the event news coverage and media recognition as yet another riot. Sporadic outbursts elsewhere in the country kept city officials tense and angered many whites.

In 1967, however, rioting was even more prevalent, with eighty-three major disturbances recorded. Blacks took to the streets in usually tranquil cities like Waterloo, Iowa, and Dayton, Ohio, and in Newark and Detroit the level of violence was ominous. The Newark uprising began in July when police arrested a taxi driver and dragged him into the central precinct station. During the next five days, New Jersey state police and National Guardsmen called in to quell the disturbance fired 13,000 rounds of ammunition. When the violence ceased twenty-three persons were dead. That same month Detroit's riot began with a routine police raid on an illegal, after-hours drinking place, the haunt of off-duty black prostitutes, pimps, and narcotics peddlers. As in Watts, Cleveland, and Newark, a crowd gathered and a week-long riot left 43 dead and over 700 injured. There were 1,680 fires set and $50 million of property damage. But in Detroit whites as well as blacks participated in the looting, and 700 of the 8,000 persons arrested were white. Detroit Judge James H. Lincoln observed that blacks and whites "looted together in the best of camaraderie. In one police precinct the white and Negro snipers had one of the best relationships."

This example of integrated, equal-opportunity lawlessness was little consolation to harried urban leaders. Detroit, like Newark and Watts, provided evidence that the urban fabric was disintegrating and that the goal of racial harmony was as elusive as ever. Throughout America the violence further polarized the races, heightening black separatist fervor and encouraging white backlash. For example, following the 1967 riot Newark's Imamu Baraka (alias LeRoi Jones) attracted new followers to his United Brothers, an organization aimed at creating a black society purified of white influences. Meanwhile, many whites on Newark's north side rallied behind the vigilante leader Anthony Imperiale, a former marine who had a black belt in karate. Imperiale's North Ward Citizen's Committee patroled the white neighborhood nightly on the alert for black invaders. With Imperiale and Baraka creating bastions of racial exclusiveness on opposite ends of Newark, there seemed little chance of a unified city.

But the full-scale riot was only one symptom of growing unrest and social tension in the city. Demonstrations, protest marches, verbal confrontations, and militant defiance of traditional authority were also signs that the urban fragments were sharpening their knives and ready for attack. Both black and white poor persons were becoming increasingly belligerent in confrontations with public officials who had previously gone unchallenged. Not only were the police the targets of this rebellion but also welfare officials, urban renewal administrators, and schoolteachers. The discontented were shouting "Power to the People," but this was a threatening cry to those people in government positions who had traditionally possessed the power.

Among the urban militants were representatives of the National Welfare Rights Organization, founded in 1966 to win more money and fairer treatment for those who needed welfare payments. In the summer of 1966 the group organized protest marches in New York City, Baltimore, Los Angeles, Boston, Chicago, and San Francisco, and one group of welfare recipients and sympathizers marched from Cleveland to the state capitol in Columbus to present their complaints. A national convention of organizers and welfare recipients met in Chicago with representatives from such groups as Mothers of Watts, Mothers for Adequate Welfare, and the Committee to Save the Unemployed Fathers of Eastern Kentucky. For many middle-class Americans who regarded welfare as a gift rather than a right, this was a disturbing sequence of events.

During the next few years the middle class was to grow even more exasperated as welfare clients became increasingly militant and hostile. In 1968 New York City's welfare department had to establish a "war room" where staff members could keep track of the constant demonstrations at neighborhood welfare offices. Throughout the city unruly agitators closed department facilities, and one group staged a three-day sit-in at the welfare commissioner's office. To pacify the mob, New York City officials handed out supplemental welfare checks, and one sit-in reportedly reaped $135,000 in additional grants. But such favors did not permanently stem the tide of violence or anger. According to the *New York Times,* "The demonstrators have jammed the centers, sometimes camping out in them overnight, broken down administrative procedures, played havoc with the mountains of paperwork, and have . . . thrown the City's Welfare program into a state of crisis and chaos." By the fall of 1968 there were two hundred incidents a month at New York City's welfare centers. In Boston welfare protesters were equally unruly. Fifty recipients attacked a welfare center in the city, ripping out twelve telephones, ransacking eight offices, verbally abusing social workers and shoving one against the wall. A police escort finally conducted the embattled center employees to safety.

Meanwhile, Boston's poor were also defying that midwife of the city's much-vaunted "rebirth," the Boston Redevelopment Authority (BRA). As the city's urban renewal agency, the BRA was dedicated to "upgrading" the South End, through the demolition of slums, the construction of new moderate-income housing, and the private rehabilitation of properties. The net result would be the uprooting of thousands of elderly lodgers and poor families, many of them black or Puerto Rican. To thwart this plan and ensure greater neighborhood control over the BRA's actions, angry South Enders formed the Community Assembly for a United South End (CAUSE). After city council hearings failed to produce satisfactory results, CAUSE members occupied the BRA South End office and jeered Boston's mayor when he told them to leave or face arrest. Twenty-three defiant South Enders were hauled off to jail. Two days later militant CAUSE members seized a parking lot that had been the site of tenements housing one hundred poor families prior to BRA demolition. Two hundred demonstrators then established a "Tent City," camping out on the property in protest of the BRA displacement policy.

Sit-ins, the seizing of offices, and verbal abuse all were part of a pattern of defiance that was becoming commonplace in America's central cities. In San Francisco black residents who opposed urban renewal plans for the Western Addition rallied behind Hannibal Williams, a fiery one-time bouncer and later minister of the New Liberation Presbyterian Church. Williams's followers picketed urban renewal offices, sat in front of bulldozers at slum clearance sites, and generally berated redevelopment administrators, who in turn viewed the protesters as "a passing flurry of proletarianism." Even in Pittsburgh, the corporate moguls who sponsored the ACTION-Housing renewal program had to confront the United Movement for Progress, a black militant group in the Homewood-Brushton neighborhood. According to the movement's leader, his organization "started at the grass roots, by the poor and for the poor. . . . Its primary power is people power. Even if it never receives a cent, the United Movement for Progress will build power to help people crash out of Nigger Hell."

Everywhere the rhetoric of defiance and confrontation was heard as many aggrieved urbanites preferred threats to diplomacy and insults to conciliation. In San Antonio José Angel Gutiérrez became the major spokesman for the Mexican-American Youth Organization (MAYO) which expressed the outrage of some Chicanos. MAYO leaders claimed that "it is the gringo who we need to fight. He is the real enemy and cause of our miserable plight. We have to be revolutionary in our demands and make every sacrifice necessary, even if it means death, to achieve our goals." The group's actions never matched its words, but its rhetoric did arouse opposition. Its bitterest critic was San Antonio's Mexican-American congressman Henry B. Gonzalez, who accused MAYO of encouraging "racial hatred" and attacked the group for styling "itself as the embodiment of good and the Anglo-American as the incarnation of evil. That is not merely ridiculous; it is drawing fire from the deepest wellsprings of hate." Although Gonzalez's views may have appealed to many, Mexican-American militancy also was evident in other southwestern cities. In Los Angeles, for example, David Sanchez served as "prime minister" of the Brown Berets, a paramilitary group that complained of police mistreatment and promoted Chicano activism in Southern California. In 1968 Sanchez was convicted of organizing a school walkout in East Los Angeles and a street demonstration, but his group survived until 1972.

The lid was off the nation's feelings and a flood of bitterness was expressing itself in bombastic rhetoric, violent actions, and antiestablishment protests. Social, economic, and ethnic fissures had long existed in the American city, but now this outburst of anger was widening the gaps separating the nation's urban fragments. By the late 1960s America's greatest cities seemed on the verge of breaking apart.

No conflict better illustrated the bitter divisions within the city than the confrontation between white schoolteachers and black residents in the Ocean Hill-Brownsville neighborhood of Brooklyn. With New York City breaking into incompatible social and ethnic sectors, demands arose for black control of the public schools in black neighborhoods. No longer should a white-dominated central board of education and a white superintendent determine policy for the city as a whole and impose white culture and white attitudes on black children. According to militants, the existing policy was a form of "educational genocide," the cultural massacre of the minority by the majority. Responding to pressure for decentralization, the central school board agreed to create three demonstration districts where the option of community control could be tested. One was the poor, black Ocean Hill-Brownsville area. In 1967 neighborhood militants accordingly organized a black school board for Ocean Hill-Brownsville, but by the spring of 1968 the black board and many of the district's white teachers could no longer tolerate one another. The neighborhood board voted to dismiss thirteen teachers and six assistant principals, and in retaliation 350 members of the teacher's union walked off their jobs in Ocean Hill-Brownsville schools. In turn, the black school board dismissed all 350. The city's superintendent, however, overrode the dismissals. When the white teachers returned to their schools, with a police escort to disperse neighborhood demonstrators blocking the doors, they were threatened and terrorized. At one school they were ordered into an auditorium where community residents flashed the lights on and off and shouted such threats as: "If you try to enter the schools we'll throw lye in your face. Some of you will be going out in pine boxes." To make their point more forcefully, some of the agitators hit or shoved the cowering teachers.

In response, the teacher's union called a citywide strike, unleashing a barrage of bitter recriminations. Many of the teachers were Jewish, and anti-Semitism tainted the black racist rhetoric of their opponents. According to the teacher's union, militants distributed leaflets that warned the Jewish teachers, "Get Out, Stay Out, . . . Shut Up, Get Off Our Backs, Or Your Relatives In The Middle East Will Find Themselves Giving Benefits To Raise Money To Help You Get Out from Under The Terrible Weight Of An Enraged Black Community." Some claimed that the teacher's union blew the anti-Semitism out of proportion in order to turn public opinion against the blacks. But no matter whether it was an accurate reflection of black attitudes, the virulent hate literature publicized by the teacher's union increased the fears of millions of white New Yorkers and widened the gap between them and the black militants.

With riots in Detroit and Los Angeles and heated confrontations in Ocean Hill-Brownsville, the American city seemed more like a battleground than a place of business or residence. Heightening this image of the city as a place of violence and disorder were reports of a soaring crime rate. Between 1962 and 1972 the nation's murder rate more than doubled from 4.5 per 100,000 to 9.4, and in such troubled central cities as Atlanta, Detroit, Cleveland, and Newark it had soared to 40 per 100,000 by the early 1970s. Detroit recorded about one hundred murders in 1960, but despite a steady decline in population it counted over five hundred in 1971. If Detroit's murder rate of the early 1970s held steady, a baby born in that city in 1974 and remaining there all his or her life would have a one in thirty-five chance of being murdered. But if the murder rate continued to rise at the same pace as in the early 1970s, then the odds were one in fourteen that he or she would die a homicide victim. In fact, if the 1970 murder rate for America's largest cities remained constant, a person born in such a city and living there all his or her life was more likely to be murdered by a fellow urbanite than an American soldier in World War II was to die in combat with Germans or Japanese.

Not only were America's cities suffering from an epidemic of murders, the incidence of other crimes also seemed to be skyrocketing. For example, the robbery rate for the nation rose from a postwar low of 51.2 per 100,000 in 1959 to 131 per 100,000 in 1968. Although Atlanta and Detroit shared the title of murder capital of America, New York City captured the crown in the field of robbery. Tales of muggings along the streets of Manhattan became commonplace and older New Yorkers lamented the new wave of crime that turned Central Park into the nocturnal haunt of thugs. Few cities, however, could gloat, for everywhere crime rates were soaring. In sunny Phoenix the crime figures surpassed those of most older northeastern and midwestern cities, and in 1964 a local newspaper warned: "The incidents of crime are already too high and increasing at an alarming rate. . . . The crime problem is here and must be dealt with firmly and decisively." But ten years later Phoenix editorials were still claiming that "the heavy and dirty hand of crime is pervading the very fiber of Arizona's urban society. . . . Drastic conditions require drastic action."

Some observers downplayed the soaring crime rates, claiming that the statistics were not accurate indicators of criminal activity. The crime rate could increase owing to more diligent record keeping by the police or because of manipulation by law enforcement officials seeking greater funding. Yet the consistent rise in crime statistics across the country seemed to indicate something more serious. And every mugging or rape victim could testify to the degree of violence and lawlessness in America's cities. No matter how experts interpreted the statistics, by the late 1960s most urban Americans believed that cities were growing increasingly dangerous, and in surveys the citizenry identified crime as the most serious urban problem.

No one could satisfactorily answer why the crime rate was soaring, but there were many suggestions. Even though the 1960s were years of prosperity and a low level of unemployment, joblessness remained a serious problem for blacks, especially black youths, and some believed this was the source of America's crime contagion. Others pointed to the changing age distribution of the nation's population. From 1960 to 1970 the number of Americans in the crime-prone group aged fourteen to twenty-four climbed from 27 million to 40 million. The pool of rebellious youth was thus expanding at an extraordinary rate, increasing the likelihood of criminal activity. Still other observers blamed the wave of crime and disorder on the rising incidence of narcotics addiction. In Boston there were less than six hundred heroin users during the early 1960s; by 1970 this number had risen tenfold. Likewise, before 1963 the estimated number of heroin users in Atlanta did not exceed five hundred, yet by the end of the decade there were over five thousand users in the city. During the 1950s New York City authorities recorded about one hundred narcotic-related deaths each year; at the close of the 1960s this figure had jumped to over twelve hundred per year. Dependence on drugs was soaring and with it a need for cash to finance this expensive habit. The result was an increasing number of robberies.

Whatever the cause, most Americans agreed that the crime problem existed, turning urban dwellers into prisoners of fear living behind double-locked doors and barred windows. Murder and robbery rates were soaring, the army of drug addicts was growing, and riots and confrontations were tearing the city asunder. The promises of the past had failed. No unifying civic ideal joined the urban populace together. No common standard of decency applied throughout the metropolis. Instead, metropolitan America remained divided and divisive, and many believed that urban life was an increasingly brutish existence, to be experienced at one's peril.

WASHINGTON'S RESPONSE TO URBAN CRISIS

As crime and riots thrust America's urban problems on the front page of every newspaper, planners and city officials turned to the federal government for salvation. From 1961 through 1968 the Democrats controlled both the White House and Congress, largely owing to huge Democratic majorities garnered in the central cities. New York City, Chicago, Philadelphia, Boston, Detroit, and Cleveland could always be counted on to march lockstep into the Democratic column on election day. Thus the Democrats owed a great deal to their central-city constituency, and during the 1960s beleaguered urban leaders turned to the president and Congress for their deserved rewards. Especially after the accession of Lyndon Johnson to the presidency in November 1963, the national Democrats were to respond generously, creating an unprecedented array of urban programs.

One urban measure after another issued from the halls of Congress during the 1960s, all transferring federal tax dollars to distressed central cities. In 1960 there were forty-four federal grant programs, allocating $3.9 billion annually to the nation's large cities. By the beginning of 1969, the number of federal grant programs for urban America had risen to over five hundred and appropriations had climbed to $14 billion. For example, in 1964 Congress enacted the Urban Mass Transportation Act, which authorized federal grants for capital improvements in bus, subway, and elevated lines. The federal government had previously subsidized suburban development and automobile travel through grants for highway construction. Now, however, Democratic legislators sought to balance the scale of federal largesse that had formerly tipped in favor of Republican suburbia.

This injection of federal funds stimulated a new wave of optimism about mass transit, and planners spoke of a happy future when noiseless underground railway cars would comfortably transport millions of Americans each day at rates of eighty miles per hour. Aided by millions of federal dollars, the Westinghouse Corporation experimented with the Skybus, a driverless, automated vehicle capable of carrying twenty-eight passengers at fifty miles an hour along an I beam in the center of an elevated roadway. The federal government also financed construction of a rapid transit line linking Cleveland's central business district with its outlying airport, and contributed capital grants for the completion of San Francisco's expensive rapid transit system. During the second half of the 1960s a wide variety of transit-related schemes received federal money. Among the first projects funded were the purchase of seventy-five new air-conditioned buses for Memphis and the construction of a transitway along a pedestrian mall in downtown Minneapolis. Detroit won a grant for the building of 500 bus stop shelters, many with fluorescent lighting and gas-radiant heating, and federal money helped finance the city of Albuquerque's purchase of two local bus lines that were on the verge of going out of business.

Throughout the mid-1960s the Democratic White House and Congress continued to commit itself to visionary promises of urban revitalization. Johnson himself set the tone in his special message to the Congress on "The Nation's Cities." The president proclaimed that "we must extend the range of choices available to all our people so that all, and just not the fortunate, can have access to decent homes and schools, to recreation and to culture." Emphasizing the need to unite the social and ethnic fragments of urban America, he argued that "we must work to overcome the forces which divide our people and erode the vitality which comes from the partnership of those with diverse incomes and interests and backgrounds."

Responding to this rhetoric, Congress enacted the Housing and Urban Development Act of 1965. This authorized $2.9 billion for urban renewal and approved the construction of 240,000 additional units of public housing. It also authorized a rent subsidy plan whereby the federal government would pay part of the rent of poor persons living in nonpublic housing. Furthermore, the measure permitted public housing authorities to lease dwelling units in private buildings. Thus the federal government was expanding the options open to local housing agencies. Housing authorities had additional funds to construct new public projects, but they could also aid the poor who lived outside such projects.

Moreover, in 1965 the legislative branch approved the creation of a cabinet-level Department of Housing and Urban Development "to provide for full and appropriate consideration, at the national level, of the needs and interests of the Nation's communities and of the people who live and work in them." In other words, the city was now clearly a national responsibility of sufficient significance to merit its own cabinet seat. Just as the Department of Agriculture had traditionally spoken for farmers and the Department of Labor had been a liaison between the unions and Washington, by 1965 the American city had its own friend and ally in the federal bureaucratic structure.

The most notable of Johnson's domestic programs, however, was his War on Poverty. Although Johnson's war was not fought exclusively in the city, it did pump millions of dollars into urban areas for the benefit of the poor. Thus the federal government financed Headstart centers, nursery schools for preschoolers from disadvantaged homes who might benefit from a "headstart" in the educational process. Likewise, federally-funded job training programs provided vocational education for thousands of the urban unemployed. But the most innovative and controversial of the federal antipoverty schemes were the Community Action and Model Cities programs. Both were intended to encourage the poor themselves to participate in the making and implementation of policy. Neighborhood councils were to coordinate the distribution of the federal funds, and the poor were to enjoy "maximum feasible participation" on these councils. The programs were, in fact, designed to enhance the political power of the disadvantaged and aid them in securing what they wanted not only from the federal government but from the local authorities as well.

For some city officials it seemed as if the federal government was subsidizing local revolutions. Mayors and councilmen welcomed the influx of federal money, but they often resented the independent authority of black and Hispanic leaders on the community action councils. Chicago's powerful Mayor Richard Daley told Congress that "any project of this kind, in order to succeed, must be administered by the duly constituted elected officials of the areas with the cooperation of the . . . [community action] agencies." San Francisco's mayor commented that the antipoverty program was "headed in a direction we don't want . . . it has the potential for setting up a great political organization. Not mine. Because I have had nothing to say about it." Syracuse's Mayor William Walsh battled a federally-funded Community Action Training Center in his city which he claimed was organized to "train agitators" and to teach "Marxist doctrines of class conflict." The center's official prospectus specified that applicants for the program "should have a controlled but intense anger about continued injustices and should be committed to hard work for people who are grappling with apparently overwhelming problems." Walsh and other local officials felt that the federal government was not aiding America's cities by subsidizing persons of intense anger. In spring 1965 Daley and likeminded mayors met with Vice President Hubert Humphrey to complain about the threat to existing local authorities, and the Johnson administration responded by attempting to curb the independence of the community agencies. In some cities, however, relations remained strained between the federally-subsidized neighborhood leadership and the municipal government, as poverty program militants tried to shake up the city's power structure while local officials defended their prerogatives.

Although community action programs could prove unsettling to the established authorities, they did offer many blacks an opportunity to wield power and learn the skills of political leadership. In the late 1960s one distinguished critic of community action programs, Daniel P. Moynihan, predicted that "very possibly, the most important long run impact of the community action programs of the 1960s will prove to have been the formation of an urban Negro leadership echelon at just the time when the Negro masses . . . were verging towards extensive commitments to urban politics." And few could deny that the programs did co-opt blacks into the existing political structure and set them on the path to power. According to political scientist Peter K. Eisinger, almost a quarter of all blacks elected to city executive posts, city councils, and the lower houses of state legislatures between 1964 and 1977 gained political experience working in community action pograms. During this period the number of black elected officials increased from approximately 475 to 4,311, and hundreds of these rising officeholders learned the three Rs of American politics in the community action classroom.

Yet as the incidence of rioting and crime mounted during the late 1960s, many Americans believed that the federal government needed to do more than co-opt minority militants; it also had to apply its vast resources to the cause of law and order. As early as 1965 Congress had created the Office of Law Enforcement Assistance, which over the next three years distributed $20 million in grants to aid local police. But by 1968 the nation's legislators believed that further action was necessary, so they adopted the Omnibus Crime Control and Safe Streets Act, which established the Law Enforcement Assistance Administration. This office was to grant federal funds to the states for distribution to local law enforcement agencies. In 1969 it distributed $100 million, the next year $300 million, and by 1973 the agency's appropriation had risen to $1.75 billion. Throughout the nation police departments won grants to purchase expensive radio communication systems and antiriot weapons and to fund training programs and drug abuse projects. The Omnibus Crime Control Act, like the mass transit act, the housing and renewal schemes, and the war on poverty, expressed Congress's abiding faith in the healing properties of millions of federal dollars. If taken annually, the funds would supposedly cure urban America's ills and realize Lyndon Johnson's dream of a decent, just, and harmonious city.

When Richard Nixon and the Republicans moved into the White House in 1969, they did not stem this flow of federal funding. Instead, federal aid to the cities rose from $14 billion at the close of the Johnson administration to $26.8 billion in 1974. But President Nixon and his Republican followers did favor a restructuring of urban aid programs. The chief target of Nixon's disfavor were those programs which emphasized neighborhood participation in policymaking and which thereby undercut the authority of elected city officials. Nixon also sought to limit the federal bureaucracy's meddling in local affairs by enhancing local government control over the spending of federal grants. In accordance with these views, in 1972 Nixon convinced Congress to terminate the Model Cities program. And that same year the legislative branch approved Nixon's revenue-sharing proposal. Over the next few years, the revenue-sharing program was to divert more than $30 billion of federal funds to state and local treasuries, and state and local officials were to use the money as they deemed proper. In other words, the nation's cities continued to tap federal funds but there were fewer strings attached to this bounty from Washington.

Under both Democrats and Republicans, however, America's municipalities became increasingly dependent on the federal government. In 1960 federal grants accounted for only 3.9 percent of the general revenues of city governments; by 1977 Washington's contribution had climbed to 16.3 percent. Meanwhile, the share contributed by local taxes dropped from 61.1 percent to 42.8 percent. State governments also were feeding city treasuries, and the combined state and federal grants to the beleaguered central city of Newark rose from 5 percent of the municipal budget in 1960 to 48 percent in 1974. The figures for other distressed urban areas were much the same. Throughout the nation cities could no longer live within their locally-generated incomes but instead had mortgaged their futures to the state and federal governments.

All the federal money and federal programs, however, seem to have bought very little. In 1975 few Americans would have regarded the targeted neighborhoods of the Model Cities program as "model" neighborhoods, districts worthy of emulation or admiration. Yet the federal government had allocated $2.3 billion for these areas. Likewise, in the mid 1970s urban crime rates remained high despite billions of dollars distributed by the Law Enforcement Assistance Administration. Sales of security systems continued to soar, and urban Americans felt no safer in 1975 than they had in 1968. By the late 1970s a few more Americans were relying on public transit than a decade earlier, but this was probably owing to the inflated price of gasoline rather than improvements in federally-subsidized bus and rail services. Only 8 percent of the new riders on Cleveland's airport transit link had formerly relied on private automobiles; most had switched from airport limousines or taxicabs. In San Francisco worktrips to major employment centers averaged forty minutes on the $1.6 billion rapid transit line but only twenty-six minutes by automobile. Thus most San Franciscans and Clevelanders still chose the automobile over the less rapid transit lines, and the overwhelming majority of Americans still opted for clogged freeways over lumbering buses. In 1965 Lyndon Johnson had described his dream of the future city, and he had asked for billions of dollars to realize that dream. Billions had been spent, but America's older central cities still appeared to be skidding toward senility.

THE FISCAL CRISIS

After 1970 a new symptom of central-city collapse drew the attention of public officials away from the social and ethnic conflicts that had earlier preoccupied them. This new disorder was labeled fiscal stress. Stated simply, municipal expenditures were rising more rapidly than municipal revenues. With sufficient federal grants the city comptroller might be able to balance the municipal books, but every year the battle over the budget seemed to grow more serious. Big-city mayors who had formerly confronted belligerent black militants now had showdowns with fiery policemen angry over personnel cuts and negotiated with hardnosed bankers for last-minute loans. The setting for the central-city's problems had shifted from the streets to the bank boardroom, but in the 1970s, as in the 1960s, there remained a sense of impending disaster.

Underlying this fiscal crunch was the declining central-city economy. In most older cities the tax base was shrinking as tax-rich businesses abandoned the urban core and migrated to the suburbs. Between 1963 and 1972 retail sales figures, when adjusted for inflation, dropped 30 percent in Newark, 20 percent in Cleveland, 19 percent in Saint Louis, and 16 percent in Pittsburgh. Between 1970 and 1975 the number of jobs in Saint Louis tumbled 19 percent, in Baltimore 16 percent, and in New York City and Philadelphia 12 percent. In 1967 New York City was the corporate headquarters for 139 of the Fortune "500" firms; by 1974 the number had plummeted to 98. Meanwhile, other major firms moved out of the traditional headquarters cities of Chicago, Pittsburgh, Detroit, and Philadelphia. Sales, income, and employment statistics all testified to the central-city's eroded economic position.

Declining population figures also indicated that the older central cities were failing. Saint Louis, Cleveland, Atlanta, Minneapolis, Detroit, Newark, Buffalo, and Pittsburgh all suffered at least a 10 percent drop in population between 1970 and 1975. And the number of inhabitants in New York City, Chicago, and Philadelphia was falling almost as rapidly. Year after year thousands of taxpayers joined the migration to suburbia or to the Sunbelt metropolises, leaving older cities with fewer people to pay for the streets, sewers, police, and firefighters. In some cities thousands of buildings stood empty, abandoned by owners who no longer were willing to pay the property taxes on their worthless holdings. For example, by the early 1970s Saint Louis had ten thousand abandoned dwelling units or about 4 percent of the city's housing stock, and in some blocks 80–90 percent of the buildings were empty. The city had condemned and demolished other structures, leaving the face of Saint Louis pockmarked with rubble-strewn vacant lots that earned nothing for the municipal treasury.

New York City's South Bronx offered the classic example of abandonment and decline. From 1970 to 1975 it lost an estimated 20 percent of its population, and 20,000 to 30,000 housing units were being abandoned each year. Landlords eager to collect insurance on their worthless properties, teenage gangs looking for thrills, "spaced-out" heroin addicts, and welfare tenants seeking to cash in on government benefits for those burned out of their homes all joined in an orgy of arson that left thousands of buildings in ruins. Some youngsters reportedly sold their services to adults, torching buildings for as little as three to five dollars a job. In 1974 there were 12,300 separate fires in the district, an average of 34 a day, and during one three-hour period in June 1975 nearly 40 blazes erupted in a seventy-block area. In 1972 the *Newsweek* columnist Stewart Alsop observed that the South Bronx "is visibly dying, as though of some loathsome, lethal disease," and "seems destined to become a rubble-filled semidesert." *Fortune* claimed that New York's derelict neighborhood "may be the closest men have yet come to creating hell on earth." As the South Bronx descended toward oblivion tax receipts from the area plummeted. One of the first expenses landlords eliminated was payment of the city's property levy. After a three-year grace period, the city could begin foreclosure proceedings against tax delinquent properties, but in the case of the South Bronx most such properties were charred, abandoned, and worthless.

Unfortunately, by the early 1970s New York City needed every tax dollar it could squeeze from declining areas like the South Bronx because nowhere did fiscal stress strike with such severity as in the nation's largest metropolis. New York City had traditionally financed a greater range of expensive services than other major municipalities. For example, New York state required its cities to shoulder a larger share of welfare costs than did other states, and during the 1960s and 1970s this burden grew increasingly heavy. In 1960 New York City appropriated only $67 million for welfare, but by 1975 it was paying $911 million for public assistance and medical aid to the poor. Moreover, in the early 1970s New York City was supporting one of the largest university systems in the nation, and no city maintained such an extensive or expensive network of public hospitals. Rising welfare costs together with the city's generous support for a broad range of services produced a 260 percent increase in the municipality's operating expenses between 1965 and 1975. During the same period, however, the total personal income in New York City rose only 79 percent. Thus municipal expenditures were soaring at more than three times the rate of personal income, a nightmarish situation for any conscientious city official.

During the late 1960s and early 1970s, New York City's charismatic Mayor John Lindsay resorted to various means to finance the mounting municipal expenditures. Under his administration few objects or activities escaped taxation, and by 1975 the city imposed twenty-two different levies, including commuter taxes, sales taxes, vault taxes, stock transfer taxes, and cigarette taxes. Lindsay also introduced both personal and business income taxes which together accounted for 19 percent of local revenues in 1973–74. Moreover, state and federal aid increased from 36 percent of New York City's total revenue in 1965–66 to 48 percent in 1973–74. Yet during most of the Lindsay years, city expenditures far outpaced revenues, forcing New York to rely on short-term loans to pay its bills. Between 1966 and June 1974 the city's short-term debt soared from $467 million to $3,416 million. Rather than retiring its short-term loans when they matured at the end of six months, the city simply refinanced them with additional short-term obligations, allowing the debt to mount ominously.

When Abraham Beame succeeded Lindsay as mayor at the beginning of 1974, New York City had just about exhausted the short-term loan gimmick. By November 1974 the city's short-term debt was $5.3 billion, an increase of $1.9 billion over the figure for June of that year. Confidence in the city's finances was waning, and as it did so the interest on New York's short-term notes rose, further burdening the depleted public treasury. In February and March 1975, the whole precarious structure of New York's finances finally collapsed. Banks refused to accept any additional short-term notes from the city and demanded a new regime of municipal austerity. In response, Mayor Beame put on a brave face and claimed that the city's credit was good. Everyone, however, knew otherwise.

Finally New York's governor intervened, relieving the Beame administration of much of its authority and placing the city's finances under the supervision of a state-controlled board. The city was forced to reduce the municipal work force and limit wage hikes, and between 1975 and 1978 the state advanced $800 million in aid. Moreover, from 1976 through 1978 the city was able to borrow $5.2 billion from the federal government. New York thus edged away from bankruptcy, and in January 1979, for the first time in four years, it was again able to sell its short-term notes to private investors. The nation's largest city was slowly regaining its financial footing, but throughout the second half of the 1970s it was never far from the brink of fiscal crisis.

New York's money problems shocked many Americans and forced wary bankers and financial experts to reconsider the wisdom of investments in municipal bonds. Municipalities had defaulted on their debt obligations in the past; thousands of units of local government had done so during the depression of the 1930s and even major cities like Detroit and Chicago had suffered severe financial distress. As the nation's largest city and the financial capital of the world, New York, however, seemed an especially inappropriate candidate for bankruptcy.

Yet in 1975 the giant municipality did topple, one more sign of the dry rot eating away at the foundations of the nation's largest cities. Moreover, New York City's fiscal crisis was not an isolated incident. During the 1970s other municipalities also faltered, and in 1978 Cleveland joined New York in the ranks of the financial cripples. Nicknamed the "mistake on the lake" by its detractors, Cleveland was a prime example of central-city decline. It had consistently lost population since 1950, and business was abandoning it just as rapidly. Lyndon Johnson's schemes had failed to salvage the city; in fact scandal wracked Cleveland's Model Cities program and its director was wounded by a hit man who soon after was found dead, floating in the Ohio River. Crime seemed to be the city's only flourishing enterprise. By July 1978 the municipal government's credit rating was so low that it was frozen out of money markets. Yet local banks had loaned the city $15.5 million that was to come due on December 15. The youthful mayor, Dennis Kucinich, promised eleventh-hour solutions, and there were rumors that German investors, or possibly Arabs, would bail out the city. It was obvious, however, that Cleveland could not raise the money to pay the banks, and on December 15 it defaulted. Angry that the banks would not renew the city's loans, Kucinich marched into the Cleveland Trust Company and closed out his personal account of $9,000. The irate mayor told reporters, "I don't want my clean money in a dirty bank." But the mayor's gesture was of little help. Like New York City, Cleveland had suffered one more humiliating blow to add to the others incurred during its long decline.

Other central cities avoided default, but they too felt the financial pinch. Detroit was never far from financial disaster, and during the first half of 1975 it laid off 10 percent of its municipal employees and further tried to slash payrolls by failing to fill 1,200 job vacancies. Moreover, the Michigan legislature allocated millions of dollars to help maintain city services. For example, the state relieved the city of the burden of subsidizing the Detroit Institute of Arts so that municipal appropriations for the museum dropped from $2.8 million in 1975–76 to $348,000 in 1976–77. In addition, the state assumed full responsibility for operating the main branch of the Detroit Public Library, saving the city much-needed tax dollars. In virtually every aging central city, retrenchment was the watchword. During the 1970s Baltimore slashed 435 positions from the police department, cut 1,200 school personnel, reduced the library staff by 20 percent and library maintenance personnel by 35 percent. In 1976, with deficits mounting, Cincinnati's leaders opted for retrenchment, cutting 893 full-time positions from the municipal payroll. They also divested the municipality of responsibility for funding the city court and transferred the city's university to the state. Philadelphia cut 15 percent from the welfare department staff, closed its municipal hospital, halted street cleaning on a regular basis, and tried to shift responsibility for road maintenance to the state by erecting signs that read: "This is a STATE HIGHWAY. For repairs call 255-1415."

Some central cities, especially in the booming Sunbelt, escaped fiscal hardship and humiliation. For example, in 1978 Houston was the only American city of over a million people to receive the highest credit rating from both of the leading bond-rating firms, Moody's and Standard & Poor's. According to Standard & Poor's, Houston deserved a triple-A bond rating because "the city's fiscal posture remains strong, aided by conservative budgeting techniques." Fiscal conservatism was, in fact, unchallenged dogma in the Texas metropolis, resulting in a $24.3 million cash surplus in the general fund at the close of 1977. But Houston enjoyed other advantages as well. Whereas Cleveland, Detroit, and Philadelphia could not add rich suburban properties to their tax rolls, permissive annexation laws in Texas allowed Houston to absorb more than one hundred square miles of outlying territory between 1970 and 1978. Likewise the city's booming economy created 72,000 new jobs in 1978 and between 1977 and 1978 retail sales rose faster in Houston than in any other major metropolitan area. Thus in terms of fiscal policy and economic resources, Houston was the opposite of the faltering cities of the Northeast and Midwest.

Phoenix, Albuquerque, Dallas, and San Antonio shared Houston's good fortunes, but in a score of other major cities public officials realized that their municipal treasuries could no longer support legions of police and no longer finance the filling of every chuckhole or the purchase of every reference book. During the 1960s race riots had drawn the attention of television cameras to the social bankruptcy of the city; now in the 1970s repeated fiscal crises exposed the city's financial insolvency. Together the social conflicts of the 1960s and the funding problems of the 1970s leveled a telling blow at the nation's central cities. New York City, purportedly the nation's greatest metropolis, had become an incompetent ward of the state and federal governments. Cleveland moved from riots to default with few intervening signs of revival. Philadelphia, Detroit, and Saint Louis all slid steadily downward. Despite the promises of a revitalized city, despite the federal government programs and panaceas, the future of the central city appeared bleak.

THE NEW ETHNIC POLITICS

Inheriting the woes of central-city government were a new breed of black politicians. The late 1960s and 1970s witnessed a rise in the political clout of urban blacks and the election of a number of black mayors. As whites moved to suburbia leaving the central city to blacks, these new leaders were able to seize the reins of power in one municipality after another. Yet when blacks entered city hall to take the spoils of victory, they found that whites had carted away the wealth of the metropolis to suburban communities beyond central-city jurisdiction. The black-ruled fragments were little more than bankrupt relics of past greatness.

In 1967 blacks scored their first mayoral victories in major American cities, conquering the aging industrial hubs of Gary and Cleveland. After a bitter struggle, thirty-four-year-old Richard Hatcher triumphed over the white Democratic machine of Gary, a city which was 53 percent black by 1970. Meanwhile, in Cleveland a young black attorney, Carl Stokes, defeated the lackluster incumbent mayor, Ralph Locher, in the Democratic primary and then proceeded to slip by his Republican opponent in the general election.

These black victories were not, however, symptoms of a new era of racial harmony, but instead both campaigns revealed a polarization of racial attitudes. For example, in Cleveland the Stokes forces knew that victory depended on an unprecedented black turnout at the polls, and they urged the black community to vote for one of their own. According to one black campaigner, "We sold blackness. . . . The only important and overriding issue was the blackness of the candidate and his interest in the black community." Stokes was able to win support from some of Cleveland's white elite, and he garnered the endorsement of the white establishment's newspaper, the *Plain Dealer*. But most of this elite lived in the suburbs and could not vote in the central city. Among the white descendants of southern and eastern European immigrants who did live in Cleveland, the Stokes campaign provoked only bitterness and hostility. On the white west side Stokes workers were physically assaulted while distributing leaflets and windows at the west side campaign office were repeatedly broken, once by a molotov cocktail. During the primary only forty Stokes workers dared canvass the west side as compared to over four thousand on the black east side. One Stokes campaigner in the white neighborhoods complained: "We were constantly harassed — threatening phone calls, signs ripped off our cars, people spitting and screaming at you." In the primary Stokes won chiefly because the black turnout was considerably higher than the white, and in the general election racial polarization was again apparent with Stokes carrying an estimated 95 percent of the black vote and only 19 percent of the white electorate.

When Stokes ran for reelection two years later, the racial division was just as evident, with Stokes again winning virtually all the black votes while capturing less than a quarter of the white ballots. Following his reelection victory, Stokes joyously announced that, "This election today saw all of the many different parts of Cleveland come together — East Side and West Side, black people and white people, Catholic and Protestant, Christian and Jew." This was conciliatory rhetoric — the election returns proved Stokes wrong. Two years of rule by a black executive had not united the racial fragments of Cleveland. Instead, the lines between black and white remained clearly drawn and strongly defended.

Kenneth Gibson was the next black to capture the mayor's seat in a major city, winning Newark's top office in 1970. And in Newark as in Cleveland, the election campaign exacerbated the divisions in the declining New Jersey metropolis. Newark's incumbent mayor, Hugh J. Addonizio, charged Gibson with being part of a "raw and violent conspiracy to turn this city over to LeRoi Jones and his extremist followers," and Addonizio's police director described the campaign as a "black versus white situation. . . . This is no longer a political battle but a battle for survival." Gibson claimed he received bomb threats, the home of a black minister supporting Addonizio was the target of a shotgun ambush, and both candidates warned of racial upheaval if the other were elected. By 1970, however, blacks constituted 54 percent of Newark's population, and thus voting along racial lines brought Gibson victory. Gibson received virtually unanimous support among black and Puerto Rican voters but carried only about 15 percent of the non-Hispanic white electorate. In 1974 when Gibson ran for reelection against the outspoken defender of white interests, Anthony Imperiale, the election returns were much the same. The black central and south wards were solidly behind Gibson and the white north ward was Imperiale's territory.

By the early 1970s blacks also outnumbered whites in Atlanta and Detroit, and in 1973 both of these cities elected black mayors. In both cities the 1973 elections again revealed a racial polarization among the electorate. Detroit's contenders conscientiously avoided the racial issue, but when the ballots were counted the black winner, Coleman Young, received 92 percent of the black vote whereas his white opponent received 91 percent of the white vote. Atlanta's white incumbent, Sam

Massell, resorted to blatant racial attacks, causing the *Atlanta Constitution* to criticize him for acting "as if he were running for mayor of a South African city which practices apartheid rather than mayor of a fully integrated American city." Massell's tactics proved unsuccessful and on election day his black opponent, Maynard Jackson, won with 95 percent of the black ballots and a surprising 24 percent of the white votes. As late as 1962 Atlanta's city hall was strictly segregated with separate restrooms, drinking fountains, and employment listings for blacks and whites and segregated use of the cafeteria. The city even had an ordinance that prohibited black policemen from arresting whites. Only a dozen years later the executive office was securely in black hands, as blacks used their voting power to win political control of the city.

In one major metropolis, the pattern of racial polarization did not apply, for in 1973 Los Angeles also elected a black mayor, Thomas Bradley. Less than 20 percent of the residents of Los Angeles were black, yet Bradley was still able to defeat the white incumbent, Sam Yorty, winning 49 percent of the white vote. Capable and conciliatory, Bradley did not arouse racial fears among the Los Angeles electorate, and his depolarizing brand of politics was to win him a second term in 1977.

The rising political clout of blacks produced some important changes at city hall. For example, the new mayors sought to reform that symbol of white power, the police department. During 1966–67 only 9 percent of Atlanta's police force was black and only 5 percent of Detroit's squad; by 1978 blacks made up 33 percent of the Atlanta police force and the figure for Detroit was 30 percent. Moreover, Atlanta's public safety director and two deputy directors were black, as were Detroit's chief of police and nine of the twenty-one district commanders. In 1973 only 2 to 3 percent of all city purchases in Atlanta and Detroit came from minority-owned businesses; five years later 33 percent of city business in both cities was going to minority firms. Black victories at the polls meant better relations between the police and the black community and more money from the public till for black businesses.

Economic realities, however, hedged the creativity of the new black mayors, for the fiscal crisis left little money with which to experiment. In fact, decaying cities like Gary, Newark, and Detroit depended heavily on the appropriations of white lawmakers in Washington and the state capitals. Blacks may have won the highest municipal offices, but they triumphed chiefly in those cities which were forced to exchange their autonomy for state and federal dollars. The governmental fragmentation of the metropolis had left blacks ruling a crippled urban core.

Meanwhile, Hispanics were also gaining political clout in the cities. At the close of the 1970s Miami's mayor, Maurice Ferre, was Puerto Rican, and in the 1981 city election he nearly lost his position to a Cuban-born challenger. By 1981 three of the five members of Miami's ruling city commission were Hispanics. Following the 1977 election San Antonio's city council consisted of five Mexican-Americans, one black, and four non-Hispanic whites, and in 1981 that city elected its first Mexican-American mayor, Henry Cisneros. In San Antonio, however, ethnic polarization was not so evident in electoral contests as in Newark, Cleveland, Detroit, or Atlanta. Cisneros carried eight of the ten council districts, including two of the four districts with the largest percentage of non-Hispanic white voters, and overall in predominantly "Anglo" precincts he won 45 percent of the votes.

Thus those groups which had migrated to America's cities in increasing numbers after World War I were winning a powerful voice in urban government. In the case of Bradley and Cisneros these victories aroused only limited ethnic hostility, but in a number of midwestern and northeastern cities the rise of black politicians focused new attention on the divisions among America's urban dwellers. Moreover, those cities in which racial divisions were most serious were the very municipalities that could ill afford any additional problems, for Cleveland, Newark, and Detroit were prizes of only limited appeal by the late 1960s and 1970s. Whites ruled the wealthy suburban fringe while blacks wrestled with the problems of these troubled central cities.

The Fragmentation of the Metropolis

Although many cities in the late 1970s still faced financial problems, some commentators were beginning to glimpse a glowing urban future through the clouds of crisis. In 1978 *Saturday Review* featured an article titled "America Falls in Love with Its Cities — Again" which waxed poetic about downtown Los Angeles, with its "teeming streetscapes tinted with colorful ethnic overtones," and which claimed that the newly renovated Quincy Market had "turned downtown Boston into *the* place to be." That same year *Harper's* printed a piece with the optimistic title, "The Urban Crisis Leaves Town." Citing the restoration of inner-city neighborhoods and the downtown building boom, this article argued that cities like Boston and Baltimore were proving "themselves to be vital human centers with futures far more promising than either their detractors or their beleaguered proponents imagined possible." In newspapers, magazines, and books, scores of writers described the return of the white middle class to renovated central-city townhouses and the consequent "gentrification" of the urban core. And publicists of the urban renaissance never failed to report on the opening of the latest Hyatt hotel with its glass-encased luxury beckoning thousands of conventioneers to the reborn central business district. Moreover, in 1976–77 Gallery I opened, the first major retail facility built in downtown Philadelphia since 1931. With 2 major department stores and 125 smaller specialty shops and restaurants the central-city mall attracted mobs of shoppers and renewed the hopes of downtown devotees. Likewise, Baltimore's Charles Center and Inner Harbor developments seemed to promise new life for that city's downtown, and Henry Ford II's Renaissance Center complex of offices, shops, and hotel was intended to bring people and money back to Detroit's central business district.

Yet while some saw signs of hope, others perceived only continued decline. Henry Ford II promoted Renaissance Center, but his brother William Ford relocated the Detroit Lions football team in suburban

Pontiac, far from the troubled urban core. Moreover, in the early 1980s Detroit's J. L. Hudson Company closed its giant downtown department store, sealing the fate of retailing in the central business district. While Gallery I was flourishing, fine stores along formerly prestigious Chestnut Street in downtown Philadelphia were giving way to pinball arcades, fast-food restaurants, and cut-rate shops. Overall, the central-city's share of retail employment in the Philadelphia metropolitan area dropped from 44 percent in 1970 to 33 percent in 1977. Despite reports of middle-class Americans returning to the central city, the population of the urban core declined at an accelerated pace during the 1970s. The population of Saint Louis dropped 27 percent, and by 1980 it had 122,000 fewer inhabitants than in 1900. Cleveland's population plummeted 24 percent, Buffalo's dropped 23 percent, and Detroit's fell 20 percent. If Cleveland's population continued to decline at the same absolute rate as it did during the 1970s, by the year 2013 there would be no one remaining in the Ohio metropolis. For all the ballyhoo about the "back-to-the-city" movement and all the publicity about glittering new downtown office-hotel-apartment complexes, the hard figures still indicated decline and decay.

In fact, the metropolitan malaise seemed to be spreading, attacking smaller cities that had earlier escaped urban ills. In 1900 or 1920 the Uticas, Terre Hautes, and Paducahs scattered across the country perceived themselves as unaffected by the divisive maladies plaguing New York City, Chicago, and Philadelphia. By the 1960s and 1970s, however, these cities also felt the destructive impact of the automobile and experienced symptoms of decay in the central business district. Derelict railroad yards, empty downtown storefronts, and bankrupt bus lines were as commonplace in the city of 50,000 to 100,000 as in the metropolis of 500,000 to 1,000,000. Some Americans may have rejoiced at the restoration of Victorian commercial blocks, but in large and small cities throughout the country obsolete mills and warehouses outnumbered renovated apartments and lofts and no perceptive observer could escape the signs of a bleak reality.

Thus at the close of the 1970s commentators predicted both new life and imminent death for the nation's central cities. Some saw hope but others perceived only gloom. Urban boosters were still erecting Renaissance Centers and detractors were still pointing their fingers at street after street of abandoned housing and vacant lots.

Yet neither the pollyannas of urban rebirth nor the grim reapers of impending death seemed to accurately understand what had happened to the central city and metropolitan America in general. During the first eight decades of the twentieth century the city had fragmented, breaking into its component parts. In the pursuit of social and ethnic separatism, Americans had abandoned the old single-nucleus city and created instead a cluster of cities, an amorphous mass with a scattering of nuclei. By the 1970s and 1980s the "central city" was no longer central to the lives of most metropolitan Americans. The historic central business district had become one of many business districts scattered about the metropolis, still retaining some vitality but no longer the one heart pumping lifeblood throughout the metropolitan area.

Thus the central city was not dead; it had simply become one more suburb, yet another fragment of metropolitan America serving the special needs of certain classes of urban dwellers. Central cities of the 1980s housed the poor and the elderly, but they also attracted young middle-class single persons and childless couples who found newly fashionable inner-city neighborhoods more desirable than child-oriented suburbia. Meanwhile, the central-city downtown remained the hub of finance, government, and business services, and these expanding sectors of the economy were fueling the demand for new office buildings that seemed so encouraging to devotees of urban revitalization. Although the central city was attracting some middle-class Americans and some businesses, it was no longer the focus of all business nor did it encompass the bulk of middle-class urbanites. It was serving those who were too poor to live elsewhere, those fond of a childless lifestyle, and those engaged in a certain segment of the economy. In 1900 Chicago, Saint Louis, Boston, and Philadelphia had included all the diverse elements of urban life. Now they were home and workplace for a more limited range of the metropolitan populace.

Meanwhile, America's suburbs had escaped the centripetal pull of the old downtown and had veered off on an independent orbit. By the 1980s they had an economic life of their own, and in many metropolitan areas the bulk of jobs were in the suburbs. In 1977, about 60 percent of the employment in the Philadelphia metropolitan area was outside Philadelphia, and the suburbs accounted for 65 percent of the jobs in the Saint Louis metropolitan region. Suburban shopping malls of the 1970s and 1980s dwarfed the pioneer centers of the 1950s. Woodfield Mall in Schaumburg, Illinois, just northwest of Chicago's O'Hare International Airport, included 4 major department stores, 230 smaller shops, and almost 11,000 parking spaces. Around such malls clustered office buildings, hotels, medical clinics, and banks, and Landerwood Plaza in suburban Cleveland even included a cemetery. According to *Fortune,* the shopping malls were "indoor piazzas" that "to an amazing degree . . . are seizing the role once held by the central business district, not only in retailing but as the social, cultural, and recreational focal point of the entire community." The wholesale and manufacturing exodus to suburbia also had accelerated, so that by the 1980s suburban industrial parks dotted the landscape. Suburbia even grabbed an increasing share of the nation's office space. For example, between 1970 and 1977 the suburbs' share of the total office space in metropolitan Atlanta advanced from 36 percent to 56 percent. Office towers were rising in the central city, but office construction in the suburbs proceeded at an even more rapid rate.

Yet suburbia was not an undifferentiated sea of shopping malls, highways, and industrial parks. Instead, distinct boundaries separated the preserve of one social class from another, and the exclusionary zoning restrictions of a myriad of municipalities reinforced the pattern of segregation. Certain suburbs like Scarsdale outside of New York City, Lake Forest north of Chicago, and Beverly Hills in Southern California were synonymous with wealth; other suburban communities like Lincoln Heights outside of Cincinnati and Kinloch in Saint Louis County were poor black enclaves. Each suburban municipality had a definite place in the social hierarchy and the community in which one lived was a prime indicator of social status. Although some still longed for consolidation or federation of the scores of municipalities within the metropolis, each city and town clung to its separate identity and pursued separate policies suited to the class interests of its residents. The federal government encouraged the creation of metropolitan advisory councils to promote regional planning, but in many areas such councils were the scene of much acrimony and little accord.

By the 1970s and 1980s, however, there was often little basis for metropolitanwide cooperation. Suburbs did not share a dependency on the central city, and the residents of one suburban municipality often had little in common with residents of another suburb or with residents of the central city. In 1978 a *New York Times* survey of suburban New Yorkers found that 54 percent did not feel that they belonged to the New York metropolitan area and 76 percent thought that events occurring in the central city did not affect them. Only 21 percent of the surveyed household heads worked in New York City, 53 percent of those interviewed visited the central city less than five times a year, and an additional 25 percent never went there. From these findings the *Times* concluded that "the suburbs have become a multicentered urban chain with surprisingly limited ties to the metropolitan core. . . . Suburban residents have established their own institutions and go about their lives in an increasingly separate world." In 1970 the census bureau reiterated these conclusions when it found that 72 percent of employed suburban residents in metropolitan areas over a million worked in the suburbs. By the last quarter of the twentieth century, the image of suburbia as a ring of bedroom communities was no longer valid. The suburbs were on their own.

Thus the American city had changed markedly during the first eight decades of the century. In 1900 diverse ethnic and social classes shared one umbrella government and a centripetal transit system made the downtown the focus of all commerce. Rich and poor, old-stock Americans and immigrants, whites and blacks – all shared the same mayor and city council which had to mediate among the divergent social, economic, and ethnic interests within the city. Some suburban municipalities existed, but the overwhelming majority of metropolitan residents lived within the boundaries of the central city. Eighty years later, however, central-city governments ruled only a minority of the metropolitan population, and each suburban municipality had jurisdiction over a small segment of the whole. There was no longer any one dominant economic, intellectual, or cultural center to the metropolis. Instead, there were many. In 1900 economic and governmental bonds had held together the diverse lot of urban Americans. By 1980 the bonds had broken and clashing ethnic and social groups had escaped from one another.

This fragmentation had occurred despite the repeated efforts of urban reformers. From the Progressive Era through the 1960s reformers had attempted to bridge the divisions within urban society and had emphasized the need for the more fortunate to assume responsibility for their benighted or unlucky brothers and sisters. Lawrence Veiller, Jane Addams, Arthur Farwell, Edith Wood, Franklin Roosevelt, and Lyndon Johnson had all claimed that what occurred in the poorer neighborhoods should concern those along Fifth Avenue and in Scarsdale. Each conceived of reform as a means of unifying the metropolis, and each sought to realize a civic ideal that ensured uniform standards of justice, morality, or opportunity throughout the metropolitan area. Thus each battled against the fragmentation of the metropolis into zones of privilege and zones of deprivation. Yet by the 1980s the gradual, persistent fragmentation of the metropolis had thwarted the reform dream, leaving behind a few partial achievements and the relics of many well-intentioned programs.

The true molders of the twentieth-century city were not Arthur Farwell, Jane Addams, or Daniel Burnham, but Al Capone, J. C. Nichols, and the Levitt brothers. These figures had catered to the social fragments with little vision of the whole, and this had proved more appealing to the urban consumer and voter than dreams of a united metropolitan community. Capone violated federal law and quenched the thirst of that fragment of the metropolitan populace that did not accept the teetotaling dogmas of an Arthur Farwell. Nichols satisfied the demands of an upper-middle-class clientele that wanted to live in a restricted, tasteful subdivision. And the Levitts served the interests of a less affluent group who also wanted to purchase homes and enjoy the good life of suburbia. Each left an indelible mark on the city because each satisfied the demands of one element of the heterogeneous metropolis but did not attempt to convert all to the lifestyle he espoused. By comparison many of those devoted to a unifying civic ideal achieved relatively little. San Francisco never adopted Daniel Burnham's visionary master plan, Cleveland only slowly implemented his civic center scheme, and Burnham's dream of a giant domed city hall serving as a focus for diverse Chicago was never realized. Yet the Levitts built sprawling cities in a few short years. Like Nichols and Capone, they accepted the social and economic realities of the city and profited from them. In contrast, the reformers recognized problems and defied realities but their successes were fewer.

At the turn of the century many had written with optimism of the future of the city. It was the hope of democracy, the testing ground where Americans would discover whether industrialization and the good life could coexist. Commentators had recognized the problems of urban America, but they also saw the promise of the city. In succeeding decades, however, reform promises had repeatedly collided with the implacable realities of social and ethnic separatism: most Americans desired not a unified metropolis but a fragmented one, where likeminded persons lived together untroubled by those of differing opinions, races, or lifestyles. Americans preferred the autonomy of the social fragment to some unifying civic ideal preached by starry-eyed reformers. Thus Americans opted for the dissolution of the city and, with the aid of the automobile, created the dispersed and fragmented metropolitan world of the late twentieth century.

Bibliographical Essay

During the twenty years since urban history became a significant scholarly field and a standard entry in the course catalogues of American universities, scores of volumes have appeared, describing and analyzing the development of the nation's cities. University presses have supplied stacks of scholarly monographs investigating special facets of the urban past, and commercial publishers have offered general surveys for the college textbook market. City government, urban planning, ethnic migration, assimilation, racial conflict, and urban reform have all been the subject of historical research, resulting in an ample bibliography on the twentieth-century American city.

GENERAL WORKS

Among the general surveys the standard text is Charles N. Glaab and A. Theodore Brown, *A History of Urban America*, 3d rev. ed. (New York: Macmillan, 1983). Detailed and accurate, Glaab and Brown's volume provides the basic facts of American urban development. Other general surveys have offered unique perspectives: David R. Goldfield and Blaine A. Brownell, *Urban America: From Downtown to No Town* (Boston: Houghton Mifflin, 1979), views the evolution of the city from a geographic spatial perspective. Howard P. Chudacoff, *The Evolution of American Urban Society,* rev. ed. (Englewood Cliffs, N.J.: Prentice Hall, 1981), incorporates findings from the new social history; and Zane L. Miller, *The Urbanization of Modern America: A Brief History* (New York: Harcourt Brace Jovanovich, 1973), reflects the author's original research on party bosses and urban political development. Blake McKelvey, *The Emergence of Metropolitan America 1915-1966* (New Brunswick, N.J.: Rutgers University Press, 1968), is an excellent survey by a pioneering figure in the field.

In addition to these general works, there are some valuable regional studies of the urban past. Blaine A. Brownell and David R. Goldfield, eds., *The City in Southern History: The Growth of Urban Civilization in the South* (Port Washington, N.Y.: Kennikat Press, 1977), contains a series of worthwhile essays; Bradford Luckingham, *The Urban Southwest: A Profile History of Albuquerque, El Paso, Phoenix, Tucson* (El Paso: Texas Western Press, 1982), offers a straightforward account of the development of four increasingly important Sunbelt cities; and Gerald D. Nash, *The American West in the Twentieth Century: A Short History of an Urban Oasis* (Englewood Cliffs, N.J.: Prentice-Hall, 1973), provides additional information on the urban West.

For those who wish to delve deeply into the history of a single city, historians have authored a long list of urban biographies. Bayrd Still, *Milwaukee: The History of a City,* rev. ed. (1948; Madison: State Historical Society of Wisconsin, 1965), is a classic example of the urban biography genre. Harold M. Mayer and Richard C. Wade, *Chicago: Growth of a Metropolis* (Chicago: University of Chicago Press, 1969), is the finest example of a photographic history of a city. Sam Bass Warner, Jr., *The Private City: Philadelphia in Three Periods of Its Growth* (Philadelphia: University of Pennsylvania Press, 1968), explains Philadelphia's past in terms of the "privatism" that dominated American urban development; and the essays in Russell F. Weigley, ed., *Philadelphia: A Three-Hundred-Year History* (New York: W. W. Norton, 1982), offer a narrative account of the city's history. David G. McComb, *Houston, The Bayou City* (Austin: University of Texas Press, 1969), describes the growth of the booming Sunbelt metropolis; and the articles in Francisco A. Rosales and Barry J. Kaplan, eds., *Houston: A Twentieth Century Urban Frontier* (Port Washington, N.Y.: Associated Faculty Press, 1983) offer new material on the Texas metropolis. A recent series on western cities published by Pruett (Boulder, Colo.) has added to the list of urban biographies: Lyle W. Dorsett, *The Queen City: A History of Denver* (1977); A. Theodore Brown and Lyle W. Dorsett, *K.C.: A History of Kansas City, Missouri* (1978); James N. Primm, *Lion of the Valley: Saint Louis, Missouri* (1981); Lawrence H. Larsen and Barbara J. Cottrell, *The Gate City: A History of Omaha* (1982).

CHAPTER 1. PROBLEM, PROMISE, AND REALITY

Among the most prominent essays on the problem and promise of the American city at the turn of the century are Josiah Strong, *The Twentieth Century City* (New York: Baker & Taylor, 1898); Richard T. Ely, *The Coming City* (New York: Thomas Y. Crowell, 1902); and Frederic C. Howe, *The City: The Hope of Democracy* (New York: Charles Scribner's Sons, 1905). The classic account of nineteenth-century urban growth is Adna Ferrin Weber, *The Growth of Cities in the Nineteenth Century: A Study in Statistics* (New York: Macmillan, 1899).

CHAPTER 2. THE CENTURY BEGINS, 1900-1919

Many literary figures offered their observations on the turn-of-the-century American city. Among these useful sources are William Dean Howells, *Impressions and Experiences* (New York: Harper & Brothers, 1909); Arnold Bennett, *Your United States: Impressions of a First Visit* (New York: Harper & Brothers, 1912); Theodore Dreiser, *The Titan* (New York: Boni & Liveright, 1914); George Ade, *Chicago Stories* (Chicago: Henry Regnery, 1963); and Henry James, *The American Scene* (New York: Harper & Brothers, 1907).

A diverse body of works describes the business core of the city at the beginning of the twentieth century. For example, Lloyd Wendt and Herman Kogan, *Give the Lady What She Wants!* (Chicago: Rand McNally, 1952), offers a vivid, popular portrayal of the history of the Marshall Field Company. Annie Marion MacLean, "Two Weeks in Department Stores," *American Journal of Sociology* 4 (May 1899):721–41, presents a more somber picture of big-city retailing and the plight of the female clerk. Paul Goldberger, *The Skyscraper* (New York: Alfred A. Knopf, 1981), offers a readable, illustrated account of the development of downtown office towers. But Carl W. Condit's works on technology and urbanization are perhaps the most valuable studies describing the physical development of the central city during the first two decades of the century. Among his excellent volumes are *Chicago, 1910–1929: Building, Planning, and Urban Technology* (Chicago: University of Chicago Press, 1973); *The Railroad and the City: A Technological and Urbanistic History of Cincinnati* (Columbus: Ohio State University Press, 1977); and *The Port of New York: A History of the Rail and Terminal System from the Beginning to Pennsylvania Station* (Chicago: University of Chicago Press, 1980). For contemporary accounts of the opening of the elegant Astoria and St. Regis hotels, see *New York Times,* 16 Oct. 1897, p. 9; 2 Nov. 1897, p. 3; and 4 Sept. 1904, p. 5.

Grace M. Mayer, *Once upon a City* (New York: Macmillan, 1958), presents a popular, illustrated account of social life, both high and low, in New York City at the turn of the century. The *New York Times,* 10 Jan. 1905, p. 9, offers a first-hand description of Mrs. Astor's annual ball. For reminiscences of social life among Chicago's elite, see Arthur Meeker, *Chicago, with Love: A Polite and Personal History* (New York: Alfred A. Knopf, 1955). Perhaps the most useful source of information on Chicago's Gold Coast apartments is Celia Hilliard, "'Rent Reasonable to Right Parties': Gold Coast Apartment Buildings 1906–1929," *Chicago History* 8 (Summer 1979):66–77. S. L. Sherer, "The 'Places' of St. Louis," *House and Garden* 5 (April 1904):187–91, is a contemporary description of the residential havens of the social elite in Missouri's leading metropolis.

The literature describing the lower rungs of the social ladder in the early twentieth century is very extensive. For information on the ethnic neighborhoods of early twentieth-century Chicago, see Edith Abbott, *The Tenements of Chicago, 1908–1935* (Chicago: University of Chicago Press, 1936); Andrew T. Kopan, "Greek Survival in Chicago: The Role of Ethnic Education, 1890–1980," in Peter d'A. Jones and Melvin Holli, eds., *Ethnic Chicago* (Grand Rapids, Mich.: William B. Eerdmans, 1981), pp. 80–139; Thomas Lee Philpott, *The Slum and the Ghetto: Neighborhood Deterioration and Middle-Class Reform, Chicago, 1880–1930* (New York: Oxford University Press, 1978); and Allan H. Spear, *Black Chicago: The Making of a Negro Ghetto, 1890–1920* (Chicago: University of Chicago Press, 1967).

Accounts of ethnic mobility and immigrant adaptation to the American city during the Progressive Era include Moses Rischin, *The Promised City: New York's Jews, 1870–1914* (Cambridge, Mass.: Harvard University Press, 1962); Humbert S. Nelli, *The Italians in Chicago, 1860–1920: A Study of Ethnic*

Mobility (New York: Oxford University Press, 1970); Edward R. Kantowicz, *Polish-American Politics in Chicago 1888–1940* (Chicago: University of Chicago Press, 1975); and Thomas Kessner, *The Golden Door: Italian and Jewish Immigrant Mobility in New York City, 1880–1915* (New York: Oxford University Press, 1977).

Jane Addams, *Twenty Years at Hull House* (New York: Macmillan, 1910) provides insight into the reform response to immigrant culture and is a classic account of the most famous of the settlement houses. Allen F. Davis, *Spearheads for Reform: The Social Settlements and the Progressive Movement, 1890–1914* (New York: Oxford University Press, 1967), offers the best overview of the work of Jane Addams and her colleagues. Robert H. Bremner, *From the Depths: The Discovery of Poverty in the United States* (New York: New York University Press, 1956) is a more general account of the problem of poverty, including information on the settlements and quotations from the writings of critics of the settlement-house movement. Roy Lubove, *The Progressives and the Slums: Tenement House Reform in New York City, 1890–1917* (Pittsburgh: University of Pittsburgh Press, 1962), describes the work of Lawrence Veiller; and Paul Boyer, *Urban Masses and Moral Order in America, 1820–1920* (Cambridge, Mass.: Harvard University Press, 1978), offers a perceptive analysis of social reform.

For contemporary accounts of the tenement-house problem and housing reform efforts, see Jacob A. Riis, *How the Other Half Lives: Studies Among the Tenements of New York* (New York: Charles Scribner's Sons, 1890); *First Report of the Tenement House Department of the City of New York* (New York: Martin B. Brown Press, 1903); Lawrence Veiller, *Housing Reform: A Hand-book for Practical Use in American Cities* (New York: Charities Publication Committee, 1910); Mary B. Sayles, "The Work of a Woman Tenement-House Inspector," *Outlook* 75 (12 Sept. 1903):116–22; Emily W. Dinwiddie, "Women Tenement Inspectors in New York," *Annals of the American Academy of Political and Social Sciences* 22 (Sept. 1903):394–96; *Housing Conditions in Baltimore* (Baltimore: Federated Charities, 1907); and Frederic Almy, "Summary Evictions from Tenements," *Proceedings of the National Conference of Charities and Correction* (1906):376–82.

A number of sources focus on the problem of the saloon and the brothel. Emmett Dedmon, *Fabulous Chicago* (New York: Atheneum, 1983), includes a lively description of the Levee; and Al Rose, *Storyville, New Orleans* (University: University of Alabama Press, 1974), is the standard work on New Orleans's red-light district. Clifford G. Roe, *The Great War on White Slavery or Fighting for the Protection of Our Girls* (n.p., 1911), reprints the findings of the Chicago vice commission and describes the battle against prostitution in other cities as well. Mark T. Connelly, *The Response to Prostitution in the Progressive Era* (Chapel Hill: University of North Carolina Press, 1980), also tackles the issue of commercial vice; and John Clayton, "The Scourge of Sinners: Arthur Burrage Farwell," *Chicago History* 3 (Fall 1974):68–77, discusses Chicago's leading moral reformer. Perry Duis, *The Saloon: Public Drinking in Chicago and Boston, 1880–1920* (Urbana: University of Illinois Press, 1983), deals with the problem of the saloon in urban America; Charles J. Bushnell, "Some Social Aspects of the Chicago Stock Yards," *American Journal of Sociology* 7 (Nov. 1901): 289–330 offers some comments on the saloons in a working-class neighborhood; and Royal L. Melendy, "The Saloon in Chicago," *American Journal of Sociology* 5 (Nov. 1900):289–306; 6 (Jan. 1901):433–464, provides an extensive account of the urban saloon at the beginning of the twentieth century and the plight of the destitute habitués of these gin mills.

The literature on Progressive-Era urban politics is especially extensive. James Bryce, *The American Commonwealth* (London: Macmillan, 1888), describes American city government as a "conspicuous failure." But the most famous account of political corruption during the period is Joseph Lincoln Steffens, *The Shame of the Cities* (New York: McClure, Phillips, & Son, 1904). Tom Johnson, *My Story* (New York: B. W. Huebsch, 1911), and Frederic C. Howe, *Confessions of a Reformer* (New York: Charles Scribner's Sons, 1925), are enlightening contemporary works by political reformers. Clinton Rogers Woodruff, ed., *City Government By Commission* (New York: D. Appleton, 1911), presents a variety of arguments in favor of the commission plan. Samuel P. Hays, "The Politics of Reform in Municipal Government in the Progressive Era," *Pacific Northwest Quarterly* 55 (Oct. 1964):157–69, is a seminal essay that has proved highly influential in the study of city government during the early twentieth century. More recent works on Progressive-Era politics and government in the city include Gerald Kurland, *Seth Low: The Reformer in an Urban and Industrial Age* (New York: Twayne, 1971); John K. Buenker, *Urban Liberalism and Progressive Reform* (New York: Charles Scribner's Sons, 1973); Martin J. Schiesl, *The Politics of Efficiency: Municipal Administration and Reform in America, 1880–1920* (Berkeley: University of California Press, 1977); Bradley R. Rice, *Progressive Cities: The Commission Government Movement in America, 1901–1920* (Austin: University of Texas Press, 1977); and Michael H. Ebner and Eugene M. Tobin, eds., *The Age of Urban Reform: New Perspectives on the Progressive Era* (Post Washington, N.Y.: Kennikat Press, 1977). Among the useful studies of political reform in individual cities are Walton Bean, *Boss Ruef's San Francisco: The Story of the Union Labor Party, Big Business, and the Graft Prosecution* (Berkeley: University of California Press, 1952); Zane L. Miller, *Boss Cox's Cincinnati: Urban Politics in the Progressive Era* (New York: Oxford University Press, 1968); and James B. Crooks, *Politics and Progress: The Rise of Urban Progressivism in Baltimore, 1895–1911* (Baton Rouge: Louisiana State University Press, 1968). For information about three powerful civil servants of the turn of the century, see R. H. Thomson, *That Man Thomson* (Seattle: University of Washington Press, 1950); George A. Babbitt, "Retirement of Dr. Samuel H. Durgin from the Boston Board of Health," *American Journal of Public Health* 2 (May 1912): 384–85; and John McLaren's obituary in *San Francisco Chronicle*, 13 Jan. 1943, pp. 1, 7.

The leading works on urban planning during the first two decades of the twentieth century are Thomas S. Hines, *Burnham of Chicago: Architect and Planner* (New York: Oxford University Press, 1974); Charles Moore, *Daniel H. Burnham: Architect Planner of Cities* (Boston: Houghton Mifflin, 1921); Judd

Kahn, *Imperial San Francisco: Politics and Planning in an American City 1897–1906* (Lincoln: University of Nebraska Press, 1980); and Mel Scott, *American City Planning Since 1890* (Berkeley: University of California Press, 1969). The most important contemporary expressions of the urban planning philosophy are Benjamin C. Marsh, *An Introduction to City Planning: Democracy's Challenge to the American City* (New York: Benjamin C. Marsh, 1909); and Charles Mulford Robinson, *Modern Civic Art or the City Made Beautiful,* 4th rev. ed. (New York: G. P. Putnam's Sons, 1918).

CHAPTER 3. PROMISES THWARTED: THE TWENTIES

The finest general survey of American urban history during the interwar years is William H. Wilson, *Coming of Age: Urban America, 1915–1945* (New York: John Wiley & Sons, 1974). Well written and thorough, Wilson's study deserves the consideration of novice and scholar alike. Blaine A. Brownell, *The Urban Ethos in the South, 1920–1930* (Baton Rouge: Louisiana State University Press, 1975), focuses on the South during this vital period in American urban history.

For information on gangsterism during the Prohibition Era, see Herbert Asbury, *Gem of the Prairie: An Informal History of the Chicago Underworld* (Garden City, N.Y.: Garden City, 1942); Humbert S. Nelli, *The Business of Crime: Italians and Syndicate Crime in the United States* (New York: Oxford University Press, 1976); and Andrew Sinclair, *Prohibition: The Era of Excess* (Boston: Little, Brown, 1962). Arthur Evans Wood, *Hamtramck: Then and Now* (New York: Bookman Associates, 1955), tells about the roaring 1920s in a seamy Detroit suburb; and Fred D. Baldwin, "Smedley D. Butler and Prohibition Enforcement in Philadelphia, 1924–25," *Pennsylvania Magazine of History and Biography* 84 (July 1960):352–68, is a thorough report on the exploits of Philadelphia's embattled public safety director.

Although generally neglected by scholars, urban politics during the 1920s has been the subject of some popular, highly readable volumes. For example, Lloyd Wendt and Herman Kogan, *Big Bill of Chicago* (Indianapolis: Bobbs-Merrill, 1953), is a vivid biography of William Hale Thompson. Written in a similar style, Gene Fowler, *Beau James* (New York: Viking Press, 1949), tells the story of New York's Mayor James J. Walker. In James Michael Curley, *I'd Do It Again: A Record of All My Uproarious Years* (Englewood Cliffs, N.J.: Prentice-Hall, 1957), Boston's irrepressible Mayor Curley expresses his views on government and recounts his long career. For contemporary accounts of Cleveland's city manager regime, see William G. Shepherd, "The City Upset the Mayor's Chair," *Collier's* 75 (14 Feb. 1925):9, 44; and Randolph O. Huus, "The Attack on Cleveland's Council-Manager Charter," *National Municipal Review* 17 (Feb. 1928):69–73. For Czech opinion on city manager rule in Cleveland, see *Cleveland American,* 7 Nov. 1927, p. 1; and 19 Aug. 1929, p. 6; for the Polish viewpoint, see *Wiadomści Codzienne,* 23 April 1928, p. 8. For black criticism of the reform scheme, see *Cleveland Gazette,* 5 Nov. 1927, pp. 1, 5; and 17 Aug. 1929, p. 1. The Kansas City experience with city manager rule is discussed in

"Partisan Government," *Kansas City's Public Affairs* (1 April 1926); Henry M. Alexander, "The City Manager Plan in Kansas City," *Missouri Historical Review* 34 (Jan. 1940):145–56; Maurice M. Milligan, *The Inside Story of the Pendergast Machine by the Man Who Smashed It* (New York: Charles Scribner's Sons, 1948); and A. Theodore Brown, *The Politics of Reform: Kansas City's Municipal Government 1925–1950* (Kansas City, Mo.: Community Studies, 1958).

The best works on the development of the black community in urban America following World War I are Gilbert Osofsky, *Harlem: The Making of a Ghetto, Negro New York, 1890–1930* (New York: Harper & Row, 1966); Allan H. Spear, *Black Chicago: The Making of a Negro Ghetto, 1890–1920* (Chicago: University of Chicago Press, 1967); Kenneth L. Kusmer, *A Ghetto Takes Shape: Black Cleveland, 1870–1930* (Urbana: University of Illinois Press, 1976); William Tuttle, Jr., *Race Riot: Chicago in the Red Summer of 1919* (New York: Atheneum, 1970); and Harold F. Gosnell, *Negro Politicians: The Rise of Negro Politics in Chicago* (Chicago: University of Chicago Press, 1935). Kenneth T. Jackson, *The Ku Klux Klan in the City, 1915–1930* (New York: Oxford University Press, 1967), offers further insight into ethnic tensions in the American city during the 1920s. Deborah Dash Moore, *At Home in America: Second Generation New York Jews* (New York: Columbia University Press, 1981), describes the success story of one ethnic group that climbed the social ladder in the years between the two World Wars. In contrast, Ricardo Romo, *East Los Angeles: History of a Barrio* (Austin: University of Texas Press, 1983), and Virginia E. Sanchez Korrol, *From Colonia to Community: The History of Puerto Ricans in New York City, 1917–1948* (Westport, Conn.: Greenwood Press, 1983), recount the problems of poor Hispanic newcomers to the city. Max Sylvius Handman, "San Antonio: The Old Capital City of Mexican Life and Influence," *The Survey* 66 (1 May 1931):163–66, is a contemporary description of one of the leading Mexican-American communities of the 1920s. For material on the Mundelein-Polish feud, see Charles Shanabruch, *Chicago's Catholics: The Evolution of an American Identity* (Notre Dame, Ind.: University of Notre Dame Press, 1981); and Joseph John Parot, *Polish Catholics in Chicago 1850–1920: A Religious History* (DeKalb: Northern Illinois University Press, 1981).

The rising popularity of the automobile was perhaps the most notable development of the 1920s, and a number of recent studies have examined the adaptation of urban America to the internal combustion engine. Chief among these are John B. Rae, *The Road and the Car in American Life* (Cambridge, Mass.: MIT Press, 1971); Mark S. Foster, *From Streetcar to Superhighway: American City Planners and Urban Transportation* (Philadelphia: Temple University Press, 1981); and Paul Barrett, *The Automobile and Urban Transit: The Formation of Public Policy in Chicago* (Philadelphia: Temple University Press, 1983). Howard L. Preston, *Automobile Age Atlanta: The Making of a Southern Metropolis 1900–1935* (Athens: University of Georgia Press, 1979), and Blaine A. Brownell, "A Symbol of Modernity: Attitudes Toward the Automobile in Southern Cities in the 1920s," *American Quarterly* 24 (March 1972):20–44, both present information on the adaptation of southern urbanites to the automobile. Similarly, Ashleigh E. Brilliant, "Some Aspects of Mass Motorization in Southern California 1919–1929," *Southern California Quarterly* 47 (June 1965):191–208, and Robert M. Fogelson, *The Fragmented Metropolis: Los Angeles, 1850–1930* (Cambridge, Mass.: Harvard University Press, 1967), describe the advent of the automobile and the decline of public mass transit in Southern California. Among the many contemporary articles dealing with problems posed by the automobile and the plight of aging streetcar lines are "Wanted — More Hitching-Posts for Cars," *Literary Digest* 80 (2 Feb. 1924): 57–60; Forrest Crissey, "No Parking, The City Planner Turns Traffic Engineer," *Saturday Evening Post* 197 (2 May 1925):32–33, 181–82, 185–86; and John A. Beeler, "What Price Fares?," *Transit Journal* 76 (June 1932):263–66.

The classic contemporary work on suburbanization in the 1920s is Harlan Paul Douglass, *The Suburban Trend* (New York: Century, 1925). John Nolen, *New Towns for Old: Achievements in Civic Improvement in Some American Small Towns and Neighborhoods* (Boston: Marshall Jones, 1927), expresses Nolen's idealistic hopes for suburbia and his plans for the model community of Mariemont. The restricted suburb of Westchester, Illinois, is described in Henry Clarke, "The Planned Community," *National Real Estate Journal* 31 (12 May 1930):25–28. For a short sketch of the suburban real estate boom in Southern California, see W. W. Robinson, "The Real Estate Boom of the Twenties," in John and LaRee Caughey, eds., *Los Angeles: Biography of a City* (Berkeley: University of California Press, 1976), pp. 276–79. Daniel Schaffer, *Garden Cities for America: The Radburn Experience* (Philadelphia: Temple University Press, 1982), provides a detailed study of the creation of the innovative Radburn suburban community; and Jon C. Teaford, *City and Suburb: The Political Fragmentation of Metropolitan America, 1850–1970* (Baltimore: Johns Hopkins University Press, 1979), offers in-depth coverage of the struggle for metropolitan government in the 1920s and 1930s. For suburban comments on metropolitan consolidation in the Saint Louis area, see Maplewood (Mo.) *News-Champion,* 8 Oct. 1926, p. 4; and *Webster News-Times* (Webster Groves, Mo.), 11 June 1926, p. 1.

CHAPTER 4. AN INTERLUDE IN URBAN DEVELOPMENT, 1930–1945

For vivid material on the plight of Chicagoans during the 1930s, see Edmund Wilson, "Hull House in 1932: III," *New Republic* 88 (1 Feb. 1933):317–22; Harold M. Mayer and Richard C. Wade, *Chicago: Growth of a Metropolis* (Chicago: University of Chicago Press, 1969); and "Blank Pay Days," *Saturday Evening Post* 206 (1 July 1933):16–17, 68–70. Jervis Anderson, *This Was Harlem: A Cultural Portrait, 1900–1950* (New York: Farrar, Straus & Giroux, 1982) includes material on the impact of the depression on New York City's leading black neighborhood. Upton Sinclair, *The Flivver King: A Story of Ford-America* (Emaus, Pa.: Rodale Press, 1937), expresses depression-era contempt for the industrial idol of the 1920s, Henry Ford. W. R. Morehouse, "Has the Public Lost Confidence?" *Bankers Magazine* 124 (June 1932):619–24, is indicative of the sense of insecurity among bankers during the depths of the depression. George H. Mayer, *The Political Career of Floyd B. Olson* (Minneapolis: University of Minnesota Press, 1951), describes the class tension that arose during the depression in the Twin Cities as exemplified by the Minneapolis teamster's strike.

The onset of economic depression in the 1930s transformed federal-city relations, and some recent studies have investigated the impact on troubled urban America. The most important are Bruce M. Stave, *The New Deal and the Last Hurrah: Pittsburgh Machine Politics* (Pittsburgh: University of Pittsburgh Press, 1970); Mark I. Gelfand, *A Nation of Cities: The Federal Government and Urban America, 1933-1965* (New York: Oxford University Press, 1975); and Charles H. Trout, *Boston, The Great Depression and the New Deal* (New York: Oxford University Press, 1977).

The literature on New Deal programs is extensive. Harry L. Hopkins, *Spending to Save: The Complete Story of Relief* (New York: W. W. Norton, 1936), expresses the CWA chief's views on the New Deal relief programs. Likewise, Nathan Straus, *The Seven Myths of Housing* (New York: Alfred A. Knopf, 1944), states the views of the first chief of the U.S. Housing Authority. *What the Housing Act Can Do for Your City* (Washington: United States Housing Authority, 1938), also presents the federal government's position on the housing issue. Edith Elmer Wood, *Slums and Blighted Areas in the United States* (Washington: United States Government Printing Office, 1935), offers the opinions of a leading housing reformer and her discourse on the negative impact of substandard housing on the morals and behavior of the poor. The federal housing and greenbelt programs also are examined in Lawrence M. Friedman, *Government and Slum Housing: A Century of Frustration* (Chicago: Rand McNally, 1968); Devereux Bowly, Jr., *The Poorhouse: Subsidized Housing in Chicago, 1895-1976* (Carbondale: Southern Illinois University Press, 1978); Paul K. Conkin, *Tomorrow a New World: The New Deal Community Program* (Ithaca, N.Y.: Cornell University Press, 1959); and Joseph L. Arnold, *The New Deal in the Suburbs: A History of the Greenbelt Town Program, 1935-1954* (Columbus: Ohio State University Press, 1971).

Relatively little has been written about urban America during World War II, but the list of studies on the subject is growing. The chief work on wartime urban policy is Philip J. Funigiello, *The Challenge to Urban Liberalism: Federal-City Relations during World War II* (Knoxville: University of Tennessee Press, 1978). Some of the essays in Roger W. Lotchin, *The Martial Metropolis: U.S. Cities in War and Peace* (New York: Praeger, 1984), provide useful information. Carl Abbott, *Portland: Planning, Politics, and Growth in a Twentieth-Century City* (Lincoln: University of Nebraska Press, 1983), offers the best account of Vanport and Henry Kaiser's impact on Oregon's largest city. Martin W. Schlegel, *Conscripted City: Norfolk in World War II* (Norfolk, Va.: Norfolk War History Commission, 1951), provides a detailed description of one of the nation's chief urban arsenals. J. Blan Van Urk, "Norfolk — Our Worst War Town," *American Mercury* 56 (Feb. 1943):144-51; and Walter Davenport, "Norfolk Night," *Collier's* 109 (28 March 1942):17, 35, 38-39, are two contemporary accounts of the Norfolk scene. Harvard Sitkoff, "Racial Militancy and Interracial Violence in the Second World War," *Journal of American History* 58 (Dec. 1971):661–81, is an informative study of racial conflict during the war; and Walter White, "Behind the Harlem Riot," *New Republic* 109 (16 Aug. 1943):220–22, is a contemporary commentary on the racial tensions of the war period.

CHAPTER 5. SUBURBIA TRIUMPHANT, 1945–1964

Urban historians have not yet written extensively about the significant years following World War II. Thus students of this period need to rely heavily on the contemporary investigations of social scientists and journalists. Two sociological studies examine life in Levittown: Herbert J. Gans, *The Levittowners: Ways of Life and Politics in a New Suburban Community* (New York: Random House, 1967); and David Poponoe, *The Suburban Environment: Sweden and the United States* (Chicago: University of Chicago Press, 1977). Edward J. Smits, *Nassau: Suburbia, U.S.A.: The First Seventy-Five Years of Nassau County, New York 1899 to 1974* (Syosset, N.Y.: Friends of the Nassau County Museum, 1974), and "The Industry Capitalism Forgot," *Fortune* 36 (Aug. 1947):61–67, 167–70, provide information specifically on the construction of Levittown, New York, and the popular response to the massive project. "Park Forest Moves Into '52," *House & Home* 1 (March 1952):114–21, offers a progress report on the Park Forest suburban community. Scott Donaldson, *The Suburban Myth* (New York: Columbia University Press, 1969), is a spirited critique of suburbia's detractors; and Peter Blake, *God's Own Junkyard* (New York: Holt, Rinehart & Winston, 1964), includes a diatribe of postwar suburbia. Zane L. Miller, *Suburb: Neighborhood and Community in Forest Park, Ohio, 1935–1976* (Knoxville: University of Tennessee Press, 1981), tells the story of one postwar suburban community in the Cincinnati metropolitan area. But the best single analysis of suburbia is Peter O. Muller, *Contemporary Suburban America* (Englewood Cliffs, N.J.: Prentice Hall, 1981).

Among the many sources on postwar retailing, see "Too Many Shopping Centers?" *Business Week* 1420 (17 Nov. 1956):136–38, 140, 142, 144; "Year-Round Razzle-Dazzle Achieves Center Dominance," *Chain Store Age* 33 (May 1957):38–39; and George Sternlieb, *The Future of the Downtown Department Store* (Cambridge, Mass.: Joint Center for Urban Studies, 1962). Carl W. Condit, *The Port of New York: A History of the Rail and Terminal System from the Grand Central Electrification to the Present* (Chicago: University of Chicago Press, 1981), includes material on the fate of New York City's giant railroad depots.

A large number of volumes describe and evaluate the postwar programs for urban revitalization. Roy Lubove, *Twentieth-Century Pittsburgh* (New York: John Wiley & Sons, 1969), describes the Pittsburgh renaissance. Roy Lubove, ed., *Pittsburgh* (New York: New Viewpoints, 1976), and Herbert Kubly, "Pittsburgh: The City that Quick-Changed from Unbelievable Ugliness to Shining Beauty in Less than Half a Generation," *Holiday* 25 (March 1959):80–87, also contain material on the supposed rebirth of Pittsburgh. For information on the Civic Progress campaign to win voter approval for the revitalization of Saint Louis, see the *St. Louis Post-Dispatch* for May 1955. John McDonald, "The $2-Billion Building Boom," *Fortune* 61 (Feb. 1960):119–22, 232–43, reports enthusiastically on the boom in office construction in midtown Manhattan; and "Boston Makes A Comeback," *U.S. News & World Report* 57 (21 Sept. 1964): 52–54, 56–58, is typical of the journalistic response to urban renewal plans in Boston. Among the collections of essays on urban renewal policy are James Q. Wilson, ed., *Urban Renewal: The Record and the Controversy* (Cambridge, Mass.: MIT Press, 1966); and Jewel Bellush and Murray Hausknecht, eds., *Urban Renewal: People, Politics, and Planning* (Garden City, N.Y.: Anchor Books, 1967).

Sharply critical of the traditional dogmas regarding urban revitalization is Jane Jacobs, *The Death and Life of Great American Cities* (New York: Random House, 1961). Especially critical of the relocation of families from Boston's West Side renewal site are Chester Hartman, "The Housing of Relocated Families," in Wilson, ed., *Urban Renewal*, pp. 293–335; and Marc Fried, "Grieving for a Lost Home: Psychological Costs of Relocation," Wilson, ed., *Urban Renewal*, pp. 359–79. For criticism of urban renewal in Buffalo, see, *New York Times*, 29 July 1965, p. 58. Criticisms of public housing in Chicago, especially of the Robert Taylor Homes, are found in *Chicago Daily News*, 10 April 1965, p. 1; and Devereux Bowly, Jr., *The Poorhouse: Subsidized Housing in Chicago, 1895–1976* (Carbondale: Southern Illinois University Press, 1978). See also, Arnold R. Hirsch, *Making the Second Ghetto: Race and Housing in Chicago, 1940–1960* (Cambridge, U.K.: Cambridge University Press, 1983). For a before-and-after critique of Pruitt-Igoe, see "Slum Surgery in St. Louis," *Architectural Forum* 94 (April 1951):128–36; and "The Case History of a Failure," *Architectural Forum* 123 (Dec. 1965):22–25.

In recent years a notable body of literature has appeared describing the growth of Sunbelt centers in postwar America. Among the useful works on urban development in the South and West are Carl Abbott, *The New Urban America: Growth and Politics in Sunbelt Cities* (Chapel Hill: University of North Carolina Press, 1981); David C. Perry and Alfred J. Watkins, eds., *The Rise of the Sunbelt Cities* (Beverly Hills, Calif.: Sage Publications, 1977); and Richard M. Bernard and Bradley R. Rice, eds., *Sunbelt Cities: Politics and Growth Since World War II* (Austin: University of Texas Press, 1983).

CHAPTER 6. AN AGE OF "URBAN CRISIS," 1964–1979

Among the many works on ethnic tension in urban America during the 1960s are Fred C. Shapiro and James W. Sullivan, *Race Riot: New York 1964* (New York: Thomas Y. Crowell, 1964); David O. Sears and John B. McConahay, *The Politics of Violence: The New Urban Blacks and the Watts Riot* (Boston: Houghton Mifflin, 1973); Hubert G. Locke, *The Detroit Riot of 1967* (Detroit: Wayne State University Press, 1969); James H. Lincoln, *The Anatomy of a Riot: A Detroit Judge's Report* (New York: McGraw-Hill, 1968); Maurice

R. Berube and Marilyn Gittell, eds., *Confrontation at Ocean Hill–Brownsville: The New York School Strikes of 1968* (New York: Frederick A. Praeger, 1969); and Tony Castro, *Chicano Power: The Emergence of Mexican America* (New York: Saturday Review Press, 1974).

For an understanding of the urban crime problem in America during the 1960s and 1970s, the best analysis is James Q. Wilson, 2d rev. ed., *Thinking About Crime* (New York: Basic Books, 1983). Another excellent study is Anne Heinz, Herbert Jacob, and Robert L. Lineberry, eds., *Crime in City Politics* (New York: Longman, 1983). Among the pertinent essays in this collection are David L. Altheide and John S. Hall, "Phoenix: Crime and Politics in a New Federal City," pp. 193–238; and Dorothy H. Guyot, "Newark: Crime and Politics in a Declining City," pp. 23–96. For an examination of the federal response to rising crime rates, see Malcolm M. Feeley and Austin D. Sarat, *The Policy Dilemma: Federal Crime Policy and the Law Enforcement Assistance Administration* (Minneapolis: University of Minnesota Press, 1980).

Government social programs of the 1960s have been the subject of a substantial body of literature. Bernard J. Frieden and Marshall Kaplan, *The Politics of Neglect: Urban Aid from Model Cities to Revenue Sharing* (Cambridge, Mass.: MIT Press, 1975), is a dry account of changing federal policy in the late 1960s; and John H. Mollenkopf, *The Contested City* (Princeton, N.J.: Princeton University Press, 1983), is a perceptive study of federal urban policy from the 1930s through the 1970s. Frances Fox Piven and Richard A. Cloward, *Regulating the Poor: The Functions of Public Welfare* (New York: Pantheon, 1971), is a polemical work by two leading sociologists. Critical of the Johnson administration social policy is Daniel P. Moynihan, *Maximum Feasible Misunderstanding* (New York: Free Press, 1969). Even more critical and provocative is Edward C. Banfield, *The Unheavenly City Revisited* (Boston: Little Brown, 1974). For information on Mayor William Walsh's battle with the Syracuse Community Action Training Center, see, "Poverty War Out of Hand?" *U.S. News & World Report* 59 (23 Aug. 1965):48–52. Roy Lubove, *Twentieth-Century Pittsburgh* (New York: John Wiley & Sons, 1969), presents information on the social reform efforts of the 1960s in one aging northeastern city. Confirming the hypothesis that the war on poverty created a new cadre of black political leadership is Peter K. Eisinger, "The Community Action Program and the Development of Black Political Leadership," in Dale Rogers Marshall, ed., *Urban Policy Making* (Beverly Hills, Calif.: Sage Publications, 1979), pp. 127–44.

As the fiscal problems of city government mounted during the 1970s, so did the number of scholarly studies on this aspect of the urban crisis. The best volume on New York City's debacle is Charles R. Morris, *The Cost of Good Intentions: New York City and the Liberal Experiment, 1960–1975* (New York: W. W. Norton, 1980). Ken Auletta, *The Streets Were Paved with Gold* (New York: Random House, 1979), offers a more polemical and popular account of New York City's difficulties. Stewart Alsop, "The City Disease," *Newsweek* 79 (28 Feb. 1972):96, and Herbert E. Meyer, "How Government Helped Ruin the South Bronx," *Fortune* 92 (Nov. 1975):140–46, 150, 154, are two of the many commentaries that describe the social and physical decay that underlay New York's fiscal problems. Charles H. Levine, Irene Rubin, and George G. Wolohojian, *The Politics of Retrenchment: How Local Governments Manage Fiscal Stress* (Beverly Hills, Calif.: Sage Publications, 1981), describes the response to fiscal stress in other localities. For information specifically on Cleveland's default, see *Cleveland Plain Dealer* for December 1978. Susan A. MacManus, *Federal Aid to Houston* (Washington: Brookings Institution, 1983), reports on the financial state of a fortunate city that escaped the fiscal crunch of the 1970s.

The body of literature on black urban politicians is growing. William E. Nelson, Jr., and Philip J. Meranto, *Electing Black Mayors: Political Action in the Black Community* (Columbus: Ohio State University Press, 1977), describes the campaigns of Gary's Richard Hatcher and Cleveland's Carl Stokes. Peter K. Eisinger, *The Politics of Displacement: Racial and Ethnic Transition in Three American Cities* (New York: Academic Press, 1980), deals with the transition to black political rule in Detroit and Atlanta.

CHAPTER 7. THE FRAGMENTATION OF THE METROPOLIS

For two optimistic accounts of the reborn central city, see Horace Sutton, "America Falls in Love with Its Cities — Again," *Saturday Review* 5 (Aug. 1978):16–21; and T. D. Allman, "The Urban Crisis Leaves Town," *Harper's* 257 (Dec. 1978):41–56. Gurney Brekenfeld, "'Downtown' Has Fled to the Suburbs," *Fortune* 86 (Oct. 1972):80–87, 156, 158, 162, describes the preeminence of the suburban shopping mall in the late twentieth century. *New York Times,* 14 Nov. 1978, p. B3, examines suburban attitudes toward the central city.

Index

THE JOHNS HOPKINS UNIVERSITY PRESS

The Twentieth-Century American City

This book was composed in English Times by
Capitol Communication Systems, Inc., from a design
by Martha Farlow. It was printed on 50-lb. Sebago
Eggshell Cream Offset paper and bound by the
Maple Press Company, Inc.